Economic Origins of the Iranian Revolution

Pergamon Titles of Related Interest

Amos ARAB-ISRAELI MILITARY/POLITICAL RELATIONS: PERCEPTIONS AND THE POLITICS OF ESCALATION
Amos THE PALESTINIAN RESISTANCE: ORGANIZATION OF A NATIONALIST MOVEMENT
Kilmarx/Alexander BUSINESS AND THE MIDDLE EAST: THREATS AND PROSPECTS
Mossavar-Rahmani ENERGY POLICY IN IRAN: DOMESTIC CHOICES AND INTERNATIONAL IMPLICATIONS
Mroz BEYOND SECURITY: PRIVATE PERCEPTIONS AMONG ARABS AND ISRAELIS

Related Journals*

ECONOMIC BULLETIN FOR EUROPE
INTERNATIONAL JOURNAL OF INTERCULTURAL RELATIONS
OPEC REVIEW
SOCIO-ECONOMIC PLANNING SCIENCES
WORLD DEVELOPMENT

*Free specimen copies available upon request.

PERGAMON POLICY STUDIES ON INTERNATIONAL DEVELOPMENT

Economic Origins of the Iranian Revolution

Robert E. Looney

Pergamon Press
NEW YORK • OXFORD • TORONTO • SYDNEY • PARIS • FRANKFURT

Pergamon Press Offices:

U.S.A.	Pergamon Press Inc., Maxwell House, Fairview Park, Elmsford, New York 10523, U.S.A.
U.K.	Pergamon Press Ltd., Headington Hill Hall, Oxford OX3 0BW, England
CANADA	Pergamon Press Canada Ltd., Suite 104, 150 Consumers Road, Willowdale, Ontario M2J 1P9, Canada
AUSTRALIA	Pergamon Press (Aust.) Pty. Ltd., P.O. Box 544, Potts Point, NSW 2011, Australia
FRANCE	Pergamon Press SARL, 24 rue des Ecoles, 75240 Paris, Cedex 05, France
FEDERAL REPUBLIC OF GERMANY	Pergamon Press GmbH, Hammerweg 6 6242 Kronberg/Taunus, Federal Republic of Germany

Library of Congress Cataloging in Publication

Looney, Robert E.
Economic origins of the Iranian Revolution.

(Pergamon policy studies in international development)
Bibliography: p.
Includes index.
1. Iran--Economic conditions. I. Title.
II. Series.
HC475.L644 1982 330.955'053 82-384
ISBN 0-08-025950-2 AACR2

Printed in the United States of America

Contents

Foreword

Jahangir Amuzegar

Revolutions are often the least understood events in human history. Even when their immediate causes can be sensibly identified, they frequently remain a mystery in the totality of their unfolding and the actual timing of their occurrence. The Iranian Revolution is no exception.

In retrospect, unbiased Iranian and foreign observers agree that the fall of the Shah was not the result of any single act of commission or ommission on his part - or on the part of his so-called "advisors" - but due to a confluence of circumstantial forces which first, collectively paralyzed the government's nerve centers, and then brought the regime down. By almost everyone's reckoning, none of those forces by itself could have been effective in causing the downfall. There is also little disagreement that the 1979 Revolution was neither a Marxian proletarian revolt of the left, nor a bourgeois uprising of the right, in the classical sense. The identifiable opposition forces were neither the "immiserized" reserve army of the unemployed; nor an angry horde of poor, landless peasants; or a group of disenfranchised bourgeois capitalists. The coalition of the red, the black, and numerous other shades of gray, which did the regime in, was in a true sense *sui generis*.

Professor Looney's study seeks to identify the *economic* origins of the 1978-79 upheaval, while not unmindful of other deep rooted sociopolitical and religio-cultural factors. The notable strength of this study lies in its avoidance of ideological angles and its rejection of the simplistic explanations routinely offered by the popular press. Unlike many burgeoning latter-day Iranologists and mushrooming shortorder analysts, the author resists the temptation to analyze the overthrow of the Iranian monarchy in familiar terms. Thus, the rise of "Islamic fundamentalism" in the region, the regime's "oppressive rule," "rampant corruption" in high places, and other such one-dimensional phenomena are discarded as the crucial causes of the revolution. The author convincingly argues that these elements had always been present at certain levels in Iran (and, one may add, to a larger degree still exist in many outwardly stable societies elsewhere). Reference to the prevalence of individual freedoms during the Shah's regime - freedom in the practice of religion; in the choice of employment, profession or trade; in the ease of travel and study at home and abroad; in the open criticism of high officials in the press, etc., - reinforces the argument. The unravelling of the Iranian crisis is correctly regarded as the end result of the convergence of a number of deeprooted and diverse elements producing a devastating force which gradually became much larger than its individual parts.

By a thorough and painstaking attention to detailed economic variables, the book traces the origins and implications of major economic policies and decisions from the early post-war step by step to the end. Along the way, it demonstrates (by implication or design), the intellectual failings of some pre-Revolution analysts who argued that neither the intelligentsia,nor the bourgeoisie, nor even Islam, but only the army could stage a coup against the regime. At the same time, the study's findings challenge the Shah's own strong conviction that his large and modern armed forces were capable of warding off <u>any</u> threat to his reign or rule. Discarded further is the "conspiracy" theory, so fondly embraced by many Iranian exiles, who put the blame for the ultimate debacle on certain Byzantine political rivalries among major powers, and on Western leaders who were presumably annoyed by the Shah's "independent" and occasionally patronizing posture toward them.

Instead, the study offers a sober and unpretentious examination of the Iranian development strategy in its strengths as well as its shortcomings. Without trying to justify or rationalize the previous regime's economic policies, it finds genuine the Pahlavis' concern with uplifting the welfare of the Iranian masses. The Shah's development strategy is considered fundamentally sound. And the final setbacks are regarded as a partial outcome of the initial success.

The study's major argument is that the dynamics of the regime's initially successful development process unleashed a number of latent socioeconomic tensions which, surprisingly, escaped the leadership's attention. Then, once these tensions appeared on the surface, the authorities' reaction was a series of hasty measures which complicated their increasingly onerous tasks, and emboldened the opposition to harrass the bureaucratic machinery into near total collapse.

The extent to which the Iranian revolution has been caused by <u>economic</u> factors may still be an open question.

Professor Looney emphatically argues that the Shah's demise can be traced "almost exclusively" to a set of economically related factors. Among these factors, too, he assigns top responsibility to the government's failure to design and implement a coherent agricultural strategy; to the large and run-away public spending which gave rise to inflationary pressures; to the misguided manner in which the authorities tried to cope with inflation; and to the widening gap in income between various strata in society.

Future historians (and the revelation of still unclassified data) may throw a different light on some as yet unanswered questions concerning the origins and causes of the Iranian Revolution. There is also the possibility that, as in many past events in history, the truth may never come out. But for the time being this study offers a good backdrop for further inquiry and analysis.

For Anne

Preface

A drastic alteration of views as to the proper methodological approach for the study of economic and political development has been precipitated by a series of disasters occurring in countries where development seemed to be vigorously underway. The civil war in Nigeria, the bloody falling apart of Pakistan, and the recent Islamic revolution in Iran are only the most spectacular instances of this phenomenon.

As a result, one reads with increasing frequency pronouncements about the bankruptcy of development economics, with its accent on growth rates, industrialization, and international assistance, and about the need for a wholly new doctrine that would emphasize income distribution, employment, and self-reliance.

The present study of Iran is not written with the intention of stemming this tide, much of which represents a refreshing approach toward current development problems. It is grounded, however, in the strong feeling that a conventional economic analysis, despite its limitations, is as useful if not more so than alternative approaches in providing an explanation as to the demise of the Shah's regime.

It is hoped that this methodology and analysis of the Iranian revolution will yield valuable new insights into the mechanisms of growth in other OPEC countries and will, in turn, provide a series of policy prescriptions as to how these countries, through better policy design and management, can avoid much of the economic dislocation that must ultimately have led to the violence and disruption of the type experienced by Iran.

At the start, it should be carefully noted that the present study is not intended to justify or even rationalize the Shah's economic policies. Instead, it is intended to shed light on the problems faced by economic planners responsible for achieving material progress in an environment of limited information and structural change.

Acknowledgments

This study is an outgrowth of a research project on the effects of arms transfers to developing countries sponsored by the Research Foundation of the Naval Postgraduate School. I owe considerable debt to the foundation for its financial assistance and, just as important, its encouragement in pursuing this broader study.

At the Naval Postgraduate School, Peter Frederiksen was particularly helpful and, in fact, co-authored the chapter on Iranian Military Expenditures. Ralph Magnus and Kamil Said were invaluable in providing insights into the socio-political fabric of Iran. Huroko Mimura deserves credit for developing the optimal control computer programs.

As always, my wife, Anne, not only typed the final manuscript and the many rough drafts that preceded it but also provided the moral support necessary for this sort of undertaking.

1 Introduction

INTRODUCTION

A question that is still being asked by Middle East observers is why the Shah fell. The answer is by no means clear. Of course, the identity of the forces opposed to his regime were well known. They embraced Islamic groups, the bazaar merchants, Mossadegh-type liberals, and the radical Left. Still, despite the fierceness of their opposition, the Shah seemed (at least to most observers) to be in complete control, even as late as a year before he was overthrown. With a large army, an ubiquitous secret police, and plentiful oil-generated funds, he seemed better equipped to thwart any attempt to upset his rule than at any time during his reign. Yet, notwithstanding its apparent strength, the royal regime collapsed less than a year after the beginning of serious riots in 1978.(1)

MAJOR QUESTIONS

What is also puzzling is the fact that the regime collapsed at a time when most observers were expressing unqualified optimism over the country's development prospects based on the following factors:(2)

- Iran's manpower shortages were not seen by most experts as long-run problems.
- The country's agricultural potential was good by Middle East standards.
- A relatively modern infrastructure had been developed during the Third and Fourth Development Plans (1963-1973).

- The country's prospects for developing non-oil mineral resources appeared excellent.
- The country had huge natural gas resources that could complement the petroleum industry as oil reserves approached their peak potential for rapid expansion.
- A base of heavy industry was developed that had the potential for rapid expansion.
- Iranian development planners had greater experience and influence over the plan formation and implementation than planners in other OPEC countries.

What is most striking about the period immediately preceding the overthrow of the regime was the profound anger manifestly permeating Iranian society. Whether it was adolescents demonstrating in the streets; mobs sacking banks, cinemas, and other symbols of Iran's Westernization; the political discussions of the intelligentsia; or the speeches of the nation's religious leaders, what burst forth in every case was rage - explosive, violent rage, and rage that was always focused on the Shah.(3)

The explanation continually put forth by the popular press was that, despite the country's favorable long-run potential, the overthrow of the Iranian monarchy was the inevitable consequence of the Shah's oppressive rule. In particular, the brutality of the secret policy (SAVAK) together with the increasing role of the regime as regional policemen led to the overdevelopment of a repressive apparatus at the expense of representative institutions. This together with the rampant corruption in the government and royal family are said to have constituted the essential ingredients of opposition.

Such arguments cannot survive critical scrutiny. It is true that the Shah's regime was authoritarian, that supreme power rested in his hands, and that the secret police actively engaged in suppressing the opposition. Yet, these elements had always been present at a certain level, and there is little evidence that the levels of any of these factors were increasing that rapidly in the years immediately prior to 1978.(4)

On the other hand, politically active Iranians were free to practice the religion of their choice; to engage in trade, industry, and profession; to travel and study abroad; and, in general, to live their lives according to their individual preferences. This was in marked contrast to the situation in Iraq, South Yemen, and several other oppressive regimes in the region.

Clearly, the intricate details behind the unfolding of the Iranian crisis cannot explain the depths of the passions that were unleashed. To understand that requires an in-depth analysis of a number of elements that characterized the country in the 1960s and particularly the early and mid-1970s.

SUMMARY OF MAJOR ECONOMIC TRENDS

It is argued in the chapters that follow that the Shah's demise can be traced almost exclusively to a set of economically related factors. While these will be examined, suffice it to say here that Iran's recent economic history before the overthrow of the Shah (1965-1977) had the following characteristics:

- This was a period of accelerated industrialization largely concentrated in Tehran where more than half of all manufactured goods were produced and 22 percent of the work force were located in the mid-1970s.(5)
- The Iranian government as well as foreign capital played a central role in financing the industrialization process.(6)
- The government's investments and financing of industrialization came largely from oil revenues which increased from $817 million in 1968 to $2.25 billion in 1972-73 and to $19.6 billion in 1975-76.(7)
- Output in the industrial and mining sectors increased by 18 percent in 1973-74, while simultaneously the number of new companies registered in the large population centers almost doubled, total capitalization rose almost threefold, and per capita income increased from $501 to $821.(8)
- The manufacturing sector increased its output each year by 17 percent between 1973 and 1976.
- Government expenditures accounted for 60 percent of all industrial investment by 1977.
- There were major demographic shifts toward an increasingly urbanized population. Migration to the cities occurred as unemployed rural laborers were incorporated into the booming manufacturing and construction sectors of the economy.
- The agricultural work force declined from 75 percent of the total economically active population in 1945 to less than 50 percent in 1966, then to approximately 33 percent by the late 1970s.(9)
- High levels of underemployment existed in the agricultural sector stemming in large part as a result of the government's decision to promote modern commercial farms in the 1960s as part of its agrarian reform program.
- Agrarian reforms created a rural middle class in the 1960s whose members were the chief beneficiaries of substantial amounts of economic and technical assistance from the government. At the same time, approximately 40 percent of the rural population received no land whatever under the agrarian reforms.(10)
- Large numbers of rural workers were made landless by the land reforms and moved to the urban areas in search

of employment. These workers accounted for 80 percent of the decline in the agricultural labor force during the 1956-66 period.

- Industrial wage labor took on a growing importance in the Iranian economy. Out of an economically active population totaling 10.4 million in 1977, an estimated 2.5 million were employed in approximately 250,000 manufacturing firms, while another 1 million found job opportunities in the construction sector.(11)
- A rapid economic transformation took place toward an industrial society based on the development of modern industries, the weakening of traditional economic forces (especially small producers and preindustrial, commercial, and religious groups), and the intensification of class and regional inequalities.(12)
- A number of government banking and financial institutions and trading companies began to displace traditional small commercial and money-lending firms in the 1970s.
- Modernization generated growing discontent in the mid-1970s within the displaced and economically weakened groups.(13)
- The government used a portion of its oil revenues in 1973-75 to placate the hostility of the bazaar entrepreneurs toward increased government intervention in the economy.
- Resentment of the regime resurfaced in 1975-76 due to corrupt practices within the government.
- The increased inability of the regime to control inflation through normal monetary and fiscal measures eventually resulted in direct state action in the form of a 1975 anti-profiteering campaign during which more than 250,000 businesses were briefly closed, over 8,000 shopkeepers were jailed, and another 23,000 shopkeepers and merchants were sentenced to deportation (later rescinded) to remote areas of the country.(14)
- Income disparities between skilled and unskilled industrial wage laborers, as well as between urban and rural workers continued to widen in the 1970s.(15)
- Increases in wages during 1973-75 barely kept pace with the rate of inflation caused, in turn, by bottlenecks and shortages created by inadequate communications, and port and power facilities.
- Stagnation in agriculture resulted in an increased dependence on food imports (from $32 million in 1973 to $1.5 billion in 1978).(16)
- Military expenditures accelerated markedly after 1973 to nearly $8 billion in 1977.(17)
- The unofficial rate of inflation averaged around 50 percent for the three years between 1975 and 1977. These price increases eroded the incomes in per capita income

and, thereby, depressed the purchasing power not only of the working class but of the middle class as well.(18)

- The government confronted a wide range of problems associated with its development strategy including the lack of competent administrators, bureaucrats, and skilled manpower; insufficient energy; an inadequate communications infrastructure; rising food prices and housing costs; faulty economic planning; a massive waste of resources; spiraling inflation; and growing regional and class socioeconomic inequalities.
- Governmental measures in 1977 to reduce inflation through the imposition of credit controls set off a deceleration of the industrialization program.(19)
- As a result of the stabilization program, the construction industry, a major source of employment for unskilled rural labor, underwent a severe contraction in 1977 with the rural migrants as a whole suffering the greatest decline in living standards because of inflation, food shortages, and the need to use a large portion of their income for rent.
- The bazaar merchants, dependent on state credits to finance many of their activities and affected by the inflation, came to feel by 1977 their economic role in society increasingly threatened by the pattern of development that was gradually narrowing their possibilities for private capital accumulation and upward social mobility.
- Local industrialists joined the merchants to express in 1977 their opposition to price controls, anti-profiteering campaigns, and an endless series of government decrees placing limits on capital accumulation and expansion.(20)

In brief, this period in Iran's economic history saw massive economic and demographic changes. Sustained urban expansion and multi-billion dollar investments were accompanied by the rapid growth of modern working and middle classes in new industries and expanded state services. The authority of older traditional religious and cultural leaders was undermined while, in some cases, agrarian reforms transferred land from religious notables to commercial farmers. The post-1973 influx of petroleum dollars led to speculation in land, high rates of inflation, and a relative decline in living standards of a large proportion of the population. The oil boom exacerbated all of the tensions inherent in the pattern of rapid and uneven development - increasingly affecting the salaried and wage earning industrial workers as much as those in the more traditional sectors.

By the time of the upheaval, therefore, the Shah had managed to antagonize the already hostile religious leadership with a cut in government subsidies, he had irritated large segments of the intelligentsia with seemingly excessive arms purchases, he had restrained the traditional bazaar merchants from receiving what they considered to be their due share of lucrative government contracts, and he had forced large firms to sell shares in their companies to their workers.

Thus, by the summer of 1977, the only sources of support for the Shah were the army, a thin layer of high government officials, and a very small segment of the upper middle class. All the others who formed the great majority of the Iranian nation actively or passively filled the ranks of the opposition. As Hirschfeld notes:

> The fall of the Pahlavi dynasty was brought about not only by the loss of mass support, but similarly by the Shah and his advisers' lack of understanding of the great political significance of this loss. They were unaware that the modernization of Iran had created a new political, social and cultural reality, which rendered the traditional Pahlavi political system obsolete. Moreover, they failed to evaluate the formidable power of socially mobilized and politically conscious popular forces.(21)

IMPORTANCE OF ECONOMIC FACTORS

In this respect, the mechanism developed below is quite different from the so-called "J curve" hypothesis which attributes revolutionary outbreaks to a sudden downturn in economic performance coming after a long upswing. Such a downturn no doubt increased the likelihood of civil strife in Iran, but was by no means the only cause. Instead, it is argued that a number of latent tensions began inevitably arising out of the development process itself which, given their nature, did not provide the authorities with any advance notice of the mass alienation developing within the country. Further, these developments were taking place at precisely the time at which the authorities should have been on the lookout for a distinctly different climate of public and popular opinion. The result of this mechanism was to lull the regime into complacency from which it could not recover once the very development process that seemed so successful and widely accepted began to be denounced en masse.

The major argument of this book is that the economic problems that undermined the regime all had one thing in common - their impact on the economy and its various social groups was very difficult to anticipate and, once identified by the government, were inevitably responded to by the authorities through a series of stop-gap, ill-conceived measures that only tended to compound the regime's difficulties.

Five major questions arise in examining the economic causes of the Iranian revolution:

1. What, precisely, was the Iranian development strategy - including its ideological foundations, rationale, and method of implementation?
2. What were the country's major economic goals?
3. What problems did the development strategy create before 1973?
4. What were the origins of the economic problems caused by the strategy and oil boom after 1973?
5. How did these problems interact to reduce the ability of the government to manage the economy?

In general, the methodology adopted for this study is similar to that of the structuralist method of analysis used successfully in examining the mechanisms of growth and stagnation in Latin America(22) but never previously applied to a Middle Eastern economy. Using this approach, we will analyze the Iranian economic crisis in terms of its preconditions (pre-1973 socioeconomic structure); the shock (the post-1973 oil-financed acceleration in spending); and the propagating mechanisms that developed (from those problems) and which eventually led to a cumulative movement toward economic anarchy and revolution.

2 Early Development Patterns

INTRODUCTION

Iran's postwar economic history falls into four rather distinct stages. The first covers the period up to 1963 and was characterized by a relatively low rate of growth of about 5.5 percent in constant prices between 1959 and 1963 with nearly zero inflation. (1959 is the starting point for most of the country's macroeconomic data.) The second period extended from 1964 to 1970 (or 1973) and was characterized by a high rate of growth, about 10.5 percent in constant prices, and increased inflation. The third phase, from 1971 to 1977, was characterized by extremely high rates of growth concurrent with a seemingly accelerating rate of inflation. The final stage, 1978 to the present, has been one of stagnation with high rates of inflation. While these dates are somewhat arbitrary,(1) they do delineate four fairly distinct periods, each with its own particular characteristics.

One thing that the first three stages seem to have in common is that, during each period, the economy, despite abundant oil revenues, began to suffer balance of payments problems that were both a cause and a consequence of political instability. The Iranian economy traditionally was able to absorb far more capital and consumer goods imports than it could support through foreign exchange earnings, thus forcing the government to sooner or later initiate fairly harsh stabilization measures. While the main interest in the chapters below is with the third stage, an examination of the first two, particularly the first, is instructive because of the insights provided as to the workings of the economy and the way in which the government responded to the economic crisis of 1959, a response which, perhaps because of its success at that time, was not altogether different from the policies implemented nearly twenty years later by the government.

THE REZA SHAH PERIOD

Although attempts at industrialization and modernization in Iran go back to the early 1920s, the idea of economic development within a planning framework did not fully materialize until after World War II.

The development policies of the government under the reign of Reza Shah (1925-1941) did not constitute development planning as the term has come to be understood in the postwar economic literature. The prewar policies were restricted to partial investment programs for the public sector only, with little consideration concerning the activities of the private sector. Furthermore, the public sector programs that did exist did not reflect any explicitly defined set of policy objectives. As a result, the allocation of resources was not determined on the basis of any particular investment criterion. A number of specific investment projects in different sectors were implemented without giving sufficient consideration to their interrelationships or their overall effects on such things as the level and distribution of national income.(2)

What is of interest in terms of the present study, however, is the fact that the framework for the development strategy the country was to follow until the time of the revolution was developed during this period. More specifically, the primary development objectives of the period were rapid industrialization and the development of the country's infrastructure, while agriculture was by and large ignored. The most important policy instruments of the prewar period, aside from the investment programs, included tax rates and wage and price controls, as well as government controls over the various aspects of foreign trade.

Economic policy under Reza Shah was also characterized by the establishment of a state monopoly over foreign trade. This was a period before oil revenues had a significant impact on government finances. Most of these early development efforts were financed through the imposition of a tax on tea and sugar.(3)

Evaluations of Reza Shah's approach to economic reform have been extremely varied, with Lambton's observation perhaps the most insightful:

> In spite of the apparent progress achieved during the regin of Reza Shah, and although Persia had become more conscious of her new role as a national state belonging to Western Society she had not yet

> found a sound basis for her new life, nor had she achieved a synthesis between the basis of Western Society and Persian tradition. The house had been swept of much of the past that remained but nothing solid had been put in its place.(4)

Variations of this theme have been expressed by others,(5) all with the general thrust that Reza Shah's reforms were carried out at too rapid a pace, and much that was old was removed with not enough that was new put in its place - a view which we will find has also been used to describe his son's, the Shah's, approach to the country's economic development.

THE FIRST DEVELOPMENT PLAN (1949-1955)

The First Seven Year Development Plan was approved by the Iranian parliament in 1949. Critics have described the plan as deficient in both basic planning methodology and objectives. While this issue is certainly debatable, it is clear that the plan was largely partial and did not take into account the role of investment by the private sector. In effect, the plan was a collection of infrastructure projects to be executed by the newly established Plan Organization. The 1951-53 crisis over oil nationalization and the subsequent loss of oil revenues made the actual implementation of the plan impossible.

The interruption of oil production during the period of political instability and unrest accompanying the premiership of Mohammed Mossadegh ended with the signing of an agreement between the Iranian government and a consortium of oil companies in October 1954. Production increased rapidly after the new agreement, but it was not until 1957 that the 1950 (the last pre-disturbance year) level was reached. The agreement between Iran and the Consortium provided the country a royalty of roughly one-half the difference between the "market value" of oil produced and the cost of production; i.e., one-half of the consortium's profits. Officially, Iran's share of the oil profits were paid in sterling but could be transferred into other currencies at the request of the government.

Because nearly all of the government's expenditures were in local currency, the oil revenues had to be converted into rials. This was done through direct purchases from Bank Melli, and the rials thus obtained aggregated with general tax revenues. Economically, rials obtained in this manner had to have an inflationary impact on the economy because they did not (as is the case with taxes) have an offsetting component elsewhere in the country's income stream; i.e., they represented net injections to expenditure. The presumption was, of course, that private sector imports would ultimately fulfill the role of offsetting income stream leakages. However, while the private sector did respond by accelerating its level of inputs, inflationary pressures soon developed.(6)

Iran's exchange rate during this period mirrored, to a certain extent, developments in the oil sector. From March 1946 to March 1956, the country had a de facto multiple exchange rate system. Both imports and exports were classified into several categories, and certificates for each class were required since the price of certificates varied from category to category (and given that Bank Melli was their sole buyer and seller); the system of certificates acted as a form of multiple exchange rates. Beginning in 1954 the rial began to strengthen and the country was able to initiate a single rate. The free market rate, except at odd times (e.g., when a decline in the price of oil was forecast) differed little from the official rate.(7)

Despite the resumption of oil production in 1954, the economy continued to languish. Commenting on the situation at the end of the first plan period, Jahangir Amuzegar noted that, despite the government's concerted efforts both before and after the war, its plans and programs did not seem to have achieved their proclaimed objective of improving the living conditions of the Iranian masses. "Although there is no statistical proof, there seems to be conclusive evidence that in the last thirty years the lot of the average individual in Iran has deteriorated and the inequalities in the distribution of wealth and income have been intensified."(8) As an explanation Amuzegar speculated that:

> Among the greatest barriers to Iran's economic development are certain aspects of the Iranian mentality. Three-fourths of Iran's population are poor, illiterate farm workers living in widely scattered villages throughout the country. Many are sharecroppers; others are mainly landless peasants and tribesmen. Protracted poverty, chronic diseases, ignorance and isolation have made these people stagnant, custom ridden, and superstitious. Their *modus vivendi* based on fear, suspicion and insecurity has begotten attitudes of subservience, apathy, and individualistic self-interestedness. Although not inherently lazy nor necessarily content with their lot, they seem to have lost individual initiative, and become apathetic to hard work and outwardly fatalistic toward discomfort.(9)

THE SECOND DEVELOPMENT PLAN (1955-1962)

After the overthrow of the Mossadegh government and the subsequent resumption of oil production and export in 1954, development efforts began anew. A Second Plan, largely financed out of oil revenues, was drawn up and initiated in 1955.

As was the case with the First Plan, emphasis was given to infrastructural projects. Similarly, investments for inclusion in the plan were chosen without any particular systematic framework in which their simultaneous impacts could be assessed and evaluated; i.e., the plan was largely a set of independent projects, whose main commonality was that they had been easy to identify. Almost all the plan's allocation to the agricultural sector went to three large dams: Karaj, Safid Rud, and Dez. Similarly, allocations in the industrial sector were concentrated in several major projects involving the construction or modernization of large textile, sugar, and cement factories. Transportation and communication projects were confined to construction of inner city highways and the extension of the railway network, with little attention given to feeder roads and other rural projects.

As revealed by actual choices, therefore, it seems that the overall tendency of the planners was to select projects with low value added returns and low employment generating effects. As a result, the investment program was dominated by the relatively few capital-intensive projects. In sum, the investment program had all the shortcomings of an unintegrated public investment program prepared on the basis of the so-called project-by-project approach characteristic of the lack of a clearly defined development policy.(10)

It cannot be denied, however, that the task of designing a good development plan in Iran at this time was indeed difficult. The lack of both statistical data and familiarity with planning methodology and techniques was a major limitation. In addition, the overriding aim of the government at the time seemed simply one of initiating an investment program of some sort and as soon as possible. It was the size rather than the composition of expenditures which received the highest official consideration. As a result, most of the basic planning issues were not even raised, and the Second Plan was destined from its very inception not to satisfy the attributes (such as efficiency and internal consistency) of a well designed development plan.(11)

More fundamentally, however, the somewhat capricious attitude of the government toward planning at this time undoubtedly stemmed from the fact that political power, the commitment of which was necessary if planned economic development was to be achieved, was difficult to locate and define.

The Shah was obviously much more than a constitutional monarch, but clearly did not have absolute power. He had to act within certain indeterminate boundaries not easily definable even for him. On the other hand, genuine democratic institutions were nonexistent. Political power appeared to rest on a very precarious set of balances among the dynasty, the feudal landlords, the army, the clergy, and the emerging new urban classes among which as yet only the merchants and intellectuals seemed to exert any major political influence.(12)

By the late 1950s, these power groups (none of which was very homogeneous) had more or less successfully kept each other in check. This type of environment was obviously not conducive to planned economic development. Further, the balance between the different groups was not only precarious but also contained a number of inner contradictions, many of which were never effectively resolved. It is little wonder, therefore, that the first two plans had vaguely stated objectives with no apparent focus.

Plan Financing

In terms of the financing of the plan, the government's oil revenues at the time were divided among three agencies: the Plan Organization, the Ministry of Finance, and the National Iranian Oil Company (NIOC), with about 80 percent going to the Plan Organization. Subsequently, the Plan Organization's share was reduced (only to be restored again in the late 1960s). The reduction in Plan Organization allocations appears to have not only reduced its implementation capability at the time but, more importantly, was an indicator of the attitudes toward development that prevailed among some of the leading government officials.

Several technical aspects surrounding the oil agreements are of interest. The consortium-oil revenue-government expenditure linkage meant that, in effect, the government agencies that converted their share of the oil revenues to rials (denominated in sterling) would, in contrast to the usual situation in developing countries, benefit directly from a devaluation of the rial; i.e., they would receive more rials for the same quantity of oil receipts. This situation created a set of incentives whereby devaluation could then increase the Plan Organization and Ministry of Finance's imports (because a smaller amount of oil revenue would be required to obtain the necessary rials). If, after devaluation, the private sector continued to buy all the foreign exchange the public sector offered, then devaluation would constitute a tax on the private sector.

A revaluation of the rial in terms of gold would, of course, produce a windfall gain; and this was, in fact, what the government did. By setting the buying and selling rates of the rial at 75 and 76.5, respectively, the authorities created a disparity in the gold-rial rate; i.e., the gold content of the rial still implied an official exchange rate of 32.25 rials per dollar. In order to bring the gold content rate into equality with the actual rate at which the currencies were exchanged, the rial was revalued in terms of gold during May 1957. The result was to release 7.1 billion rials ($95 million of gold) from note cover; i.e., approximately $95 million in gold which, at the previous gold content exchange rate of 32.25 rials per dollar, was required under existing law to be as note-cover was, under the new gold content exchange rate of 75.75 rials per dollar, released for other uses. Most of the revaluation windfall was allocated for loans to agriculture and industry for the purchase of equipment.

It has been argued that the revaluation of the rial was used to provide the rationale needed by the authorities to accelerate the expansion of the money supply (by the amount equivalent to the rise in the rial value of the country's stock of gold and foreign exchange).(13) In any case, the change in the rial rate did mean a considerable once and for all rise in rial revenues of the government and a subsequent rise in its level of expenditure. It is clear, of course, that the so-called revaluation financed projects were no different than the government undertaking its increased expenditures by simply printing money.

Whatever its motives, the net effect of the government's manipulations was to facilitate the expansion of credit to the private sector. Loans extended to the private sector increased by 46.1 percent in 1957, 60.5 percent in 1958, and 32.4 percent in 1959. The industrial loans financed through the banking system were limited to one-third of the total investment of the project in an attempt to attract a significant amount of personal and business savings into productive capital formation.

Rising government expenditures together with the unprecedented expansion in private sector credit produced Iran's first major economic boom during this period. Expansion was most pronounced in urban housing and industry. Private sector investment in construction in Tehran, for example, rose by 85 percent and 130 percent in 1958 and 1959, respectively.

In addition to the government's fiscal actions, the expansion was aided by a major liberalization of restrictions on the importation of capital equipment. Rising aggregate demand, cheap loans, and increased imports combined to sustain the investment boom for several years. The most rapidly expanding areas for investment appear to have been the more traditional ones of textiles, cement, sugar refining, leather, bricks, etc. Furthermore, investment during this period was largely for plant expansion or new plants built by individuals or concerns that already were operating similar ones.

It is significant that few firms owned or controlled by new entrepreneurs came into existence during the investment boom, suggesting that the type of entrepreneurs willing to venture into new areas or take great risks were in short supply at this time. The failure of the system to induce diversification and greater private sector response to new productive investment opportunities exposed what was to become the major shortcoming inherent in the country's economic system.

Inflationary Pressures

By the late 1950s, the point had apparently been reached where even the expanded growth of imports could not prevent inflation from increasing at rates significantly over its historical pattern (although at a rate still somewhat below that experienced by many other countries at the time).

Since the economy still had a relatively simple structure, it is tempting to explain this inflationary surge as simply one of excess demand. A closer examination of available information indicates that, while the demand pull mechanism was important, other factors were also at work. For instance, if excess demand were the sole cause of inflation at that time, imports should have increased even more than they did. Prices rose by only 1 percent in 1959, partially because imports increased by roughly one-third during that year. A year later, however, the price level had risen by 10 percent, yet imports had expanded by only 10 percent. Given the limited data covering this period, one can only speculate as to the reasons for the deceleration in import growth. Clearly, the drop in foreign assets of the banking system did contribute to the decline, falling as they did from 16.41 billion rials in 1959 to 11.40 billion in 1960.

Another contributing factor could have been the effect on demand of changes in the distribution of income that was taking place at the time. Employment was increasing rapidly in urban areas. In 1960, the lower range of wage rates for urban jobs averaged from 20 to 60 rials per day. Given the relatively high price level of most imported goods, however, an increase in wages at rates of even 10 to 20 percent would probably be sufficient to significantly shift this income group's profile of demand from domestic to foreign goods. Instead, the increased demand originating in the upward movements was likely to remain concentrated in domestic consumer goods, thus preventing excess demand from spilling over into imports.

On the other hand, increases in incomes of the upper and middle income groups seem to have resulted in increased demand for consumer durables, higher quality textiles and food products, much of which were imported. As already noted, most new investments during this period relied on imported capital equipment. If rising incomes of the higher income groups and the acceleration in private investment did, in fact, cause the import boom of 1959, a deceleration in investment activity, thereby reducing not only imports but also upward pressure on the lower end of the wage scale, would be expected to lessen the upward pressure on prices. If these patterns were at work, unused capacity, i.e., unused foreign exchange, would likely materialize. In fact, foreign assets of the banking system increased from 11.40 billion rials at the end of March 1960 to 15.88 by the end of 1961.

Balance of Payments Problems

Beginning in 1959, the total balance of payments deficit accelerated rapidly. The cumulative short fall for 1958-61 amounting to around $276 million, therefore, had to be financed through the running down of reserves. Indeed, the four-year deficit was $51.6 million greater than the surplus built up during the preceding four years. By the end of 1960, the country had only enough foreign exchange to finance several week's essential imports.

The main source of this mounting payments deficit was clearly the rising trade deficit which, in turn can be traced to the uncontrolled expansion of imports and the stagnant level of exports (table 2.1), the combination of which led to deficits much higher than their historical levels.

Table 2.1. Excess of Imports Over Non-Oil Exports

	Percent
1900-1905	82
1910-1914	61
1925-1929	63
1935-1939	16
1946-1948	97
1955-1960	263
1957-1960	363

Source: George Baldwin, Planning and Development In Iran (Baltimore: Johns Hopkins University Press, 1967), p. 59.

How did the situation reach this state? As George Baldwin notes, it was not because no one realized what was going on.

> The trade and payments statistics were certainly good enough to have warned what was happening. Nor was it because there were no Iranian officials who recognized the danger signals and argued for more prudent policies toward imports and the casual assumption of foreign debt. The 1958-61 payments slide was essentially one more symptom of the general condition of Iranian politics during this period: a few sensible people who understood were not in positions of political control, and the people in positions of control either did not understand or would not listen. If real trouble developed, the authorities seemed to think new loans would always be arranged or that the American Government would buy the country back from the brink, or the oil revenues might be pushed up by pressuring the Consortium for higher prices. As a last resort officials could resign and turn the mess over to someone else. All these remedies were tried. The Iranian talent for ingenious maneuver under pressure succeeded in confining the financial crisis and avoided the rupture with her principal foreign creditors which clearly threatened.(14)

By the end of 1960, therefore, the monetary-induced boom had come to its inevitable end with the country facing both excessively rising prices and a large and growing current account deficit. The government was forced to embark on a now famous economic stabilization program initiated by the International Monetary Fund. This program consisted of a set of standard IMF measures including direct control of private sector credit, the raising of interest rates, the restriction of imports, and forced reductions in government expenditures.

As a result of these measures, the boom of 1957-60 was soon turned into a deep recession. Real private sector gross domestic fixed capital formation declined by 7.7 percent and 9.5 percent in 1961 and 1962, respectively. Public sector investment also dropped by 11.6 percent in 1962. The more traditional sectors, such as agriculture, construction, and domestic trade, were most seriously affected by the recession. Domestic trade (which covers the economic activities of the bazaar) probably suffered the most because it bore the full brunt of the plan's import and credit restriction measures. In fact, the value added in trade actually declined by 2 to 3 percent in 1961, while showing only a marginal increase in 1962.

The modern sector, it appears, faired much better during the recession with the value added of manufacturing and mining (excluding oil) increasing in real terms by 8.4 percent and 13.6 percent in the depressed years of 1961 and 1962, respectively.

The asymmetrical impact of the stabilization program upon the traditional and the modern sectors of the economy inevitably created a number of social and economic problems. Most serious in this regard was the growing mass discontent among both low income urban groups (a large proportion of whom were unemployed migrant construction workers) and the bazaar merchants (who as a group had been the most severely affected by the government stabilization program).

The administration's response to the deteriorating conditions was the introduction of a number of reforms including: land reform, profit sharing in industry, female suffrage, nationalization of forests, return of state industries to private enterprise, and the formation of a literacy corps. These reforms were clearly a real threat to the interests of the landed upper and propertied middle class and certainly perceived that way by them. Thus, instead of relieving the social tensions, the economic and political uncertainties created by their initiation may have aggravated certain groups to the point of reviving old alliances, particularly between the ulma and the bazaar merchants, especially in regard to their joint opposition to the regime. The culmination of unrest was a series of mass demonstrations against the regime in June 1963. In contrast to those nearly 15 years later, these were quickly and brutally suppressed.

EMERGING DEVELOPMENT PATTERNS

The late 1950 to early 1960 period is of interest because several patterns emerged from the country's first attempt at accelerated growth during this period that were ultimately to be repeated on a much larger scale in 1978-79. Of special note in this regard is: (1) the role of the oil sector in the economy, and (2) the rigidity of indigenous institutions to economic growth.

Role of the Oil Sector

The main characteristic of the oil sector at this time (and to this day, as far as that is concerned) was that it was in no sense indigenous to the economy but, rather, superimposed on it. Although output was increasing rapidly and investment in the sector was also accelerating in the industry, it did not provide the nucleus around which the entire economy could develop. While this pattern is typical worldwide, it was undoubtedly intensified in Iran due to the country's predominantly rural agricultural village-oriented social and economic system. Because most village inhabitants had no contacts beyond their immediate village, whatever potential spread the oil sector may have had was quickly dissipated. Since farming methods with several exceptions were primitive, levels of income in rural areas remained very low. As a result, most of the economy imposed few demands on the oil industry, and responded little if at all to increases in the supply of oil or to the demands for skilled labor and other inputs generated by that industry. In fact, after six decades of operations, the petroleum sector remained a virtual appendage to the Iranian economy, with little direct impact on the industrialization of the economy. The bulk of the requirements of the oil industry consisted of capital goods which were imported duty free including parts and equipment required in the operation of the refineries, the oil fields, and pipeline transportation. Thus, for the period 1962-66, 88.3 percent of the total purchases of the consortium of foreign oil companies and an estimated 90.7 percent of those of the National Iranian Oil Company (NIOC) were foreign.(15)

In short, the oil industry did not play a leading sector role similar to that played by the textile, iron and steel, railroad, and automobile industries in the earlier stages of the development of some of the Western nations. The industry was important, therefore, in Iran's development program largely because it provided a source of easily controlled and easily mobilized revenue for the government and a supply of foreign exchange greatly in excess of what the indigenous Iranian industries could possibly earn and not because it imparted its dynamism directly to the rest of the economy.

Institution Building

In terms of its institutional development, it is clear the country was not at the "take off" stage at this time. Not only was the economy extremely rigid and unresponsive but, perhaps just as significant, the country's social arrangements remained deeply engrained in forms that were the virtual antithesis of those required to facilitate economic growth. Those more perceptive in the government undoubtedly saw as an immediate goal not one of sustained equilibrium growth but, more realistically, a limited one of uprooting and eventually replacing a mode of behavior and set of institutions that had become established over centuries of static economic performance.

More specifically, while the rural groups remained tradition bound, most of the urban population living as they had for centuries through successive periods of invasions, civil wars, and political instability had become distrustful, self-interested, and cynical. Iranian businessmen had grave misgivings about prospective partners and generally minded their own business, often withdrawing from large-scale cooperative endeavors. Conservatism, drive for quick profits, and a high discount of the future were their common characteristics.

On the other hand, while the bureaucrats and the ruling intelligentsia were informed, educated, and ambitious, they often tended toward pessimism and despair. Living in their country's glorious past and disappointed with its plight at the time, they frequently sought scapegoats, and tended to blame their troubles on anything and anyone but themselves. Fearful and suspicious, they questioned the motives and mistrusted the counsel of others. An extreme sensitivity to defeat and failure made them fearful of trying new things. The majority lacked initiative for constructive action, risk taking, and free enterprise.(16)

Based on its actions at the time, the government seems to have opted for a development strategy that would attempt to achieve high growth with institutional change, i.e., its strategy was apparently designed so that the process of accelerating economic change would also undermine many if not all of these institutions. The ultimate goal of this institution-destroying phase was undoubtedly the creation of an atmosphere that would permit rapid development of modern Westernized groups possessing progressive attitudes toward change and with access to positions of importance. For example, projects that resulted in increasing inconsistencies with respect to the prevailing social and economic arrangement - a road building program that made tribal life a little more bearable, a rural credit program that reduced the dependence of the peasant on the landlord, a village electrification program that relieves a bit of the drabness of the daily routine - were seen by the authorities as ultimately transforming existing attitudes and socioeconomic relationships in the country toward arrangements more compatible with increases in material well-being.(17)

CONCLUSIONS

Despite its increased oil revenues, Iran began to experience a number of difficulties during the Second Plan period, including strong inflationary pressures and a rapid fall of official foreign exchange reserves. Interestingly enough, these problems do not seem to have been caused exclusively by the government's excess spending but, instead, appear to have their origin in more fundamental structural problems characterizing the economy at that time.

There is no doubt that the sharp reversal of 1960-62 was crucial in fermenting not only increased revolutionary action but also in the creation of a fairly broad-based opposition to the regime. The recession of 1960-62, however, could not have brought about the level of 1962-63 internal strife by itself. Clearly, the role of the religious groups in the organization of political opposition and their mobilization of the masses was a crucial element.(18) As in 1978, it was the development of adverse socioeconomic conditions that provided the appropriate environment for the ulma's particular brand of opposition to flourish and eventually succeed. The government's harsh suppression of the 1963 demonstrations undoubtedly enhanced the position of the leading religious groups giving the impetus to the ulma's opposition to the Shah's regime which was to be so crucial in the February 1979 revolution and its aftermath.

The general conclusion that emerges from this discussion as to the progress made by the country toward development by the early 1960s depends very much on how one views the development process. The growth in output that took place in the late 1950s and early 1960s was limited to a handful of traditional Iranian products and industries. At the same time, the major sector of the economy, agriculture, remained virtually stagnant. No new, dynamic sector had been stimulated by the increase in oil revenues and the unwillingness of entrepreneurs to assume risks in undertaking new productive investments cast some doubt on the contribution the private sector was willing and able to make to future growth. Inflation was also beginning to be associated with the country's growth process and had reached levels that were quite likely inconsistent with long-term continuous growth. Worse yet, instead of being eliminated by the availability of foreign exchange, price increases seemed at times to be fostered by that availability, in that increases in foreign exchange permitted expanded employment and wage bill. The resulting distribution of income caused the demand for domestically produced commodities to expand at a rate faster than supply. This situation was to be repeated a number of times over the years.

Despite the far-reaching impact that the resumption in oil revenues was to have on the economy, the process of oil-induced economic development had certain ramifications. As oil came to be the initiator of the country's economic development, the accompanying structure of production and trade began to evolve in a very artificial environment - one in which certain built in distortions not only seemed inevitable but were at the time looked upon by many in the government as beneficial to the whole modernization process. In the general overview of the 1962-73 period and the industrialization process, an attempt is made to show how oil-induced distortions not only impeded the process of diversified economic development but actually created a productive structure that was inherently stagnation prone.

3 Formulation of a Development Strategy, 1964-1973

INTRODUCTION

With the upturn in economic activity following the stabilization program of the late 1950s to early 1960s, it looked as if the country was in a position to begin the conscious integration of agriculture and industry into a modern structure. Between 1963 and 1969, government revenue from the oil sector had grown at a high average annual rate of 18 percent, and the contribution of oil revenues to capital formation had reached a level of over 60 percent by the early 1970s. The significance of these developments lay in the fact that, for the first time, the government actually possessed the financial capability it had always dreamed of. Oil revenues enabled the authorities to launch a series of ambitious development projects and plans that the government's planners and economists had previously relegated to the role of wishful thinking.

By its very nature, the country's development strategy and, particularly, that of import substitution industrialization as it unfolded in the 1960s and early 1970s is treated here in a very general manner, the main purpose being to develop a framework in which a number of technical problems associated with several of the more specific governmental actions can be examined.

THE THIRD DEVELOPMENT PLAN (1962-1967)

The Third Plan was to be Iran's first comprehensive development plan. This anticipated broadening of the planning scope had come about as a result of the main findings of the Second

Plan's evaluation undertaken by the Economic Bureau; i.e., that most of the country's economic problems during the Second Plan period had been caused by: (1) lack of coordination between the activities of the various government agencies, and (2) lack of a comprehensive view regarding the availability and use of resources in the whole economy.(1)

These warnings do not seem to have been taken seriously by the planners for, as a practical matter, many of the plan's details were never worked out. The plan, as its predecessors, was essentially an investment program for the public sector, together with several forecasts of private sector activity. In terms of priorities, it is clear that economic growth (targeted at 6 percent in real terms) was the dominant objective of the plan, with employment and income distribution objectives receiving relatively low marginal considerations. In fact, the planners clearly stated the Third Plan should not be expected to create a large number of jobs, employment opportunities, nor be counted on to alter the distribution of income. Despite the problems encountered by inflation during the period of the Second Plan, the goal of price stability was hardly mentioned. Concern over the balance of payments was at least expressed, but this goal was also relegated to minor importance compared to growth.

In terms of actual developments, especially those relating to the balance of payments, the Third Plan period can be divided into two subperiods: 1962-63 and 1964-67. During the earlier period, the recessionary conditions prevailing in the economy and the implementation of the stabilization program of the early 1960s combined to produce a favorable balance of payments. During this period, the import restrictions placed on the private sector were successful in bringing that sector's foreign exchange use more in line with the country's ability to earn foreign exchange.

Following the economic recovery, especially after 1965, both investment and imports began to increase again. As a result, despite increased foreign exchange earnings of the oil sector, the balance of current payments deficits soon appeared, growing from $58 million in 1964 to $212 million in 1967. Foreign loans, although substantial, were not really adequate to cover the growing deficits. As a result, the country's foreign exchange reserves declined. Cumulative balance of payments deficits on current account amounted to $421 million during 1962-67, of which only $274 million (65 percent) could be covered by foreign loans.(2)

Because of a number of initial criticisms of the Plan's potential inflationary impact, the authorities made a genuine effort to keep the money supply under control. Factors recognized which tended to make the economy vulnerable to inflation included:(3)

1. Basic economic development problems and the structural characteristics of the systems of production which tended to augment any inflationary tendencies;
2. Agrarian reform which was felt by many as quite likely to have an adverse effect on agricultural output during transition;
3. The urbanization and the consequent increase and changes in the composition of demand for consumption which tended to raise consumption levels and thus possibly led to disequilibrium between savings and investment;
4. The likely increase in nondevelopment expenditures and thus effective demand due to political and other pressures, and finally
5. The long gestation period of a major proportion of public investment which would tend to increase the effective demand without simultaneously increasing wage goods.

The money supply was kept under control and the overall level of prices remained relatively stable during the Third Plan period. While the first two years of the plan period were years of recession, the subsequent economic recovery together with increase in development outlays resulted in a substantial increase in the domestic supply of goods and services during the latter part of the period. A significant portion of this increased output resulted from fuller utilization of previously idle capacity. In addition, production began as several of the capital intensive plants initiated in the Second Plan came on stream. The government actively pursued a price stabilization policy during the last two years of the Plan by directly importing those products for which significant domestic shortages had occurred. The combination of all these factors helped stave off an aggregate supply/demand balance of the type that had undermined the Second Plan.

THE FOURTH DEVELOPMENT PLAN (1968-1972)

In contrast to the Third Development Plan, the Fourth Plan contained several overall objectives: (1) an increase in economic growth (by gradually increasing the relative importance of industry, raising the productivity of capital, and introducing advanced techniques of production); (2) a more equitable distribution of income; (3) a decrease in dependence on foreign countries and diversification of exports, and (4) improvements in administrative services by the introduction of basic changes in the administrative system and the extension of advanced managerial techniques to all ministries and public and private organizations.

The objective of the plan regarding employment was the creation of maximum full-time productive employment for the purpose of (1) absorbing those seeking employment who would enter the labor market, and (2) gradually converting unproductive or low productive jobs into stable and productive employment. Quantitatively speaking, total employment was to rise from 6,932,000 in 1967 to 7,898,000 in 1972, or an increase of 966,000. On the other hand, open unemployment was expected to decline only to 61,000 by the end of the period. The government was pursuing what must be termed a quasi-full employment policy (4) since, if successful, the Plan's programs would reduce unemployment to about 7 percent of the labor force.

In terms of performance, the actual rate of growth during the period amounted to about 11.6 percent (thus indicating an overfulfillment of the target rate by about 2 percentage points). With the exception of agriculture and construction, all the sectoral value added targets were either attained or surpassed. Agriculture had the lowest growth at 3.9 percent per annum; oil and services achieved the highest rates at 15.2 and 14.2 percent, respectively, with the service growth almost twice the planned rate (mainly due to the rapid expansion of government services). Industry grew at an average annual rate of almost 14 percent in real terms.

In general, the employment targets were also overachieved with actual employment increasing by 1.2 million versus the target of only 966,000. Agricultural employment, however, declined by 202,000 compared with a planned increase of 226,000. On the other hand, industrial employment increased more than its planned target (737,000 as against the planned figure of 417,000). Perhaps most significant, employment in the services sector increased by 720,000 or 60 percent of the total increase in employment during the period.

Price stability, a major objective, was not fully realized over the period. The GNP implicit price deflator rose at an average annual rate of 4.3 percent during this time as compared to 0.6 percent for the Third Plan period. Between 1968 and 1970, the overall level of prices remained relatively stable; however, in the final two years of the Plan, prices increased at about 6 percent per annum. More specifically, the wholesale and consumer price indices rose 7.1 and 5.5 percent, respectively, in 1971, and 5.5 and 6.3 percent 1972. All in all, during the Fourth Plan period, the general price level was positively correlated with the overall shortage of supply, especially in agriculture and construction sectors, and with movements in world prices.

While most of the Fourth Plan targets were met, the overriding fact remained that, by the early 1970s, the country's development prospects were not good. Oil production was reaching its capacity level, foreign debt repayments and interest were a major drain on the country's foreign exchange holdings, and both development and military costs were growing rapidly. Relative stagnation in the agricultural sector, rising income levels that produced growth of demand for food in the urban centers, and increased urbanization aggravated the problems. Food requirements had to be increasingly met by imports, thus further reducing the availability of foreign exchange. Incremental oil price adjustments between 1971 and June 1973 temporarily relieved the balance of payments pressure. But the long-run problems did not significantly improve, and, by the end of the Fourth Development Plan, the government was anticipating a major balance of payments crisis to occur during the Fifth Plan period.

For the period (1964-73) as a whole, the country's economic goals, while not always attained, had at least remained stable. First, economic development was pushed at the expense of all programs (except defense). During the 1960s, this involved investment in import substitution industries and subsidization of public credit for industrial and manufacturing projects. Second, Iran's leaders stressed continued government investment in infrastructure. In practice this entailed heavy public sector investment in infrastructure and social capital projects. Third, the country's leaders sought better utilization of its oil and gas resources. By the 1970s, oil production was approaching capacity. No major discoveries had been made for years and prospects for significant increases of proved reserves were limited. Also, the foreign oil companies had not exploited natural gas in secondary recovery for foreign sale. Moreover, the government was unable to control the rate of oil production and exports. Consequently, greater control over operation of the oil industry was a major government goal.

During this period, the government sought to strengthen the country's defenses. Iran began to develop its military capability rapidly during the Third Plan period (1962-1968). Before that, increases in military spending had been sporatic and relatively low. In 1968, however, Great Britain announced its intent to withdraw its military presence from the Persian Gulf. This move, coupled with the growing intensity of the rebellion in Oman, provided the impetus for a major shift in the government's budget toward defense. Between 1966 and 1973, military-related expenditures rose from \$370 million to over \$2.6 billion, a seven-fold increase that was accompanied by nearly \$2 billion in armaments imports.

OVERALL STRATEGY - IMPORT SUBSTITUTION INDUSTRIALIZATION

Ironically, the economic stabilization program that was responsible for the sharp reversal of 1960-62 embodied an important stimulus to the economy throughout the rest of the 1960s and into the 1970s.(5) The restriction of imports of nonessential items, which was intended to solve the country's balance of payments problems, laid down, perhaps inadvertently, the foundation of an import substitution industrialization strategy.

The policy of import controls was later complemented with generous fiscal incentives, exclusive industrial licensing, low or nonexistent profit taxes, and easily accessible low interest loans for investment in the manufacturing sector. In short, Iran began to follow a strategy of import substitution similar to that adopted at the time by a number of other developing countries. But there was one major difference: many of the other newly industralizing countries, in addition to relying on primary exports and foreign loans, promoted their manufacturing exports to pay for a proportion of their imports of capital and intermediate goods. However, Iran continued to rely heavily and almost exclusively on oil exports. Between 1963 and 1972, foreign exchange receipts from oil and gas accounted for 76 percent of the country's total export earnings, and the average annual rate of growth of oil and gas revenues during the Third and Fourth Plans amounted to 14.5 and 25.0 percent, respectively.

Much concern and apprehension was expressed by Iranian economists and government officials at this time about the plight of non-oil exports. Their policy response seems to have been designed largely to: (1) vitalize exports, (2) make the terms of trade more favorable, and (3) lower the rate of increase in imports. In practice, the government's program in this area was essentially one of providing incentives to diversify exports (by enlarging the export of technically simple manufactures) and substituting domestic production for a wide variety of imports at any cost, regardless of efficiency considerations.

The ever-increasing oil revenues and foreign loans and aid may partly explain the previous lack of enthusiasm on the part of the government to modernize and diversify the non-oil export sector. Agriculture in Iran was a good example of the "fossilization" thesis.(6) Neither the cultivators nor the public authorities had felt compelled to innovate or adopt modern farming techniques. On the one hand, cultivators clung to their ancient patterns of activity and institutions. Over the years, they adapted themselves to primitive techniques and static patterns of capital replacement. On the other hand, government officials had never experienced the crunch stemming from a prolonged foreign exchange shortage except during the oil nationalization disputes (1951-53) when they had no alternatives but to promote non-oil exports. It is no wonder, then, that by the mid-1960s Iran's per capita non-oil exports and its non-oil export share of gross national product were both the lowest in the Middle East.

In addition to general official neglect and lack of interest, cultural attitudes and value systems also seemed to have impeded the development of manufactured exports and processed agricultural profits. Fatalism, bazaar mentality (quick profits), "personal government" rather than abstract law and impartial administration, nepotism, and aversion to planning all affected the country's commercial relationships in adverse ways. Unfortunately, unethical practices of some producers and exporters went on without much official concern but with considerable damage to the reputation of the country's exports. For instance, to make the weight of exports heavier, it was not uncommon to add dirt to dried fruits; or to put bricks, stones, and scrap metals in bales of cotton and wool, or in the sacks of almonds or beans. Increasing the amount of moisture in cotton or filling the top of a bag or case with good quality and the bottom with low quality commodities were also common practices. These characteristics of Iranian business no doubt explain the lackluster performance of the non-oil export sector and also why at any time there were usually large quantities of rejected Iranian commodities in the Western European warehouses.(7)

Perhaps because of these and other impediments conceived by the authorities during this period, the government looked more and more to the establishment of entirely new industries, using Western technology and modern management techniques. These would be superimposed on the existing industrial structure which for all practical purposes was written off as a means of not only diversifying exports but also of enabling the country to become a modern industrial nation by the early 1990s.

THE PROCESS OF IMPORT SUBSTITUTION INDUSTRIALIZATION

The process of import substitution began in the 1960s and was initially confined to consumer goods. Protective measures for the domestic market were the chief stimulus with firms expanding eventually into import substitution of intermediate and capital goods.

At least ten distinctive features characterized the sector's subsequent growth during this period.(8)

1. Industrialization proceeded at an extremely rapid pace and in a wide variety of industries.
2. Immediately following or even parallel with the growth of the light consumer goods manufacturing (primarily food processing, textiles, footwear, and similar industries), intermediate and capital goods industries were begun.
3. Investment in intermediate products industries was concentrated in steel, fertilizers, chemicals, and transport equipment. Capital goods expansion was primarily in construction materials and electrical equipment.
4. The normal time lag usually experienced in moving from light to heavy industry was drastically shortened.
5. Almost all industrial growth was oriented for the domestic market as a process of pure import substitution. Most industries were started in response to already existing or anticipated demands on products previously imported.
6. Industries were given generous incentives by the government. These consisted of tariff protection or import prohibitions.
7. Both domestic and foreign private capital participated in the industrialization, with a domestic entrepreneurial class evolving out of import trade businesses.
8. The demand for labor increased selectively. Although there were large masses of underemployed in the rural areas, shortages of skilled and semiskilled labor resulted from the industrialization process.
9. While a policy of geographical deconcentration was pursued by the government, industry became increasingly concentrated in Tehran.
10. Although most of the industrial growth took place in the private sector, the government continued to exercise a major influence on investment and output. Some projects such as in petrochemicals were government owned, as was the integrated steel mill in Isfahan.

COMPOSITION OF PRODUCTION

During the 1960s it appears that, as a proportion of total industry sales, domestic production rose most rapidly in the consumer durable area. The domestic production of capital goods also expanded rapidly during this period with Iranian firms gaining an additional 25 percent of the domestic market in this area. Domestically produced electrical equipment, for example, accounted for under 5 percent of domestic sales in 1960, but by 1969 its share had risen to almost 40 percent (of an expanded market). Vehicle assembly was another area in which rapid growth took place. By 1969 domestic firms supplied over 70 percent of the market compared with only 40 percent in 1960.(9)

Expansion of domestic output of intermediate goods was much more uneven with production products such as paper, printing, rubber, and chemicals, increasing very rapidly with only limited expansion in metal products and nonmetallic minerals (although domestic producers did manage to increase slightly their share of the local market). As noted earlier, imports of capital goods such as machinery were very significant. By the end of the 1960s, imports of these goods still accounted for over 90 percent of the domestic market, amounting to about 25 percent of the country's total imports.

Apparently, the degree of interdependence and reliance of various sectors of the economy upon each other and not on the foreign sources of intermediate goods declined during the period under consideration. This occurred at the same time the manufacturing firms enjoying the protected home market became less competitive in world markets. At least this is the picture one obtains by comparing the country's input-output tables over time. In 1962, for example, the manufacturing sector's sales to other sectors was about 31 percent of the sector's sales. However, by 1970, this ratio had fallen to only 19 percent (table 3.1). Although direct comparisons with other countries are difficult, 19 percent is quite a low percentage by any measure and is indicative of the economy's very weak linkages.(10)

Along these lines and reflective of the decline in linkages in the economy was the fact that, by 1970, consumer goods output had increased to 68 percent of manufacturing goods over the 1962 figure of 62 percent. A similar pattern developed in exports, with exports accounting for only 4.7 percent of the sector's output in 1962, falling to 2.3 percent in 1970. The failure of manufacturing to develop any sort of non-oil exports was occurring at the same time that the imports were accounting for a higher and higher proportion of inputs into the manufacturing sector.

Typical of the lack of market planning was the target for automobiles contained in the Fifth Five Year Plan. According to the Plan, priority was given to the production of 2 million passenger vehicles by the early 1980s. Even under the most favorable circumstances, however, it was unlikely that the situation whereby (in the early 1970s) nearly half the country's population was living in near subsistence conditions in rural areas would change to the extent necessary to create a market for this number of cars. Moreover, with 72 percent of the country's rural families having an income below subsistence level at the time the decision to expand the automobile industry was made draws one to conclude that little or no economic considerations underlay the industrial selection process.(11)

This criterion is even more telling in light of the fact that the income distribution at the time was not only quite unequal and becoming more so but was also being adversely

Table 3.1. Structure of Iranian Economy 1970 and 1962
(Figures are in 1959 prices - bil. rls.)

Sector	Interindustry Demand		Final Demand: Consumption		Final Demand: Capital Formation		Exports	
	Value	%	Value	%	Value	%	Value	%
1970								
Agriculture	52.48	29.86	117.65	66.95	0	0	5.59	3.18
Oil & Mining	42.87	70.65	16.71	27.54	0	0	1.10	1.81
Other sectors	114.34	38.72	88.81	30.08	87.94	29.78	4.18	1.42
Manufacturing	47.91	19.07	170.76	67.97	26.87	10.70	5.67	2.26
1962								
Agriculture	22.70	23.10	72.30	73.70	--	--	3.20	3.20
Oil & Mining	8.70	12.70	4.50	6.60	--	--	55.30	80.80
Other sectors	38.20	26.10	77.50	52.90	30.70	21.00	--	--
Manufacturing	28.40	31.30	56.60	62.40	1.40	1.60	4.20	4.70

Sources: 1970 figures are derived from G. Pyatt et al., Employment and Income Policies for Iran, Mission Working Paper No. 12, Methodology for Macroeconomic Projections (Geneva: International Labor Office, 1973), Table II.2 (mimeo); 1962 figures are derived from A. Sh. Shaheen, The Input-Output Table for the Iranian Economy (Tehran: The Ministry of Economy, 1962), mimeo.

Notes: 1. Contribution of the "rest of the world" to the modern manufacturing sector has been 43.74%.

2. "Oil & Mining" in 1970 Table contrary to 1962 Table reflects "domestic oil" and mining lumped together as one single sector.

affected by the import substitution process itself. One study indicated that, whereas the gap between rural and urban sectors had fallen from 2.13 in 1959 to 1.91 in 1965, it had increased to 3.21 by 1972. This deterioration coincided with the period when the import substitution phase of consumer durables was getting underway on a large scale. Apparently, as the economy began to implement the import substitution strategy, the intersectoral distribution of income between urban and rural areas began to widen at an alarming rate.

On the basis of these figures, one can characterize the manufacturing sector as: (1) becoming more heavily oriented toward the production of consumer goods; (2) one whose linkages within the sector and with other sectors, were not only weak but also were becoming weaker over time; (3) becoming more reliant on imports for sustaining production, and (4) a declining export capability. These patterns were undoubtedly an outgrowth of the incentives provided by the government. The lag in capital and intermediate goods production was clearly due to the lack of restrictions on the importation of these goods together with the high tariffs afforded consumer goods. The result was that, even to many sympathetic observers, Iran's industrialization strategy seemed lopsided, ill-conceived, and devoid of any long-run comparative advantage.

One fundamental criticism of the strategy was the nature of the industries that were being established which, rather than reducing the country's vulnerability to international market movements and pressures, instead dictated that the country would be increasingly dependent on imports of foreign technology, skilled manpower, and capital goods. Equally damaging was the observation that the whole strategy concentrated its attention on productivity and was devoid of any realistic assessment as to markets for the proposed industries. Clearly, the industries would all have to be dependent on the internal market for sales. For all practical purposes, however, the size of this market was too small for many of the products completed for the import substitution industrialization. Even into the 1980s, with high and steady rates of GNP growth, it was unlikely that Iran would have expanded its internal markets to absorb many of the type of goods produced and contemplated. The internal export market which might have provided an outlet to these goods was slow to develop and had limited possibilities in any case due to the competitive edge possessed by many of the other developing countries.

As noted earlier, an additional criticism of the manner in which the import substitution strategy developed in Iran, unlike that of most developing countries, was the fact that the industrialization process did not generate foreign exchange to finance its own intermediate and capital goods requirements. Together with the high level of protection, this meant that the whole process of importing capital and intermediate goods and producing finished consumer goods for the domestic market could go rather smoothly only as long as the oil revenues kept expanding. The whole industrial process was effectively isolated from any type of competitive checks.

Labor costs and productively in the oil sector did not, of course, determine the level of oil exports. This fact would not have been a particular problem for the country outside of equity considerations except for the fact that there was a certain amount of spillover in wage increases from the petroleum to the manufacturing sectors. Because of the lack of competition in both the petroleum and modern manufacturing sectors, there were no real constraints to stop the process of wage-price-wage increases once it became established.

The implications of this situation were serious. First, the economy could not benefit from any market signals that might have warned producers that wage increases or the prices of the finished products were becoming way out of line with those in foreign countries. Second, there was no self-terminating pressure on wage-price inflation. Third, if and when oil revenues slackened and, with that, domestic demand, there would be no other source of demand to sustain sales of the marginal firms; i.e., large-scale unemployment and underutilization of capacity would likely occur. In short, the oil sector became the pivotal link in the economy upon which the manufacturing sector was able to prosper. Since the whole environment in which industry developed was extremely artificial and not based at all on efficiency considerations or profit maximization under relatively competitive conditions, any shock such as a drop in the world's demand for Iranian oil would likely result in an immediate decline not only in the country's level of production but employment as well.

PROBLEMS ASSOCIATED WITH TECHNOLOGICAL CHANGE

The nature and speed of technological change in Iran was greatly influenced by the industrial strategy and, in turn, shaped the direction that strategy took. In general, technological change during this period (even up to 1978) was characterized by the increasing importance and wider range of activities in which there were economies of scale, the increasing degree to which capital was used relative to labor at given factor prices, and the decreasing flexibility in production processes, especially in the increased difficulty of substituting plentiful factors of production (such as semiskilled and unskilled labor) for scarce ones (such as skilled labor).

The degree to which these tendencies applied, of course, varied from industry to industry. Indeed, these tendencies were far more typical of technological change in intermediate goods areas than for consumer or capital goods or services, although in the early 1970s the development of agribusiness was bringing the same kind of changes to agriculture.

While technical efficiency (output per unit of inputs) generally increased in the process, the overall effects of these changes were not altogether favorable. As noted, the limited size of the domestic market was not supplemented by the potentially large size of foreign markets. Even the larger domestic markets were sufficiently fragmented so that many industries had to choose between producing for the domestic market in small-scale, high-unit-cost plants or in larger but underutilized ones. At the same time, the other two characteristics of technological change combined to guarantee that even rapid rates of industrial growth would generate minimal increases in industrial employment.

Although these effects may not have been completely inevitable, the costs of avoiding them (given the country's desire to industrialize) may have been sufficiently high to make it rather unlikely that they could have been completely avoided. One obvious alternative would have been to develop alternative small-scale technologies more appropriate to the conditions of the country. Except for a few relatively unimportant production processes, however, such technologies were not widely available at the time and the cost of their development might well have been prohibitive.

Another alternative would have been to rely on the multinational corporations which could have supplied the needed skilled labor, managerial talent, and international marketing expertise. While the country did this to a large extent, limits were undoubtedly being reached in terms not only of the foreign exchange cost and dependence but also of the political and social ramifications of a large expatriate labor force in the country becoming increasingly the chief beneficiaries of the oil boom. Moreover, the high degree of dependence on multinational firms undoubtedly reduced the spread effects and linkages from these activities to the rest of the economy (and, of course, thereby greatly reducing their potential benefits).

Changes in technology appear, therefore, to have played an inherently disequilibrating role, accentuating the scarcity of skilled labor and supervisory talent (and the abundance of unskilled labor), and reducing the potential competitiveness of the country's products in industrial markets. Most industries tended to pressure the government for continued protection, thus reducing the potential benefits that might conceivably have been introduced by the new technology. Existing productive structures were made more rigid, inflexible, and less innovating as a result of the inefficiency increasing effects of the monopolistic structure of domestic production created by the barriers to international trade. Thus, as the potential for lower labor costs went up with new equipment, output per worker may have decreased in some areas due to increases in inefficiency; i.e., the dependence of domestic industries on protection diverted scarce entrepreneurial activity from positive sum activities like management and supervision to zero or negative sum activities like bribing government officials for special favors and further protection from competitors both foreign and potential domestic.

In sum, domestic production, together with the underpricing of foreign exchange, reduced the profitability of exporting and thereby limited opportunities for taking advantage of economies of scale. In addition, because (1) the structure of tariffs tended to discriminate against older equipment, (2) international transport costs were more closely connected to product weight than value and hence were higher in relation to total cost for older equipment, (3) there were shortages in supervisory personnel, and (4) the costs of night labor were considerably higher than day labor, many firms were not able to take advantage of second best alternatives such as longer production runs and older but more labor-intensive equipment.

Even the potentially favorable effect of increased world energy (and hence transport) prices in limiting the economic advantage of large-scale production techniques (and hence in increasing the dynamic viability of small-scale production techniques) was dissipated by the failure of the government to raise the domestic price of fuel and other forms of energy in step with their international trend.

The implications of these distortions were to reduce the level of employment below what it should have been. This was a point never conceded by the authorities who steadfastly maintained that the manufacturing industry employed around 2.5 million people or nearly 25 percent of the total labor force. But there is reason to believe this estimate to be highly misleading. In reality, of the 250,000 manufacturing firms in Iran, only 6,000 employed 10 or more people, thus placing manufacturing employment in the range of 17 percent of the labor force.(12)

CONSEQUENCES OF THE IMPORT SUBSTITUTION STRATEGY

Industrialization was the long-standing objective of Iran's development ambitions, the symbol of progress, and it was considered by many in the government as the only way of assuming prosperity status once oil production began to dwindle. Expenditure on industry as a proportion of total public outlays began to fall in the mid-1970s as attention shifted to those parts of the economy that constrained further expansion of productivity, particularly to the transport and communication infrastructure. But industry was always the first consideration when it came to allocating funds, and remained so until the fall of the government in 1979.

By the mid-1970s, it was clear that Iranian industry was not justifying the priority treatment it was enjoying in terms of investment. By 1975, it was still generating only 18 percent of GDP in fulfilling its objectives of generating export income and substituting domestically produced goods for an increasing proportion of imports. In the years following the oil boom, the industry failed to do both as the increased national wealth produced a corresponding surge in domestic demand. The proportion of imports in the aggregate supply of goods rose from 20.6 percent in 1973 to 26.9 percent in 1975, and the trend was not checked in 1976. Meanwhile, the effect of rising domestic demand on non-oil exports was predictably detrimental, and these were lower in 1975 than in the two previous years.

The problem of the roles to be played by the state and private sectors was at the forefront of many industrialists' minds. The task of distributing the country's oil wealth took the government deeper and deeper into the productive sector with the corresponding danger of declining initiative on the part of the private sector. With the additional uncertainty over government intentions aroused by such steps as the share participation program, there was an increasing tendency for a process of capital flight and falling investment.

Thus, the pattern of import substitution industrialization initiated in Iran not only presented a seriously distorted way of development, high social cost, unemployment, underemployment of resources, inequitable distribution of income and wealth, and relatively neglected agricultural and handicraft sectors, but also involved problems associated with the building of overcapacity in key industries such as petrochemicals, fertilizers, steel, and refineries. The limited size of the internal market coupled with the skewed income distribution pattern in the country further impeded the full utilization of productive capacity already built, or the planned capacity being contemplated in the various development plans. The consequences of import substitution industrialization were the high costs of production, a decrease in quality of products because of heavily protected domestic industry, and perpetual dependence on world markets, both to build new production capacities and to maintain existing capacities.

It is easy to sketch out a sequence of events whereby growth took place during the 1960s and 1970s. Government investment out of increased oil revenues in the 1960s began to induce increasing rates of migration to urban areas, increasing labor force participation rates, and savings rates change in the composition of demand toward industrial consumer goods. This process, in turn, induced increased investments in these activities, increasing urban employment, etc. As the country became increasingly urbanized, the urban population came to carry larger and larger weight in the decision-making process. New urban-oriented institutions were created (banks, credit and financial institutions, and government agencies) and oil institutions transformed the rural-oriented ones into urban entities. Monetary fiscal trade and exchange policies and social overhead expenditures became urban and industrial biased. Buttressed with positive feedbacks of this sort, an import substitution industrialization and urbanization strategy became a process that fed upon itself, generating ever-increasing income inequalities.

With the leveling off in oil revenues and cutbacks in government expenditures in the mid-1970s, momentum began to slacken. The strategy became self-defeating and sterile. Domestic savings could not be generated to finance the social overhead capital and it was necessary to resort to deficit financing which was inflationary. The government-imposed controls began to reduce subsidies; groups had become accustomed to increased standards of living. This led to political pressures for more controls which led to further distortions in the allocation of resources. Zero sum activities - such as avoiding controls, capital flight, and speculative investments in urban real estate - became common. Without momentum, the country quickly became mired in a vicious cycle of financial repressions, distortions, social conflict, and political instability from which it was impossible to break out.

On a speculative note, a number of observers have contended from time to time that the system of industrial controls, licensing, tariffs, etc. was set up so that the Shah's family and close business associates would have an easy source of monopoly profits and political influence. Further, it was felt that the Pahlavi family used their unrestrained political level to ensure: (1) that they became business partners of most major manufacturing enterprises, hotels, banks, and insurance companies; and (2) that by resort to bribery, arm twisting, and enforcement of changes in the country's trade and banking regulations, they created an appropriate environment for their own purposes which often proved contrary to the objective of achieving balanced growth and a more equal distribution of income. In fact, this belief became one of the intellectual's main rallying points in the revolution. As the argument goes,(13) the establishment of new banks by close business associates of the Pahlavi family paved the way for easy access to private sector deposits as well as public sector funds (loans and credits from the Bank Markazi of Iran), much of which was alleged to have been transferred abroad; and, finally, that these banks were also used to grant loans to companies (often in excess of their worth) which belonged to the Pahlavi family or their close associates.

Certainly some of these things must have happened, but it is unlikely that most of the industrial regulations and the whole strategy itself was created with this purpose in mind. A careful reading of the industrial history of this period shows that, in many respects, Iran's import substitution strategy was similar to that taking place in a number of other countries.

A more accurate description of the country's strategy is that it evolved first by necessity out of the crisis in the early 1960s and later largely by whim and emulation of other countries. George Baldwin sums up this situation best. (14)

> In contrast to the powerful stimuli periodically contributed by the government's unpredictable monetary, fiscal and credit activities has been the weakness of most of its administrative programs - e.g., any kind of direct controls, direct services, institution-building of almost any kind. It was because of this long standing institutional weakness of the government that the planners relied primarily on helping industry indirectly through credit programs based on a fast growing banking system.

CONCLUSIONS

The adoption of an import substitution strategy, together with the rising oil revenues and the country's political stability, produced high profit expectations and thus ensured a high and sustained growth of the industrial sector through the 1960s and into the 1970s. Manufacturing value added grew on average by 12.3 percent per annum over the 1963-72 period, increasing its share in total domestic value added from 12.6 percent to 14.5 percent. This high degree of industrialization was achieved by a considerable amount of investment in construction and imported machinery and equipment. The average annual growth of gross domestic fixed capital formation reached 16 percent and that of fixed investment in machinery and equipment amounted to over 20 percent during the Third and the Fourth Plan periods. Increased imports of intermediate and capital goods also reflected a shift away from imports of consumer goods (as a percent of total imports). In fact, as evidence of the success in replacing imports of consumer goods, these imports in total nonmilitary merchandise imports declined uniformily from 30 percent in 1959 to less than 11 percent in 1969.

Unfortunately, many of the mechanisms that from a neoclassical vantage point should have been equilibrating, became quite disequilibrating in the Iranian import substitution context. Disequilibrium caused growth to feed upon itself for a time but, with the slackening momentum, the same disequilibrium forces pushed the economy to stagnation.

Import substitution industrialization as implemented in Iran created several severe sectoral imbalances. As the terms of trade turned against agriculture (due to increased cost of manufacturers to the agricultural sector), agricultural production fell. Normally, over time, this process would be self-correcting and eventually short agricultural supplies would reverse the declining price trend. Oil revenues permitted almost unlimited food imports at constant prices, however. As a consequence, Iran was not only a net importer of agricultural commodities including grains in the 1970s, but the gap between consumption of foodstuffs and domestic production was increasing at an alarming rate. This disequilibrium process whereby the agricultural sector became marginalized is examined in the next chapter.

4 Developments in Agriculture

INTRODUCTION

As Iran's development strategy evolved during the 1960s and formalized after 1973, it envisioned the building of an industrial society on a par with those of the developed countries by the end of the century. Implicit in this strategy was a favorable international trade position and the availability of essential resources and commodities. The desirability of a consumption-oriented, largely urban society was seldom publicly questioned nor were the problems of agriculture seriously addressed by the government. In retrospect, Iran's policymakers were slow to recognize that their national aspirations would be seriously undermined by a dislocated rural society and stagnant level of food production.

There are numerous explanations of what went wrong with the government's rural policies. In fact, there are so many plausible answers that it is difficult to draw consistent conclusions. The profusion of negative factors allows observers of diverse persuasions to use the Iranian case to bolster their own ideological arguments just as it allows Iranian historians sometimes to argue that, once the government's policies were in force, nothing could have diverted the economy from its path of rural chaos, economic failure, political disorder, and violent repression.

Part of the problem lies in the fact that Iranian agricultural development is difficult to fathom without knowing how political factors were intertwined with the technological, economic, and social options open to the authorities. No doubt, these interactions underscore the incompatability that seemed to exist during the period under consideration between the country's long-term national goals and the government's tendency in the short run of placating various groups - particularly the larger landowners and the new urban working class.

As has become apparent when all of the errors involved in implementing the country's development strategy are examined, the most serious mistakes of all were made in agriculture - particularly the resettlement policies beginning with the Fourth Plan period, but carried to an extreme during the Fifth Plan period.

MAJOR DIFFICULTIES

Generalizations about Iranian agriculture can be misleading. The quality of agricultural land in the country varies considerably from the deserts of Sustan and Baluchistan to the perennially wet slopes facing the Caspian Sea. As might be expected, incomes from farming vary considerably. A low of $8 per capita was earned in 1975 by those farming the poorest lands of Baluchistan; while $576 was the average farm income in Gilan, Azerbaijan, and Mazanderan. In view of such variations, one of the most difficult decisions that confronted the government planners all through this period was whether or not resources should be concentrated in relatively productive regions, where investments were able to earn high returns, or in poor regions, where incomes were low and poverty needed to be eradicated. Given the country's increasing food deficits, the incentives for both the public and private sectors was to shift the capital to the more productive areas.(1)

As noted previously, the gap between domestic agricultural production and consumption in general, and food in particular, began to develop around 1959. The supply demand gap widened over time with the continuous expansion of incomes made possible by the oil revenues while, at the same time, supply tended to lag for a number of the reasons outlined below.

Precise figures on the food shortfall are not available. However, a fairly realistic estimate based on plausible assumptions as to demand and supply can give some idea as to the likely magnitudes.(2) If the average annual growth of real non-oil GDP was 9 percent and that of the population was 2.8 percent (roughly coinciding with the official figures during this period), and the income elasticity of demand for food was equal to 0.8 percent, then the demand for food would have grown at around 10 percent per annum. If a slight deficit existed in 1959 (the starting point of the exercise) and if the government did not want this to deteriorate any further, then agricultural output and productivity would have had to grow at around 10 percent and 7 percent, respectively, to maintain the constant deficit. In actuality, the growth of productivity was near zero and agricultural output about 3 percent. It is easy to conclude, therefore, that after eleven years or around 1970, peasants would still be living in poverty (if not worsening conditions) while urban groups would simultaneously be increasingly dependent on imports. This is, in fact, what happened.

Equally sobering in this regard was the sharp increase in world food prices in 1972 and 1973 together with the uncertainty concerning future prices and availabilities. The world food price index increased from 100 in 1970 to 278 in 1974. From 1971 to 1974, U.S. prices per bushel increased from \$1.58 to \$4.68 for wheat, \$1.67 to \$3.92 for maize, and \$3.06 to \$6.68 for soybeans. Many of the country's leading planners felt this upswing in prices would continue with dire long-term implications for the country. For example, the Iranian Minister of State in Charge of Planning and Budget noted in 1977 that a shift in priorities toward agriculture was necessary because:

> The world food situation is anticipated to worsen over the next twenty years as population pressures begin to make themselves felt anew. This in turn will create scarcity conditions whereby food, even if available, will sell for very high prices. While such a scenario is by no means certain, it should be clear that from this vantage point in time there are distinct repercussions on present and future overall agricultural policies for Iran. Most important is the fact that in the face of such world uncertainties and bearing in mind the limitations (physical, climatic, social, cultural and economic) presently existing in the agricultural sector, the policy for Iran is to try and attain self-sufficiency in grains. This is indeed a challenge in that rapid industrialization must be accompanied by the maximum growth in the agricultural sector.(3)

The fact that agriculture had been given a low priority in the first four development plans had finally caught up with the government. Even though the authorities had given more emphasis to agriculture in the Fifth Plan (it allocated \$18 billion to the sector), it was too late to reverse the adverse trends that had already become established.

A final and related problem was that of rural-urban migration. This process actually had been underway since the 1930s, but was accelerating rapidly by the early 1970s. According to estimates, the yearly movement of rural workers to the cities in the mid-1970s was around 8 percent of the rural population. A widening economic gap between urban and rural dwellers stimulated much of this drift. Urban-rural differentials in average per capita income had grown over five to one during the mid-1970s. Educational opportunities, social services, and status factors given the lack of amenities in most rural areas added to the attractiveness of the urban environment.(4) These problems can ultimately be traced back to the government's programs for the rural sector in general and agriculture in particular.

LAND REFORMS

Iran's agrarian policies have usually been discussed mainly in terms of land reform. To a certain extent, therefore, much of the literature on Iran has given a distorted picture of the government's policies toward agriculture. Land reform was only one part of a more general agrarian policy which, in turn, was an outgrowth of the country's industrial strategy. Nevertheless, since the dilemmas encountered by the government in developing a consistent policy for the sector are best illustrated by its attempts at land reform, these programs are also given a relatively large amount of attention below.

Initial Conditions

For centuries, Iranian agriculture was based on a system whereby owners received a proportion of the crop from their tenants. As late as 1960, around 70 percent of the cultivated areas was farmed directly under this arrangement, with wages and other costs of the remaining 30 percent being indirectly affected.

A major criticism of the old system was that it held both landowners and peasants within set patterns, thereby slowing the introduction of better methods of farming, while the preponderance of customary holdings hindered the free transfer of land. In addition, the excessive level of rents (usually ranging from 40 to 50 percent of the crop) transferred capital badly needed by the peasants to the owners who, more often than not, used most of it unproductively or transferred it to urban investments. In short, the crop sharing practices together with many of the existing and traditional tenant-landlord relationships were impeding the sector's integration into the country's modern and rapidly expanding non-oil sector.

What is even worse is the fact that, as late as 1960, approximately three-fifths of the country's population still lived in semipoverty in the country's rural areas. Landowners possessing five hectares or less made up the largest peasant group (about 65 percent of all the landowners). This group averaged only 1.3 hectares under crop and owned the equivalent of 5 cattle. About 48 percent of these holders had no draft animals. Their productivity was thus extremely low and, as a result, they were usually in great debt with little if any surplus to market.(5)

Available estimates indicate that in 1956 the nutritional level of this group was very poor with an average caloric intake of 2,140 calories or 86 percent of their estimated daily requirements. At the same time, the protein in their diets averaged only 18 percent of their nutritional needs. This group also lived in substandard housing, heavily in debt, and at the mercy of money lenders for credit and middlemen for disposal of their crops. Their life had shown no real improvement for a number of years and, with industrial goods rising in price due to higher levels of protectionism, they actually faced an increasingly difficult time in purchasing bare necessities.

In 1960 there were 5,932,000 families with less than 5 hectares, and together with families which had livestock but no land, comprised two-thirds of the agricultural population.(6) Those in this group who found employment were usually hired as manual laborers. Thus, together with the small land holders, better than two-thirds of the rural inhabitants lived in poverty.

The next largest rural group consisted of the relatively well-to-do peasant landowners. This group accounted for about 12 percent of the landowners and farms between 10 and 20 hectares, averaging 7.5 hectares. They owned the equivalent of 11.8 cattle and had draft animals. Their incomes averaged 2.5 metric tons of grain (after their deduction of rent). In general, they averaged around three times as much land under commercial and permanent crops as did the poor peasants.

The First Two Phases

To alleviate these conditions, the first phase of the land reform program (initiated in 1962) proposed that the ownership of land per person should be limited to one village (or an equivalent amount of land scattered among a number of villages), with the rest to be distributed to the peasants. The government agreed to pay for the distributed land and the peasants were to repay the government in annual installments over a fifteen-year period. As part of the agreement, the new owners were required to accept membership in a multipurpose agricultural cooperative. There is a dispute about the exact number of villages affected by this stage of the program, with the number probably as low as only 15 percent.(7)

The second phase of the land reform program began in February 1965. A number of options were provided to the landowners in the remaining villages at that time. These included: (1) leasing their land to the peasants; (2) dividing their land with the peasants according to the ownership of labor, land, water, seed, and oxen; (3) selling their land to the peasants; (4) forming agricultural units with the peasants with shares of each group determined on the basis of the ownership of the factors; or (5) buying the peasants' rights and employing them as wage laborers.

In addition, limits were placed on the size of individual ownership except in the case of orchards, tea plantations, and existing mechanized farms up to 1,240 acres which operated without tenants. According to Lambton:

> The first state was favorable to the peasant as against the landowner and the propaganda and publicity accompanying it was uncompromisingly pro-peasant and anti-landlord. This was not the case with the second stage. When the additional articles were drafted, it was intended to regulate the relations between the peasants and the landowners, and in particular to improve the lot of these peasants who cultivated the land in villages not subject to purchase by the government under the first stage. A secondary object was to protect the position of the small landowner whose condition deteriorated under the land reform, because the peasants were in many cases withholding from them their share of the crop and who unlike the large landowners lacked the influence necessary to obtain redress or the power to coerce the peasants.(8)

A major objective of this land redistribution program was to create a rural middle class which the government would begin to use as a political base. The government also hoped that the compensations paid to the landlords would provide funds for investment in industry, thus eventually creating a modern, urban middle class upon which the country's growth would be oriented.

Rural cooperatives (in which membership was mandatory for peasants receiving land) had been envisaged by the designers of the program as productive units that would replace the traditional marketing institutions. The original intent was for the cooperatives to be run by the peasant shareholders with a certain amount of managerial assistance provided by the state. As things worked out, the appointed managers eventually dominated the decision-making process in most of the cooperatives.

The first two phases of the land reform program affected about a million households; i.e., less than one-third of the peasant households acquired land (either through the implementation of the first phase or through the second or third of the above options). About a million households (44 percent of the peasant households) became tenants and about 81,000 households (2.5 percent of the peasant households) acquired shares in the newly formed agricultural units. More than 20 percent of the rural households were, therefore, totally bypassed by the land reform program.(9) In addition, about a million landless households were excluded from the categories of persons to whom land might be transferred. Aside from these limitations, the first two phases of the land reform program represented a positive move toward the creation of tenancies in place of the old peasant landlord system. The program also represented a significant attack on the power of large landowners. In fact, the first two stages of the land reform are generally credited with eliminating the landlord class as a political and social force in rural Iran.

The economic impact of the land reform, however, seems to have been unfavorable. Production was disrupted as some of the best lands were divided into small holdings, and agricultural investment may have fallen in the 1960s. In fact, because the economic aims of the reform were not explicitly specified, government agencies and departments never agreed on a target model of agricultural organization to replace the village system.

In terms of the redistributive effect of the land reform program, it is clear that, over time, a number of factors would come into play to determine the ultimate distribution of rural income and wealth. The process would most likely be quite complex but, as an approximation of the impact of the reform, a practical approach using existing data is to estimate the discounted income streams of the peasant and landlord based on: (1) the final price of the distributed land, (2) the amount of distributed land, and (3) the terms on which the former landlord was compensated and the new peasant owner obligated to pay the government. From this information, Askari made a rough estimate of the relative attractiveness of different income streams to the original landowner. Using a discount rate of 15 percent (the assumed opportunity cost of capital), he found that the landowner was better off before land reform, but that the redistributional impact of the Iranian land reform was quite mild compared with several others in the Middle East.(10)

The Third Phase

The third phase of the land reform program began in January 1966. Its major objective was to set guidelines for establishing private farm corporations. As such, it was an extension of the fourth option mentioned above (in conjunction with the second phase). Emphasis in the third phase was on the modernization of agriculture through mechanization, better seeds, the increased use of chemical fertilizers, and the creation of agro-industrial enterprises. When examined in conjunction with the previous phases, it is clear the third phase marked an abrupt shift of emphasis from the break-up of large landholdings (the proposed goal of the first two phases) to a reconsolidation of the small peasant holdings for the purpose of creating farm corporations.

Although the third phase of the land reform program was largely an attempt to eliminate the tenancy relations which the second stage had failed to deal with effectively, it happened to coincide with the government's move toward creating farm corporations to facilitate mechanization of farming and increased agricultural productivity. As things worked out, the conflict between these two objectives caught a number of peasants in the middle. These farmers were actually forced to transfer the use of their land permanently to the corporation in exchange for shares equivalent to the value of their land and other farm assets. This was seen by many observers as a reversal of the land redistribution program. The peasants resented the fact that they had not only ceased to be landowners but were reverted to their previous social status of being mere agricultural laborers.(11)

The Fourth Phase

Finally, a fourth phase (1966) anticipated that the leaseholds created by option one above should be either divided between landowner and peasant according to the fourth option in the second phase or sold to the peasants. Part of the problem lay in the fact that, while the third phase had set the guidelines for establishment of the farm corporations, the results of the first two phases of the land reform program meant one-third of the peasant households remained eligible as potential shareholders of the proposed farm corporations. Forty-four percent of the households had reached tenancy agreements with their respective landlords and, as such, were not eligible to form farm corporations. It was against this background that the fourth phase of the land reform program was formulated and introduced.

The task of the fourth phase was to increase the number of peasant households that could form a farm corporation. Two points about farm corporations should be particularly noted. First, the exchange of the peasants' permanent farming rights for ownership of paper shares paved the road for the concentration of shares because the large shareholders could buy the shares of the less well-to-do peasants. Second, the fact that these corporations had been controlled by paid employees of the government created much doubt about the whole program among the peasants who traditionally had been suspicious of the government.

As the fourth phase unfolded, a major shift from the original land reform strategy became apparent. Originally, the reform was to be followed up by the provision of marketing and technological services. By the time of the fourth phase, however, the government decided that small-scale farming was inefficient. Traditional small farms and land reform farms began to be combined into large farm corporations run by the government, and large central towns were to concentrate services and administration for all the farming units. Villages which were not considered adequately productive were left out of the plan and no investments were allocated to them. The intent of the government was to let these villages simply collapse economically releasing their workers for jobs in more productive areas.(12)

In any case, the corporations themselves were designed to be more labor efficient than traditional farms, releasing even more peasants for urban industrial employment. On virgin lands and especially on land made available below the new dams, private foreign and domestic investors were encouraged to establish new agro-industrial complexes. Inducements such as the exemption from income taxes, easy credit, and grants covering up to 85 percent of irrigation system costs, 50 percent of the cost of wells, and 20 to 60 percent of reclaiming land were available. Finally, there was no limit placed on the size of these farms. Eventually, fertilizer costs were subsidized, generous price supports were introduced, and guaranteed government purchase of commodities was implemented.

The government's policy, therefore, finally evolved into one subjecting the small holding peasantry to bureaucratic control, while driving large numbers of farm families off the land,(13) thereby emptying whole villages while encouraging foreign agricultural investment on the choice irrigated lands and (on a selective and political basis) even offering lavish inducements to some of the large owners who still remained to increase the capitalization of their farms.

The land reform laws can be summarized as follows(14):

1. For the first time in history, the boundary of the Persian village as a complete and integrated social and economic unit was to be broken for corporations which included more than one village.
2. The ownership of land was converted into the ownership of paper shares - the peasant had no right to dispose of his land, only his shares.

3. They paved the way for concentration of share ownership so it would be only a matter of time before small shareholders began to sell to the large ones. Hence,a refrom policy that had begun with the express purpose of breaking up large ownership of land was, in a few years, converted to one of favoring concentration.
4. They made absenteeism once again possible. The large shareholder could now afford to live in the nearby town making money while the army of landless peasants (unaffected by the terms of the reform) would provide labor for cultivation.
5. They made it easier for the government departments to extend their control over productive activity and rural life in general. For, in spite of the unusual constitutional trimmings - shareholders' meetings, boards of governors, etc. - the corporations were run by urban bureaucrats appointed by the state.

Craig, in his case study of a village before and after land reform in the Fars Province, concluded that:

> The While Revolution undeniably changed the status quo between 1965 and 1973; land titles changed hands, the kadkhuda (the village headman) and the landlord were excused from village affairs, and new institutions were established. However, in many ways the changes came full circle and several of the pre-reform problems remained unsolved 10 years after the reform. While at the outset there had been optimism and cooperation on the villager's part, there was now factionalism, stratification and disenchantment with the government. What the political impact of these frustrated expectations will be remains to be gauged.(15)

How did these things happen? Was it by government design or did things just evolve? The evolution theory seems the most accurate explanation. The reform laws contained many loopholes. In all phases, choice land was exempted; many landlords succeeded in transferring land to family or friends; however, a few had enough influence to escape reform entirely, and much land was wrongly declared "mechanized" allowing landlords to retain ownership. Hence, only a small segment of Iranian land belonging to large owners was brought up by the government for redistribution.

By the end of the reform period, noncultivating owners had held on to almost half of Iran's cultivatible land. If the spirit of the first phase of reform, promoted by the agriculture minister Arsanjani, who favored "land to the tiller" and effective rural cooperative societies, had been carried through its later phases, Iran's reforms might have been successful.(16) Instead, it brought villagers few economic benefits, it did not improve production, and it allowed bureaucrats to replace landlords as local authorities.

There were at least two paths which the reform could have followed while still remaining within the framework of a market economy. The first, which would have largely served the interest of the peasantry, was to nationalize all landed property or, somewhat less drastic, transfer the large estates to the cultivators with nominal compensation payments to the previous owners. Presumably, the new owners given technical and financial support by the government would be the foundation for a modern, efficient, market-oriented agricultural sector. Other countries that have pursued this approach have, in quickly eliminating all remmants of the past, experienced falling production during the transition period of adjustment and institution building. In the longer run, their agricultural sectors have often been more dynamic than would have been the case with a more cautious approach.

The second and more conservative approach would have been to make some concessions to the peasants without fundamentally altering the power of the large landowners or their role in affecting the allocation of resources in rural areas. Rhetoric aside, in retrospect it appears this was the strategy the government either decided to adopt or allowed to evolve.

OTHER MEASURES OF PERFORMANCE

A number of other agricultural policies have been referred to such as price controls, credit, and the like. The details of individual programs are not particularly important at this time, having been covered in detail elsewhere.(17) Their impacts or outcomes are of interest, however, and include productivity, innovations, distribution of rural income, distribution of credit, farm debt, and rural urban organization. These are examined in greater detail below.

Productivity Change

Arable farming in Iran at this time was dominated by the production of staple food crops. In particular, production of wheat covered about 60 percent of the sown area; and wheat and barley together accounted for 75 percent of the area under cultivation. It follows that the performance of wheat and barley production was a decisive factor in determining the overall performance of this sector. The remaining 25 percent of arable land was planted in a wide variety of crops including rice, cotton, tobacco, pulses, oil seeds, fruits, vegetables, and the like, each accounting for a relatively small share of the total. From the point of view of peasant welfare, and productivity performance in general, therefore, improvements in wheat and barley production were of major importance.

Unfortunately, there are no figures for labor productivity or total productivity change for those two crops. There are, however, statistics on land productivity. These show that, during the period in which land reform was taking place, there was little if any increase in the output per acre in either of these crops between 1950 and 1975. This pattern persisted even though markets were expanding rapidly and the introduction of modern inputs into the sector was proceeding systematically.

In terms of the efficiency of large agricultural units, a 1977 study indicated that in that year the large units occupying 100 hectares and more comprised 2 percent of the land and produced 6 percent of the agricultural output.(18) At the same time, however, medium sized units of 10 to 100 hectares comprised less than half the available land, but produced three-fourths of the country's agricultural output.

As noted above, cooperatives were seen as a vehicle to provide technical assistance, subsidized inputs, and credits to small (under 10 hectares) and fragmented units. However, the cooperative movement was not adequately funded or staffed nor was it backed by market incentives. Many small holders remained unaffiliated or only nominal members. These farmers continued to rely on noninstitutional sources of credit and commercial outlets for both their production and purchases. The rural cooperatives were also slow to adopt new techniques or to increase their use of modern inputs. In fact, the performance of these organizations was a major factor responsible not only for the stagnation in improved yields but also for yields well below those in most other Middle Eastern countries.

In marked contrast to the large rural cooperatives, a flourishing subsector consisting of 400,000 medium to large-sized farms (10 hectares and larger) had developed by mid-1970s. These farms produced for the market and tended to respond quickly to market conditions. While including fewer than 15 percent of the families owning farms, these farmers cultivated 50 percent of Iran's agricultural lands and accounted for 70 to 80 percent of the country's marketed surplus of agricultural goods. These independent commercial farms were quick to adopt new fertilizers, sink deep tube wells for an assured water supply, and to employ mechanical equipment - and this in the face of neglect by the Iranian government in determining price, credit extension, and other policies.(19)

Innovations

The government, nonetheless, continued to experiment with different forms of new rural organizations. The three that received the most lavish attention were agribusiness, farm corporations, and production cooperatives. Agribusinesses were envisaged by the government as becoming large-scale, centrally directed, and vertically integrated farms, employing wage labor and using advanced techniques and scientific planning. Four were actually established on 68,000 hectares in the Dez irrigation project in Khuzestan province. They were foreign-owned, and receiving assured supplies of water and subsidies denied to smaller private projects. They were rationalized largely on the grounds that they offered the best chance for creating employment, assuring rapid increases in output, and they were also expected to serve as a catalyst for modernization in rural areas. The agribusiness experiment was abandoned in 1976 as being complex, too costly, and unsuited to local physical and social conditions.(20)

Farm corporations were formed from amalgamations of smaller farms. The aim, as in the agribusiness model, was to establish units large enough to benefit from centralized management, efficient use of farm machinery, and other economies of scale. Members were to yield permanent use of their lands in return for shares in the corporation. In addition to dividends, shareholders would receive wages for their labor time. The corporations were usually established only in districts in which good land and water were available.(21) Again, the efforts of the government to promote this concept were not really successful for, by 1976, only 89 farm corporations with a membership of 33,663 (1 percent of the rural households) had been established. As noted above, the peasants who chose to join them received shares in the profit (if any) of the corporation in exchange for giving up their farming right to the land. While the former farmers were supposed to be employed as wage laborers by the corporation, this proved impossible in the areas where modern irrigation, cultivation, and harvest techniques were being increasingly adopted. The result was to aggravate the already widespread unemployment.

The production cooperative was the final innovation designed during this period to attain benefits of scale and centralized planning. In this scheme, members retained ownership and the right to use their lands, buying their own inputs and services and marketing output on their own financial account. As in the traditional village, cooperative members would collaborate in seeding and harvesting while leaving routine daily operations to the individual unit. As a testament to their lack of acceptance by the peasants, less than 30 of these units were in operation in 1976.

In general, therefore, despite repeated attempts, the government failed to create a viable, economically profitable farming organization that was generally acceptable to the peasants. All their efforts failed on one or more of the above counts.

In general, the experiments were disastrous both politically and economically. Agricultural production lagged and there were many bankruptcies. At the end of the Fifth Plan period, Iranian agriculture was in a shambles with many small holding peasants now seriously deterred from improving their farms and many others, just as bewildered, crowding the streets of the Iranian cities.

Distribution of Income

The land reform program did not really bring about a more equal distribution of land among the rural population. For one thing, as noted above, the program did not apply at all to at least a million landless peasant households. Even those affected remained relatively far behind the more affluent landlords. When the program had been completed, the cultivated land (about 8.6 million hectares in 1974) had been distributed among 3.6 million production units, i.e., about 2.4 hectares per unit. Out of this total, 150,000 hectares (about 1.7 percent) consisted of land cultivated by 320 large agricultural units (including the agribusinesses formed by private foreign and domestic investors, farm corporations, government projects, production cooperatives, and large commercial farmers). The large commercial farms in this group were mostly owned by the landlords not affected by the land reform program. At the other extreme were around 800,000 landless peasants and about a million small farmers who cultivated on the average about one hectare of irrigated and dry lands each. In the middle there were around 645,000 medium-sized production units. While representing about 18 percent of the agricultural production units, these farms accounted for more than 58 percent of the total irrigated land and 52 percent of the total cultivated land of the country.(22) While income distribution data is not available by farm size, it could not have differed significantly from this very unequal pattern of land ownership.

Distribution of Credit

Immediately after the implementation of the land reform program, peasants who received land were required to become members of rural cooperative societies. One of the benefits of membership was supposedly the financial assistance. By 1976, 2,886 rural cooperative societies with a membership of about 2.9 million peasant households had been formed.

Despite the growth of cooperatives, agribusinesses received about 18 percent of the government's disbursements to agriculture during the 1968-76 period. The share of rural cooperatives and farm corporations, while encompassing more than 90 percent of peasant households, declined from 16 percent in 1973 to 9 percent in 1974 and finally to about 8 percent of the disbursements in 1978.

The unequal distribution of total agricultural credit shows up clearly in the distribution of farm capital between the corporations and the cooperatives with the average capital per household in a corporation over 400 times greater than that of a household member of a cooperative. In 1976 about one-third of total agricultural capital was owned by about 1 percent of the landholding peasants. This is not only a reflection of gross unevenness of the distribution of government credit but the concentration of ownership where 1.2 percent of cultivating households owned the shares of 10 percent of the sown area.(23)

Farm Debt

From the official figures shown in table 4.1, it is clear that there was no real peasant savings in the years for which we have data (1971, 1972). Even if the entire government credit was spent on consumption in 1971, there was still a deficit of consumption over income for this group and clearly a mounting debt burden.

Table 4.1. Iran: Peasant Consumption and Deficits

(1,000 million rials)

	1970	1971
(1) Total value added in agriculture (current prices)	163.1	177.8
(2) Aggregate peasant consumption	160.5	191.2
(3) Difference (1) - (2)	2.6	- 13.4
(4) Total government credit to peasants	8.9	10.3
(5) Total capital availability (3) + (4)	11.5	- 3.1
(6) Minimum credit required for productive	70.0	70.0
(7) Total income deficit	- 58.5	- 73.1

Source: M. A. Katouzian, "Land Reform in Iran: A Case Study in the Political Economy of Social Engineering," Journal of Peasant Studies (January 1974).

Rural-Urban Migration

As noted several times, the land reform process undoubtedly hastened the movement of population from rural to urban areas. First, a large number of the peasants excluded from the land redistribution chose to become urban rather than rural workers. Second, many other peasants given title to parcels of land too small to be profitable sold their property and migrated. In addition, the children of better off farmers increasingly preferred the opportunities of Iran's population centers to the drab life of the village.

While the land reform stabilized the position of small landholders and created a new rural middle class, it tended to polarize the social structure of the rural society more than ever.

> [The rural wage laborers or Khosheneshins] have always been the poorest, most insecure and dispossessed group in the peasant class and they have suffered severely from the lack of steady employment. The land reform programme was formulated to assist the nasaqadars, who were the only peasants to receive land. The Khosheneshins were left outside the entire plan and as a result their situation has steadily deteriorated where that of the new peasant proprietor has to some degree improved.(24)

Not surprisingly then, the Khosheneshins were the first rural group to migrate to the cities. However, other groups began to follow them as a result of the increase in urban jobs created by the government's industrialization strategy.

The regime's failure to effectively fill the organizational and physical vacuum created by the half-hearted land reforms combined with its neglect of agricultural investment created many disenchanted and disappointed landless peasants with little option but to look for work in the fast growing industrial centers. Unfortunately, reliable figures for the rate of rural-urban migration are not available. However, if we assume that the population of urban areas would have increased at the country's rate of population, the annual number of rural-urban migrants can be calculated as growing by 78 percent during 1966-76 as compared with the 1956-66 period. In other words, while migrants comprised 44 percent of the increase in population of urban areas between 1956 and 1966, the migrants accounted for as much as 50 percent of the increase in the urban population during the 1966-76 period.

Other factors responsible for rural-urban migration in Iran included:

- population pressure in the villages caused by high birth rates and relatively low death rates, resulting in outmigration when the amount of cultivable land and/or the level of productivity was remaining constant;
- technological advance and the mechanization of agriculture, causing unemployment or underemployment among farmers;
- soil erosion, drought, and the ownership system increasing rural poverty;
- the development of transport, mass media, and the increase in literacy making more information available about alternatives to rural life and increasing dissatisfactions among the rural population;
- the concentration of employment opportunities in city-based industries and services, widening the economic gap between the city and countryside.

The consequent shortage of field hands and especially tractor drivers and mechanics in some areas forced wages to go up for those who remained but not enough to really slow migration. In turn, manpower deficits helped to boost the costs of agricultural production.

CONCLUSIONS

Only belatedly did agricultural production and food policy gain prominence in the development planning of the country. Either because national prosperity was linked to oil exports or officials saw the path to development largely in terms of rapid industrialization, the agricultural sector rated only minor attention at best, and until around 1960 was largely allowed to languish. The government seemed to accept the vision of a consumption-oriented urban society as the key to national prosperity and power which would sustain the country into a future of declining oil income. With this long-run strategy in mind, the planners apparently expected the agricultural sector to play, at most, a supportive role in supplying needed raw materials, manpower, and food.

Massive poverty, general dissatisfaction with prevailing conditions, and the sluggish growth of agricultural production, however, made unrest in the rural areas an imminent danger, forcing the government in 1961 to initiate a land reform program with the twofold objectives of: (1) modernizing Iranian agriculture, and (2) removing the danger of a peasant uprising.

Under the government's programs, the organization of agricultural production in Iran became increasingly complex and unsatisfactory all the way up to the time of the revolution. The land reforms effectively undermined the village system of organization, but the government did not attempt to shape developments in the rural area to an overall strategy or plan. Rather, a number of conflicting organizing principles were introduced by design and some by default. If one were to choose only one economic factor that led to the revolution, it would have to be the government's failure to design and implement a coherent strategy for this sector.

The political consequences of the country's agricultural policies were not entirely due to the disappointment of expectations or the reaction to waste. The most serious political consequences were due to particular aspects of the government's development policy and its administration.

> In the most general sense, Iran's development policy was in the image of Saint-Simon and Pareto. Future shock was considered virtuous, the goal of rational modernization, to be pressed forward ruthlessly by means of science, technology, planning and despotic authority. No element of tradition, no personal desire, no aesthetic value, no religious qualm, no philosophic hesitancy was to stand in the way.(25)

And as Binder concludes:

> I am inclined to believe that the extent of the opposition to the Shah was not primarily because of his repressive treatment of the opposition, but because of the outrageous simplemindedness of his modernization programs which attacked the quiescent and made political activists of them. The Shah had gone out and created a mass opposition and therewith a responsive audience for the small groups of extremists on the right and the left who had taken up arms against the regime.(26)

5 Momentum and Decline

INTRODUCTION

In contrast to neoclassical predictions that economic growth would spread throughout the world as the advanced countries grew, the record has shown that relatively few developing countries have managed to sustain respectable rates of growth in per capita income, let alone to achieve rates sufficient for narrowing the gap between themselves and the more advanced countries.(1) Iran, of course, was an exception to this pattern throughout most of the period under consideration, sustaining high and even accelerating rates of real economic growth after the stabilization program of the early 1960s.

Industry, which was the leading sector in the rapid expansion of the non-oil economy, seemed to have lost its dynamism by the latter 1970s, however, while the growth of agriculture did not attain rates to either counteract or stem the reduced industrial expansion. Logically, at least two alternative explanations are possible. The first attributes industry's slowdown mainly to short-run phenomena, largely of a political nature, while the second theory views the stagnation tendencies in the late 1970s as a natural result of the development strategy adopted by the government particularly during the period of high growth.

This view stresses that the type of industries selected and the inducements used to channel investment into various areas created an environment whereby it was impossible to sustain the momentum built up in the 1960s and further stimulated by the oil price increases in 1973-74. By 1977 the economy began what was to be an irreversible deceleration toward stagnation.

In large part, the chapters that follow are an attempt to determine the mechanisms underlying the demise of the Iranian economy. As an initial step in this direction, a macroeconomic framework is developed below to identify some of the more important economic trends at work both before and after the oil price increases of 1973.(2) Despite the very aggregate nature of the data, several patterns identified are suggestive of the broad forces underlying the country's growth and decline.

CHANGES IN NATIONAL INCOME AND PER CAPITA INCOME

Iran was one of the world's fastest growing countries in terms of gross national product during the 1959-77 period.(3) In current prices, GNP increased from 282.6 billion rials in 1959 to 1,231.5 billion rials in 1972 and 5,342.6 billion in 1977 or a rate of annual increase of 6.3, 14.6, and 30.7 percent per annum for the periods 1959-63, 1963-72, and 1973-77, respectively (see table 5.1). The corresponding figures for GDP in constant 1959 prices were 5.6, 11.5, and 12.6 percent for the initial, middle, and latter periods. Per capita urban income in constant prices also showed a steady increase of 2.1, 6.1, and 3.2 for those periods. Rural per capita income, on the other hand, showed the least satisfactory expansion with average annual rates of 1.5, -0.03, and 3.0 for each of the three subperiods. Several patterns stand out.

1. As a result of rapidly increasing oil revenues, the share of non-oil GDP in the gross national product fell from around 90 percent in 1959-63 to 81 percent in 1972, 70 percent in 1973, and finally 66 percent in 1977.
2. High growth was also associated with increases in the standard of living as indicated by the rapid increase in per capita urban consumption.
3. The stagnation of rural incomes was particularly pronounced in the 1963-72 period when, as noted, per capita rural income actually showed a 0.03 percent average annual decline.
4. As a result of rapidly expanding urban incomes, the urban-rural income gap widened rapidly during this period, with the ratio of urban to rural incomes increasing from 2.13 in 1959 to levels of 3.81 in both 1973 and 1976.
5. Since the rate of rural-urban migration was rapid during this period, the rate of urban consumption was expanding even more rapidly over that in rural areas than the per capita figures indicate.
6. By 1976 the rural sector was producing 9.4 percent of the country's GNP with 56.0 percent of the population, while

Table 5.1. National Income Trends, 1959-1977
(billions of rials)

	1959	1963	1972	1973	1977	Average Annual Growth 1959-1963	1963-1972	1973-1977
Gross Domestic Product (current)	299.1	394.2	1,268.4	1,868.6	5,393.3	7.2	13.9	30.3
Gross National Product (current)	282.6	360.3	1,231.5	1,832.7	5,347.6	6.3	14.6	30.7
Non-Oil GDP (current prices)	256.6	323.5	1,001.4	1,281.1	3,549.8	6.0	13.4	29.0
Gross Domestic Product (constant prices)*	299.1	371.5	985.7	1,372.7	2,208.8	5.6	11.5	12.6
Non-Oil GDP (constant prices)	256.6	304.8	635.8	735.7	1,453.8	4.4	8.5	18.6
Per Capita Consumption (urban) (constant prices)	14.923	16.213	27.542	31.843	40.789**	2.1	6.1	3.7
Per Capita Consumption (rural) (constant prices)	7.012	7.443	7.423	8.351	8.706**	1.5	-0.3	3.0
Non-Oil GDP/GNP	0.91	0.90	0.81	0.70	0.66	-0.3	-1.2	-3.6
Urban/Rural	2.13	2.18	3.71	3.81	3.81	0.6	6.1	0.0

*Gross Domestic Product at constant prices = GDP deflated by export price deflator industrialized countries
**Figures for 1976.

Source: Computed from data in Bank Markazi Iran, Annual Report, various issues.

the urban sector produced 53.6 percent of the GNP with only 44.0 percent of the population. The petroleum sector produced 37.0 percent of the GNP with an insignificant proportion of the population.

7. If we assume that the contribution of each sector to national output is roughly equivalent to its income, then the average income in rural areas would have been around $250 whereas that of urban areas was $1,830.
8. If the urban sector were assumed to receive the entire contribution of oil as its income (which of course was not the case), then income per head in that sector would have been as high as $3,079. Because a considerable portion of the oil revenues did wind up directly or indirectly as additional urban income, a rough estimate of urban income as ten times as high as that in rural areas in 1976 is fairly realistic. The distribution of this income is, of course, most important and is dealt with in more detail below.

In sum, it appears that there was a great improvement in the average standard of living in the urban areas. Increased incomes more or less kept up with the growth in GNP. In spite of substantial migration toward the urban centers, however, rural income increases were still well below the increases in GNP. The result was a widening gap between incomes in urban and rural areas.

PATTERNS OF DEMAND

A number of macroeconomic relationships can be used to characterize the various subperiods under consideration. These relationships are based on the Keynesian theory of effective demand and income determination, whereby ex post over actual aggregate supply is equal to aggregate demand.

In symbols these relationships are depicted as:

$$(1) \quad Y + M = C + I + X(4)$$

where Y = gross domestic product; M = imports of goods and services; C = aggregate (private plus government) consumption of goods and services; I = aggregate investment (private plus government including net increase in stocks); X = exports of goods and services. The left side of (1) is aggregate supply (Y + M). This term depicts the total resources available to the economy at any given time. The right hand side (C + I + X) is aggregate demand or the sum of claims on available resources during the same period. Implied in the relationship is some sort of adjustment process so that ex post supplies will equal demand. Rearranging (1) yields:

(2) $Y = C + I + (X - M)$

where (X - M) is a summary of the economy's balance of payments.

The balance of payments are, in turn, equal to the sum of: (1) net transfers, and (2) the net change in the foreign balance (or the nation's portfolio of foreign assets), or

$X - M = TR + F$

where TR = net transfers and F = net change in the foreign balance. Substituting into (1) yields:

(3) $Y = C + I + TR + F$

where (C + I) = domestic absorption, and (TR + F) = external absorption. With (Y + M) = aggregate supply, the patterns of domestic absorption, external absorption, public expenditure (government investment plus consumption), and private expenditure (private consumption plus investment) underwent several significant changes during the 1960s and 1970s.

CONSUMPTION AND SAVINGS

Both consumption and savings underwent significant changes during the period under consideration, the most noticeable of which included:

- the acceleration in real private expenditures from increases of 4.2 percent per annum for 1959-63 to 8.3 percent for 1963-72 and finally to 11.1 percent for 1973-77 (table 5.2);
- the even faster expansion of real government consumption expenditures from an average annual rate of increase of 5.7 percent per annum from 1959 to 1963 to 19.3 percent from 1963 to 1972, and finally at 19.6 percent per annum from 1973 to 1977;
- since both gross national product and non-GDP increased at rates faster than private consumption, the latter declined as a proportion of GNP from 74.1 in 1959 to 72.7 in 1963 to 55.8 in 1971, and all the way down to 48.0 percent in 1977;
- with the decline of consumption savings increased from 15.1 to 59.5 percent of GNP by 1977 with the greatest gains coming between 1973 and 1977 (a 5.0 percent average annual increase in percent of savings to GNP).

Table 5.2. Patterns of Consumption and Saving, 1959-1977 (billions of rials)

	1959	1963	1972	1973	1977	Average Annual Growth 1959-1963	1963-1972	1973-1977
Private Consumption (current prices)	209.4	262.1	686.6	879.7	2,160.8	5.8	11.3	25.2
Government Consumption (current prices)	30.5	40.3	252.6	325.4	1,073.8	7.2	22.6	34.8
Total Consumption (current prices)	239.9	302.4	939.2	1,205.1	3,234.6	6.0	13.4	28.0
Private Consumption (constant prices)	209.4	247.0	504.4	580.9	885.0	4.2	8.3	11.1
Government Consumption (constant prices)	30.5	38.0	185.6	214.9	439.8	5.7	19.3	19.6
Savings	42.7	57.9	292.3	627.6	2,113.0	7.9	19.7	35.5
Private Consumption/GNP	74.1	72.7	55.8	48.0	40.4	-0.5	-2.9	-4.2
Government Consumption/GNP	10.8	11.2	20.5	17.8	20.1	0.9	6.9	3.1
Private Consumption/Non-oil GDP	81.6	81.0	68.6	68.7	60.9	-0.2	-1.8	-3.0
Government Consumption/Non-oil GDP	11.9	12.5	25.2	25.4	30.2	1.2	8.1	4.4
Savings/GNP	15.1	17.9	23.7	49.0	59.5	4.3	3.2	5.0
Government Consumption/Private Consumption	14.6	15.4	36.7	37.0	49.7	1.3	10.1	7.7

Source: Computed from data in Bank Markazi Iran, Annual Report, various issues.

From these trends it appears that the government, as the sole recipient of oil revenues, was able to increase its command over resources faster than the private sector was able to increase its expenditure out of wage income. It is not apparent from these why the decline in private sector consumption (as a proportion of total income) took place so fast.(5) One plausible explanation is that the private sector was not able to adjust to the inflation that was building up in the 1970s as rapidly as was the government. On the other hand, the expanded scope of import controls in the 1960s and early 1970s, together with increased physical impediments to imports after 1973, may have hindered the ability of consumers to adjust consumption to their growing incomes. On both grounds, it is easy to see why the share of private consumption to non-oil income fell so drastically in the mid to late 1970s.

INVESTMENT

Several of the more important patterns of investment include:

1. Government investment expenditures rose from 20.1 billion rials in 1963 to 143.4 billion in 1972 to 1,055.1 billion in 1977 (table 5.3). The ratio of government investment to GNP also increased from 8.6 percent in 1963 to 14.5 percent in 1977. Of special note is the higher rate of government over private investment expenditures.
2. Private investment increased from 31.1 billion rials in 1963 to 144.0 billion in 1972 to 776.8 billion in 1977. The share of private investment to GNP remained fairly stable between 8.9 and 11.7 percent over the period 1963-72 then rose to 14.5 percent in 1977. Similar trends were apparent for the private investment/non-oil GDP ratio.
3. The ratio of private investment to public investment declined substantially from 1.53 in 1963 to 1.00 in 1972 to 0.74 in 1977. The ratio of machinery to construction investment increased considerably from 0.37 in 1963 to 0.65 in 1972 only to fall to 0.54 in 1977.
4. The above figures suggest a major structural change around 1963 in the role of the public sector. Thus, during the post-1963 period, the growth of both government investment and government consumption were for the first time considerably greater than their private sector counterparts and undoubtedly a result of the rise in government oil revenues during this period.

In fact, oil revenues enabled most of the expenditure components of GNP to increase at not only rapidly but at accelerating rates during the 1963-77 period. Further, the public

Table 5.3. Patterns of Investment (billions of rials)

	1959	1963	1972	1973	1977	Average Annual Growth 1959-1963	1963-1972	1973-1977
Total Investment (current prices)	49.8	51.5	287.4	363.3	1,831.9	0.8	21.0	49.9
Total Private Investment (current prices)	31.9	31.1	144.0	160.4	776.8	-0.6	18.6	48.3
Total Government Investment (current prices)	20.8	20.4	143.4	202.9	1,055.1	-0.5	24.2	51.0
Total Investment: Machinery (current prices)	31.4	37.7	174.5	223.2	1,192.2	4.7	18.6	52.0
Total Investment: Construction (current prices)	21.3	13.8	112.9	140.1	639.7	-10.3	26.3	46.2
Total Investment (current prices)	49.8	48.5	211.1	239.9	750.3	-0.7	17.8	33.0
Private/Government Investment	1.53	1.52	1.00	0.79	0.74	-0.2	-4.5	-7.3
Private Investment/Non-oil GDP	11.3	9.6	14.4	12.5	21.9	-4.0	4.6	15.0
Government Investment/Non-oil GDP	8.1	6.3	14.3	15.8	29.7	-6.1	9.5	17.1
Construction/Machinery	0.68	0.37	0.65	0.63	0.54	-14.1	6.5	-3.8
Private Investment/GNP	12.4	8.6	11.7	8.8	14.5	-8.7	3.5	13.3
Government Investment/GNP	7.4	5.7	11.6	11.1	19.7	-6.3	8.2	15.4

Source: Computed from data in Bank Markazi Iran, _Annual Report_, various issues.

sector was able to sustain a much higher overall rate of growth during this period than the private sector, again undoubtedly attributable to the increased resources at the government's disposal. The economic analysis in later chapters indicates that expansion of government expenditures further stimulated the growth of the private sector through the 1963-77 period, especially with regard to private investment.

EXPORTS AND IMPORTS

The export sector experienced several notable trends.

1. Total exports of goods and services rose very rapidly in the 1963-73 period and especially in 1973-74. They leveled off at over 30 percent of GNP in the latter 1970s (table 5.4).
2. Both oil exports and non-oil exports had similar growth paths during the 1959-73 period. In particular, both experienced growth rates that doubled during 1967-72 over those achieved in the 1962-67 period.
3. While non-oil exports were able to expand in line with those of the oil sector during the period up to 1973 (albeit from a much lower base), they did not play a significant role after 1973.
4. The inability of non-oil exports to make a major contribution to Iran's foreign exchange earnings, given the emphasis placed on developing alternative sources of non-oil exports, began to cause many observers to question the viability of the country's long-term development strategy.
5. The ability of the oil and non-oil exports to finance imports declined in the period 1963-67 only to climb slightly in the period 1967-72 before reaching its post-1973 plateau.

While the non-oil export performance of Iran was acceptable up to 1973, it was clear that manufacturing was not moving in the direction of establishing a comparative advantage in any of the major industries that the government counted on as eventually replacing oil exports, a matter of serious concern given the fact that both oil production and revenues were expected to begin declining in the mid-1980s.

The growth of oil revenues during the period up to 1973 was a result of a rapid rate of reserve depletion rather than higher oil prices. The rise in per barrel oil revenues during 1960-70 was meager indeed, increasing from $0.80 in 1960 to $0.86 in 1970. Nevertheless, as a result of OPEC's actions, Iran's per barrel revenues increased to $1.25 in 1971 and to $1.36 in 1972.

Table 5.4. Patterns of Imports and Exports
(billions of rials)

	1959	1963	1972	1973	1977	Rates of Growth 1959-1963	1963-1972	1973-1977
Exports (current price)	60.2	80.0	308.5	654.9	1,815.2	7.4	16.2	12.0
Total Imports (current price)	50.8	39.7	266.7	354.7	1,488.4	-6.0	23.6	43.1
Intermediate Good Imports/Total	49.2	55.5	62.1	60.8	54.2	3.1	1.3	-1.3
Capital Good Imports/Total	20.6	20.3	25.0	24.2	27.2	-0.4	2.3	-3.0
Consumer Good Imports/Total	30.2	24.1	12.9	14.9	18.6	-5.5	-6.7	5.7
Exports (constant price)	60.2	75.4	239.7	481.1	743.4	5.8	13.7	11.5
Imports (constant price)	50.8	38.9	195.6	216.8	600.9	-6.5	19.7	29.0
Exports/GNP (current price)	21.3	22.2	25.1	35.7	33.9	1.0	1.4	-1.3
Imports/GNP (current price)	18.0	11.0	21.7	19.4	27.8	-11.6	7.8	9.4

Note: Constant price exports and current price exports deflated with the price index of exports from the industrial countries. Real imports are current price imports deflated with the Iranian wholesale price index.

Source: Based on data from Bank Markazi Iran, Annual Report, various issues.

Imports were characterized by:

1. An initial decline in the recession years of the late 1950s and early 1960s, followed by an expansion somewhat faster than GNP during the rest of the decade. They accelerated at a much faster pace than GNP in the 1970s, especially after 1973.
2. A sharp increase in capital and intermediate goods imports between 1963-67, leveling off to the GNP growth rate during 1967-77.
3. The relative importance of capital and intermediate goods imports in the country's trade reflecting the extended efforts made during this period toward import substitution over a wide range of consumer goods products.
4. Consumer goods imports rising very slowly during the period 1963-67 and then accelerating in the period after 1967. Thus the ratio of this category to GNP declined from 2.6 percent in 1963 to 2.0 percent in 1967, and then rose slightly to 2.5 percent in 1973 and 4 percent in 1977. The increased importance of consumer goods imports after 1973 was due in large part to the growth of foreign supplies of basic food items.
5. Net imports of services rising at a very rapid pace, averaging at an annual rate of over 40 percent for the period after 1963. These imports were associated not only with stepped up military purchases abroad but also reflected the growing sophistication of the country's technology and productive structure.

In sum, the composition of imports shifted rather markedly over the 1959-77 period as the share of consumer goods imports first declined with the rise in capital and intermediate goods, then rose in the post-1973 period along with net imports of services. Overall, the country's import pattern over time suggests that the government's policy of consumer goods import substitution through heavy protectionist policies was being implemented on a large scale. The large increase in imports of capital and intermediate goods reflected the positive response of the private sector to government inducements encouraging the domestic production of consumer goods. On the other hand, the large increases in the net import of services was a reflection of the need to import many of the complementary technical skills required to operate these new industries (such as the buildup in military capabilities).

SHIFTS IN PATTERNS OF DEMAND

The trends in GNP, investment, consumption, and imports and exports are all reflected in the movements of the major demand aggregates - domestic absorption, total supply, and private-public expenditure. Domestic absorption increased rapidly over time growing (at current prices) at an average rate of 5.1, 14.8, and 34.1 percent for the periods 1959-63, 1963-72, and 1973-77, respectively (table 5.5). Domestic absorption grew more rapidly than non-oil GDP, and it increased from 109 to 122 percent of non-oil GDP by 1973 and was 143 percent in 1977, indicating: (a) that the country was largely financing its expansion out of oil revenues rather than indigenous production, and (b) the increased vulnerability of the economy to shortfalls in oil revenues. Domestic supply also increased rapidly during this period following a pattern similar to that of domestic absorption, again indicating the ability of the economy to finance a rapidly expanding level of import expenditures. While private expenditures (at constant prices) increased rapidly at 3.4, 9.2, and 15.0 percent per annum for the subperiods 1959-63, 1963-72, and 1973-77, respectively, they could not keep pace with total government expenditures which expanded at 2.8, 19.8, and 25.7 percent during the same periods. As a result, government expenditure which had averaged slightly over 20 percent of private expenditure from 1959 to 1963, doubled to 48 percent in 1972, and by 1977 was 72 percent of private expenditure. Again, this pattern coincides with the expansion in oil revenues and the fact that they accrued directly to the government.

CONSTRAINTS ON GROWTH

Using the framework beginning with equation (1) (p. 62), it is possible to say something about the nature of the overall constraints on the country's growth during the period under consideration.

If imports are now defined to include net factor services, Y in equation (1) becomes gross national product instead of gross domestic product. Along with GNP two additional identities can be created:

(2) $Y = C + S$ and

(3) $F = I - S$

and from (1) with $Y = GNP$, $F = M - X$. It is now possible to estimate an ex post savings function of the form

Table 5.5. Trends in Aggregate Expenditures
(billions of rials)

	1959	1963	1972	1973	1977	Average Annual Growth 1959-1963	1963-1972	1973-1977
Domestic Absorption (current prices)	289.7	353.9	1,226.6	1,568.4	5,066.5	5.1	14.8	34.1
External Absorption (current prices)	9.4	40.3	41.8	300.2	526.8	43.9	0.4	2.1
Total Supply (current prices)	349.9	433.9	1,535.1	2,223.3	6,881.7	5.5	15.1	32.6
Private Expenditures (current prices)	241.3	276.3	610.2	686.9	1,203.1	3.4	9.2	15.0
Government Expenditures (current prices)	51.3	57.2	290.9	348.9	871.9	2.8	19.8	25.7
Domestic Absorption/GNP	1.03	0.98	1.00	0.86	0.95	-1.2	0.2	2.5
Domestic Absorption/ Non-oil GDP	1.13	1.09	1.22	1.22	1.43	-.09	1.3	4.1
Total Supply/GNP	1.24	1.20	1.25	1.21	1.29	-.08	0.5	1.6
Private Expenditures/ Non-oil GDP	0.94	0.91	0.96	0.93	0.83	-.08	0.6	-2.8
Government Expenditures/ Non-oil GDP	0.20	0.19	0.30	0.47	0.60	-1.3	5.2	6.3
Government Expenditures/ private expenditures	0.21	0.21	0.48	0.51	0.72	0.0	0.7	9.0

Source: Computed from data in Bank Markazi Iran, <u>Annual Report</u>, various issues.

$$S = a1 + b1Y + c1F$$

and an ex post import function of the form

$$M = a2 + b2Y = c2F$$

Several possible constraints to the country's growth can now be identified within the context of the so-called "two gap analysis"(6) where GS = the savings gap or (I - S), and GT = the trade gap or (M - X).

If the trade gap had been a binding constraint on the country's growth during the period under consideration, an ex ante deficiency of (desired) foreign exchange would have existed in excess of required investment over potential savings for the level of income existing at the time. It can be shown that, under these circumstances, the estimated coefficient cl in equation (2) above would assume a value between -1 and 0.(7) On the other hand, if the savings gap had been binding, foreign capital would have implemented rather than acted as a substitute for domestic savings.

In terms of the equilibrating process, it is unlikely that adjustments reflecting ex ante deficiencies in the two gaps would have been alleviated by changes in exports since actual exports could have fallen short of their potential only if the goods and services exported could have been consumed in significant amounts domestically (there were, of course, limitations on increased domestic oil usage, especially in the short run), and some imports required for producing exports could be employed in the production of goods for the internal market. Here, the specialized nature of the oil industry and the limited range of areas to which the factors in this sector could be transferred in the short run precluded this type of adjustment in Iran during the period under consideration.

The constraints on exports facilitating an equilibrating role meant that increases in imports over their desired level would have been the likely mechanism of adjustment in those years in which the savings gap was constraining the expansion in income. During those periods, actual and desired levels of savings would be equal, resulting in the estimated value of cl = 0.0. Again, the theoretical literature has demonstrated that, if, in fact, imports exceeded their minimum required levels (in the presence of relatively abundant amounts of foreign exchange), estimates of c2 would yield a positive number. Given Iran's situation whereby the inputs used by the oil sector were highly specialized and the domestic use of exportable (petroleum) products relatively low (and price inelastic), it can also be shown that c2 should have been close to (GS - GT)/GS, indicating that part of the country's foreign exchange would have gone to increasing imports.

The above considerations can be used to derive a fairly precise method of identifying the nature of the macroeconomic constraints under which the Iranian economy operated during this period. For example, a value of cl close to -1.0 together with a value of c2 not significantly different from 0.0 would imply that the trade gap posed the greatest hindrance on increased output. On the other hand, if estimates of cl were close to 0.0 and c2 was significantly positive, it is likely the savings gap had been binding.

Finally, if estimates of cl were significantly negative (but with an absolute value less than unity) while those of c2 were significantly positive, the country probably experienced periods of alternative savings and trade constraints, with neither dominating the period as a whole.

This conclusion is further supported when the 1959-73 period is examined separately. Here:

$$S = \underset{(19.3)}{\overset{(b1)}{0.22}} - \underset{(-21.3)}{\overset{(c1)}{1.03}}$$

$$M = \underset{(19.89)}{\overset{(b2)}{0.21}} + \underset{(1.03)}{\overset{(c2)}{0.05}}$$

A value of cl for all practical purposes equal to -1.0, together with the very low and insignificant value of c2 implies that the trade gap was binding. The lower value of cl (-0.78 as opposed to -1.03) for the period as a whole indicates that the post-1973 oil boom did, in fact, lessen the trade gap, but perhaps not to the extent commonly believed.

Clearly, while the country had a lot of foreign exchange, it also spent huge sums very quickly. Apparently, the government's very ambitious programs resulted in its being geared to budgets set to spend oil revenues nearly as quickly as they accrued. The results are also in conformity with the fact that by 1975 the government was back in the international capital markets seeking to borrow funds to cover its deficits. Clearly a longer run, more well thought through government expenditure strategy, complete with contingencies for foreign exchange fluctuations would have gone a long way toward relaxing the binding trade gap. As shown later in an optimal control simulation of the country, the result would have been a much smoother development path than the one actually experienced during the 1970s.

Conventional wisdom would suggest that, given the size of Iran's oil revenues and hence exchange earnings, the savings gap (i.e., the country's inability to mobilize supporting domestic resources to combine with the foreign exchange) had limited growth during this period. The results for 1959-77 (with "t" statistics in parenthesis under the coefficients) indicate differently, however:

$$S = \underset{(5.38)}{\overset{(b1)}{0.59Y}} - \underset{(-2.61)}{\overset{(c1)}{0.78F}}$$

$$M = \underset{(6.01)}{\overset{(b2)}{0.45}} + \underset{(0.33)}{\overset{(c2)}{0.07F}}$$

With c1 close to -1.0 (-0.78) and c2 not significantly different from zero (a "t' value of 0.33), the trade gap was clearly binding for the period as a whole.

SECTORAL GROWTH PATTERNS

The distinctive patterns of sectoral growth include:

- the relatively low growth of the agricultural sector causing it to decline from 33.3 percent of non-oil GDP in 1959 to 13.7 percent by 1977 (table 5.6);
- the eratic movement of construction with growth rates of 4.1, 15.5, and 58.2 percent per annum (at current prices) for the subperiods 1959-63, 1963-72 and 1973-77, respectively;
- the rather steady growth of manufacturing over time with real growth of 10.0, 13.2, and 15.4 percent per annum for the 1959-63, 1963-72, and 1973-77 subperiods, respectively;
- the expansion of public services over private services throughout the time period covered.

These movements are reflected in the relatively low income (both GDP and non-oil GDP) for agriculture and the higher elasticities for services and manufacturing shown in table 5.7.

In a broader context, it is interesting to compare the sectoral growth patterns of Iran (and other OPEC countries) with those that are usually found in countries with a similar per capita income and population.(8) Drawing on the analysis of population-income-sectoral composition developed by H. Chenery, it is possible to see not only how closely Iran followed a normal pattern of development but, perhaps more importantly, in what ways the country significantly differed from what might have been expected based on the experience of other countries at a comparable level of development. It is clear (table 5.8) that, while manufacturing grew rapidly during the period under consideration, the sector still fell far

Table 5.6. Sectoral Patterns of Growth, 1959-1977
(billions of rials)

	1959	1963	1972	1973	1977	Average Annual Growth 1959-1963	1963-1972	1973-1977
Agriculture (current price)	85.4	98.4	201.8	234.4	485.0	3.6	8.3	19.9
Oil (current price)	42.5	70.5	267.0	587.5	1,658.0	13.5	15.9	29.6
Manufacturing (current price)	30.9	45.4	171.5	231.9	638.1	10.1	15.9	28.8
Construction (current price)	13.3	15.6	58.4	78.9	494.8	4.1	15.8	58.2
Transportation-Communications (current price)	27.5	30.8	53.8	67.6	113.2	2.9	6.4	13.8
Trade (current price)	22.8	28.5	90.7	116.1	229.9	5.7	13.7	26.8
Public Services (current price)	23.3	33.0	140.5	167.1	587.7	9.1	17.5	36.9
Private Services (current price)	13.0	16.4	50.0	66.8	161.3	6.0	13.2	24.7
Agriculture (constant price)	85.4	90.3	134.4	142.1	168.2	1.4	4.5	4.3
Manufacturing (constant price)	30.9	45.2	138.1	162.4	287.7	10.0	13.2	15.4
Agriculture/GNP	30.2	27.3	16.4	12.8	9.1	-2.5	-5.5	-8.2
Agriculture/Non-oil GDP	33.3	30.4	20.2	18.3	13.7	-2.3	-5.4	-7.0
Manufacturing/GNP	10.9	12.6	13.9	12.7	11.9	3.7	1.1	-1.6
Manufacturing/Non-oil GDP	12.0	14.0	17.1	18.1	18.0	3.9	2.2	-0.1

Source: Computed from data in Bank Markazi Iran, Annual Report, various issues.

Table 5.7. Sectoral Income Elasticities
1959-1977

	GDP	Non-oil GDP	r^2	F
Agriculture	0.43	0.39	0.871	80.79
	(8.99)	(7.57)	0.827	57.41
Manufacturing	1.26	1.23	0.989	1,306.49
	(36.15)	(44.40)	0.992	1,971.07
Construction	0.92	0.90	0.911	152.94
	(12.37)	(13.38)	0.923	179.15
Transportation and Communications	0.95	0.92	0.896	103.64
	(10.18)	(18.97)	0.968	359.76
Trade	0.99	0.93	0.961	298.55
	(17.28)	(18.18)	0.970	330.83
Housing Rentals	0.82	0.77	0.969	372.06
	(19.47)	(19.71)	0.970	388.39
Government Services	1.42	1.38	0.989	1,285.53
	(35.85)	(23.20)	0.973	538.33
Private Services	1.16	1.12	0.983	843.02
	(29.03)	(18.97)	0.968	359.88
Banking	2.00	1.96	0.983	885.14
	(29.75)	(31.74)	0.985	1,007.65

short of the relative importance one might have expected given the country's population and per capita income.

The low proportion of manufacturing output is consistent with the findings reached by Chenery and Taylor.(9) They interpret this pattern as stemming from the fact that many resource-rich countries allow the private sector to obtain foreign exchange at relatively low cost. The availability of the foreign exchange made possible by the export of resources together with their underpricing act to shift comparative advantage away from manufacturing.(10) In other words, by artificially cheapening foreign manufactures, these countries stimulate imports to the point where the country tends to be industrially underdeveloped in comparison with countries at a similar level of development.

Table 5.8. Percentage Distribution of Actual Output by Sector Compared with the Normal Output by Sector for the Major Oil Exporting Countries (1970, excludes Oil and Mining)

	Iran		Iraq		Libya		Kuwait		Saudi Arabia		Venezuela	
Sectors	Normal	Actual	Normal	Actual	Normal	Actual	Normal	Actual	Normal	Actual	Normal	Actual
Agriculture	19	18	25	23	4	6	11	1	16	10	10	9
Manufacturing	29	13	22	13	31	4	30	9	28	18	37	20
Construction	5	5	7	4	8	17	8	8	6	10	6	5
Transportation and Communication	7	5	7	8	12	8	14	9	9	15	9	12
Services including Commerce	40	59	40	52	45	49	37	73	41	47	38	54

Source: Ahmad Kader "The Contribution of Oil Exports to Economic Development: A Study of the Major Oil Exporting Countries," The American Economist (Spring 1980), p. 50.

This interpretation certainly seems consistent with the situation in Iran where very little encouragement had been given industry before the 1960s. One might argue, therefore, that in principle Iran's choice of import substitution strategy in the early 1960s was fundamentally sound in that it created an environment necessary to stimulate that amount of investment needed to make up the ground lost over the years because of the relative ease most individuals had in meeting their manufactured requirements through imports rather than domestic production.

The adoption of an import substitution strategy, together with the rising oil revenues and the country's political stability, produced high profit expectations and thus produced the high and sustained growth of the industrial sector noted above. In fact, the country's manufacturing sector grew about twice as fast as the average growth of this sector in other developing countries, reflecting the historical lag in developing industry in Iran together with the incentives given for investment in the sector at this time. The result was an average annual growth of gross domestic fixed capital formation reaching 16 percent and that of fixed investment in machinery and equipment amounting to over 20 percent during the Third and Fourth Plans. As noted above, the rise in imports or intermediate and capital goods was associated with a shift away from imports of consumer goods.

While manufacturing prospered, the high tariffs on consumer goods, overvaluation of the rial, and controls of food prices in the politically sensitive urban areas made possible by liberal food import policy and government-sponsored food subsidies were undoubtedly critical factors causing the deterioration of agricultural terms of trade and the relatively slow growth of agriculture. In fact, real investment in agricultural machinery and equipment during 1963-71 grew by only 6.7 percent per annum as compared with an average annual rate of 20 percent for the total investment.

HISTORICAL PATTERNS OF GROWTH AND MOMENTUM

At least for the period before the 1970s, the general tendency among developing countries was for the aggregate growth rates of individual countries to be rather similar from one decade to the next. Drawing on data for the 1950s and 1960s, Jeffrey Nugent(11) found that the majority of developing countries were either consistently higher or consistently lower than the average for the group as a whole during each decade. More precisely, 15 of the 42 countries examined in his study had GNP growth rates less than the (population weighted) average for the group during both time periods. On the other hand,

21 countries sustained growth rates above the 42 country group average for both the 1950s and the 1960s.

From these results, it appears that, once a certain degree of growth momentum has been attained, continued growth is relatively easy to maintain. Without such momentum, however, the growth process seems relatively difficult to initiate and to sustain. Thus, Nugent concluded that countries that are not able to generate much growth in one decade have a low probability of doing significantly better in the next; i.e., incomes that are growing tend to keep growing while those that are stagnating tend to remain in that condition.(12)

The Iranian experience of declining growth in the late 1970s seem to be an exception to Nugent's findings. However, using data for the 1970s(13) and regressing the growth rates of various macroeconomic aggregates - industrial production, manufacturing output, and government consumption - on their growth rates in the 1960s, no statistically significant results were obtained. Relatively high growth such as that obtained by Iran in the 1960s did not assure similar performance for developing countries in the 1970s.

The apparent shift between 1950-1960 and 1960-1978 in the growth patterns of less developed countries is of interest in itself. As indicated below, the causes underlying this shift yield several interesting insights into the decline in growth experienced by the Iranian economy in the late 1970s.

A MODEL OF GROWTH AND MOMENTUM

A number of factors could have caused the disruption in the historical pattern found by Nugent - sudden balance of payments problems faced by previously high growth non-oil exporters, changing comparative advantages, shifts in foreign aid, and so on. Of course, it might well be that the sustained pattern observed by Nugent still existed in the 1970s but was masked by a number of situations where extreme shifts in foreign exchange earnings and/or domestic savings took place. These cases, while relatively few in number might, still have been sufficient enough to eliminate any statistical correlations between performance in the 1970s and 1960s for the group as a whole.

To determine if, in fact, this problem might have occurred, cluster analysis was used in an attempt to place countries into groups possessing more homogeneous characteristics than for the sample as a whole.(14) While any number of variables could have been used in dividing the sample countries into two groups, variables were selected on the basis of their likelihood of splitting the entire sample into groups, one of which would presumably reflect the forces observed by

Nugent, while the other would comprise a set of countries a large number of which had perhaps experienced a set of constraints no longer permitting them to sustain growth for a significant period of time.

Logically, growth once established should have a greater chance of being sustained in an environment relatively free from either savings or foreign exchange shortages,(15) necessitating perhaps the introduction of harsh credit rationing and/or widespread import controls.

Since, a priori assumptions as to which constraint may have dominated during a given period can be incorrect in the light of statistical testing, two cluster exercises were performed. The first cluster grouping was based on measures of savings and investment performance, with the presumption that countries in the high savings-investing group should have a better chance than the countries in the low savings-investment cluster of repeating good economic performance from one decade to another.

The second cluster exercise selected variables reflective of the relative constraint placed on countries by foreign exchange-balance of payments difficulties. A priori countries that are able to sustain high growth rates (or levels) of exports should be able to finance their import requirements(16) and, once attained, sustain high growth in such aggregates and private consumption.

Although an original sample of 95 countries was used in the cluster analysis, a number of countries did not have complete data sets. The computer program used for the clustering simply omitted these countries from the analysis. Somewhat fewer than 95 countries were, therefore, left in the final grouping.

The savings-investment cluster exercise yielded two quite distinct groups (based on the difference in the means of each group for the clustering variables (table 5.9), where SA,SB = gross domestic savings as a percentage of gross domestic product for 1960 and 1978, respectively, and IA,IB = gross domestic investment for 1960 and 1978, respectively.

As expected, countries in cluster 1 were in general relatively low savers and investors over this period, while those in cluster 2 had for the most part higher savings and investment rates (as a percentage of GDP).

The export-import growth was also formed with four variables (all for the 1970-78 period) with ZGB = average annual growth of imports, EGB = average annual growth of exports, IGB = average annual growth of investment, and PCGB = average annual growth of private consumption. Three distinct clusters were formed (table 5.10) with Saudi Arabia the only country in the third group. (Saudi Arabia was subsequently placed in group 2 for the regression analysis.)

Again, a pattern similar to the first cluster groupings appears - countries are apparently fairly consistent in that the good performers (such as most of the countries in group 2) tend to rate high in all four categories while those in group 1 did poorly in terms of attaining high levels of growth in all or most of the four clustering variables.

As noted above, when the growth rates of GDP, manufacturing and other macro variables indicative of income growth during the 1970s were regressed on their growth rates, no statistically significant results were found (table 5.11). Growth in the 1960s, contrary to the momentum thesis, did not ensure relatively high rates of expansion in their respective series for the 1970s.

However, regressions utilizing only the good performers in either the savings-investment cluster or the export-import clusters yielded results in conformity with Nugent's momentum thesis. For these countries, relatively high growth in GDP, manufacturing, agriculture, and government consumption in the 1960s seems to be a good predictor of their continued success in the 1970s. Countries in the relatively lower group in each cluster did not follow this pattern. In fact, no statistically significant results were obtained for any of the macroeconomic growth rates for the 1970s regressed on their respective growth in the 1960s. The results imply that momentum built up in one time period is not per se sufficient insurance for success in the next time period. The countries successful in achieving high growth rates in manufacturing and/or GNP have tended to simultaneously generate relatively high levels of savings and investment and/or relatively high rates of expansion in exports and imports. While the adage "nothing succeeds like success" is undoubtedly a good first approximation to predictability from one decade to another, it did not hold all that well for the 1960s to 1970s. The successful countries during this period seem to be ones that were able to sustain performance in key aggregates such as savings and investment which allowed their built up momentum to continue. In contrast, the unsuccessful countries as a group were unable and/or never did attain relatively above average performance in savings-investment and/or exports-imports. As a result, whatever growth they did have in the 1960s seems to have been limited in the 1970s by their inability to overcome the obstacles these deficiencies must impose. In any case, for this group of countries, it appears that whatever growth they may have in one time period provides no assurance as to what will continue in the future.

Table 5.9. Savings-Investment Cluster

	Country	1YA	1YB	SYA	SYB
Cluster 1	Ethiopia	12.0	9.0	11.0	6.0
	Afghanistan	16.0	13.0	13.0	10.0
	Chile	17.0	11.0	14.0	7.0
	Angola	12.0	9.0	14.0	18.0
	Uruguay	18.0	14.0	12.0	14.0
	Uganda	11.0	4.0	16.0	2.0
	Ghana	24.0	5.0	17.0	6.0
	Sri Lanka	15.0	22.0	11.0	17.0
	Turkey	16.0	21.0	13.0	17.0
	Senegal	16.0	23.0	15.0	11.0
	Costa Rica	18.0	25.0	13.0	15.0
	Portugal	19.0	23.0	12.0	12.0
	Niger	13.0	19.0	12.0	12.0
	Burma	12.0	20.0	11.0	13.0
	El Salvador	16.0	20.0	11.0	12.0
	Bolivia	14.0	21.0	7.0	13.0
	Egypt	13.0	28.0	12.0	14.0
	Morocco	10.0	24.0	11.0	11.0
	Zaire	12.0	19.0	21.0	12.0
	Tanzania	14.0	20.0	19.0	7.0
	Central African Republic	20.0	20.0	9.0	8.0
	Israel	27.0	24.0	14.0	6.0
	Mali	14.0	17.0	9.0	5.0
	Sudan	9.0	16.0	9.0	2.0
	Pakistan	12.0	18.0	5.0	7.0
	Haiti	9.0	18.0	7.0	9.0
	Somalia	10.0	16.0	3.0	2.0
	Mozambique	10.0	10.0	8.0	-1.0
	Rwanda	6.0	10.0	8.0	4.0
	Burundi	6.0	14.0	5.0	5.0
	Chad	11.0	17.0	5.0	-7.0
	Benin	15.0	22.0	9.0	-5.0
	Upper Volta	10.0	25.0	-4.0	-3.0
	Malawi	10.0	32.0	-4.0	16.0
	Togo	11.0	37.0	4.0	14.0
	Hong Kong	19.0	26.0	1.0	15.0
	Tunisia	17.0	30.0	7.0	20.0
	Nigeria	13.0	30.0	7.0	28.0
	Korea	11.0	32.0	1.0	28.0
	Singapore	11.0	36.0	3.0	27.0
	Guinea	5.0	15.0	6.0	16.0
	Indonesia	8.0	20.0	8.0	22.0
	Guatemala	10.0	22.0	8.0	17.0

(continued)

Table 5.9. Savings-Investment Cluster (continued)

	Country	1YA	1YB	SYA	SYB
Cluster 1	Madagascar	11.0	16.0	5.0	21.0
	Papua	13.0	19.0	2.0	16.0
	Mauritania	37.0	52.0	-3.0	7.0
	Congo	45.0	20.0	-21.0	8.0
Mean		14.4	20.5	8.0	11.0
Cluster 2	India	17.0	24.0	14.0	20.0
	Thailand	16.0	27.0	14.0	22.0
	Paraguay	17.0	27.0	16.0	20.0
	Honduras	14.0	27.0	12.0	20.0
	Colombia	15.0	25.0	12.0	19.0
	Panama	16.0	28.0	11.0	22.0
	Kenya	20.0	28.0	17.0	18.0
	Cameroon	11.0	24.0	14.0	21.0
	Dominican Republic	12.0	23.0	19.0	18.0
	Zimbabwe	23.0	19.0	22.0	24.0
	Brazil	22.0	23.0	21.0	21.0
	Spain	21.0	20.0	23.0	21.0
	Mexico	20.0	25.0	18.0	25.0
	Nicaragua	21.0	24.0	21.0	25.0
	Argentina	22.0	25.0	20.0	30.0
	Philippines	16.0	30.0	16.0	24.0
	Ecuador	14.0	26.0	16.0	26.0
	Ivory Coast	15.0	31.0	17.0	30.0
	Taiwan	20.0	26.0	13.0	33.0
	Greece	19.0	27.0	11.0	27.0
	Jamaica	30.0	15.0	26.0	16.0
	Peru	22.0	15.0	24.0	17.0
	Liberia	28.0	22.0	35.0	18.0
	Zambia	25.0	31.0	41.0	31.0
	Venezuela	21.0	40.0	33.0	34.0
	Yugoslavia	37.0	33.0	32.0	28.0
	Malaysia	14.0	25.0	27.0	31.0
	Iran	17.0	33.0	21.0	39.0
	South Africa	22.0	24.0	27.0	30.0
	Trinidad	28.0	26.0	30.0	33.0
	Algeria	42.0	51.0	34.0	37.0
Mean		20.5	26.6	21.2	25.2

Data Source: The World Bank, World Development Report, 1980 (New York: Oxford University Press, 1980), pp. 118-19.

Table 5.10. Export-Import-Investment-Consumption-Growth Cluster

	Country	ZGB	EGB	IGB	PCGB
Cluster 1	Bangladesh	-2.90	-4.70	-1.40	3.10
	Ethiopia	-0.20	-5.40	-1.60	3.70
	Tanzania	-1.00	-6.00	1.90	5.80
	Peru	3.10	-3.80	4.20	4.10
	Chad	1.70	-3.00	3.10	1.80
	Uruguay	2.30	-5.00	4.80	-1.20
	Portugal	4.70	-5.90	0.70	4.80
	Ghana	2.70	-0.10	-8.30	1.70
	Central African Republic	-0.90	1.80	0.70	4.30
	Panama	-3.40	2.20	0.90	1.40
	Chile	-0.90	6.50	-2.70	-0.40
	Argentina	-0.10	6.80	1.20	2.40
	Trinidad	-4.40	-1.30	5.30	-0.30
	Sierra Leone	-4.00	-3.10	5.60	0.50
	Sri Lanka	-2.70	-3.80	3.60	2.50
	Burma	-4.60	0.50	4.20	3.70
	Madagascar	-4.00	-0.90	-2.50	-2.20
	Zambia	-6.90	-4.70	-2.90	-2.70
	Zaire	-10.40	-4.10	0.60	-0.70
	Angola	-4.70	-8.90	-10.90	-8.80
	Jamaica	-5.90	-2.70	-10.40	0.50
	Uganda	-7.60	-5.30	-13.80	1.60
	Mozambique	-13.40	-15.90	-9.60	-2.70
Mean		-2.76	-2.90	-1.19	1.00
Cluster 2	Congo	6.70	14.70	-0.10	4.30
	Greece	5.90	13.10	1.90	4.60
	Niger	5.50	13.20	5.20	1.60
	Israel	4.50	10.60	0.70	5.70
	Spain	3.30	11.00	3.00	4.20
	Mali	5.00	7.70	1.80	6.00
	Upper Volta	9.40	8.50	1.80	0.80
	Hong Kong	3.20	4.80	10.20	8.80
	Dominican Republic	4.50	6.70	13.20	7.60
	Brazil	6.60	6.00	10.70	9.00
	Malaysia	6.80	5.20	10.20	6.40
	Costa Rica	4.70	5.90	9.30	4.90
	Nicaragua	4.20	5.60	8.60	4.90
	Philippines	4.70	5.40	11.10	4.30
	Afghanistan	8.10	2.40	12.40	3.80
	El Salvador	8.40	0.60	11.10	5.70
	Turkey	8.10	2.50	10.20	6.60
	Guatemala	7.10	3.40	11.30	5.40

(continued)

Table 5.10. Export-Import-Investment-Consumption-Growth Cluster (continued)

	Country	ZGB	EGB	IGB	PCGB
Cluster 2	Taiwan	9.10	9.30	8.20	6.80
	Singapore	8.10	9.80	5.50	7.10
	Thailand	5.60	12.20	7.80	6.70
	Ecuador	12.70	9.50	10.20	8.40
	Ivory Coast	10.60	8.50	14.0	8.20
	Somalia	13.70	7.80	8.50	2.70
	Bolivia	12.20	1.70	6.40	7.40
	Mauritania	6.40	-0.80	5.40	4.40
	Pakistan	5.90	-1.30	4.80	3.80
	Sudan	6.40	-3.20	9.80	4.30
	Honduras	2.60	2.90	4.90	4.20
	Liberia	2.0	1.50	6.10	3.30
	Colombia	-0.70	1.20	6.30	5.90
	Yugoslavia	4.90	4.50	7.20	6.10
	Cameroon	6.70	2.40	7.00	4.80
	India	3.20	6.00	6.10	3.00
	Mexico	4.00	5.20	7.10	3.80
	Senegal	4.70	4.40	2.50	2.10
	Malawi	4.20	2.40	1.10	6.40
	Paraguay	8.00	7.60	20.60	6.90
	Syria	15.50	7.10	18.20	10.40
	Indonesia	15.80	7.20	15.30	7.60
	Algeria	16.60	-0.80	11.70	11.30
	Morocco	13.70	2.60	17.40	4.40
	Rwanda	11.60	3.60	17.10	3.90
	Togo	12.40	0.30	16.0	1.90
	Iran	22.90	-1.20	22.00	10.00
	Nigeria	25.0	-.50	23.30	4.00
	Egypt	16.60	-2.30	23.30	6.10
	Venezuela	14.90	-10.10	11.80	7.10
	Benin	6.80	-13.60	8.40	3.90
	Libya	18.70	-7.00	10.90	21.20
	Tunisia	30.30	21.10	11.90	8.80
	Korea	13.50	28.80	13.70	7.50
Mean		9.06	4.91	9.68	5.94
Cluster 3	Saudi Arabia	41.50	6.20	51.00	16.50

Data Source: The World Bank, World Development Report, 1980 (New York: Oxford University Press, 1980).

Table 5.11. Indicators of Momentum
(based on savings-investment cluster)

Gross Domestic Product Growth (GDPG)

Total Sample:

GDPG (1970s) = 0.73GDPG (1960s) - 0.21
(1.96) (-0.10)

r^2 = 0.125
F = 4.01

High Group:

GDPC (1970s) = 0.69GDPG(1960s) + 0.47
(2.66) (0.26)

r^2 = 0.335
F = 7.06

Low Group:

GDPG (1970s) = 0.37GDPG(1960s) + 1.11
(0.36) (0.20)

r^2 = 0.011
F = 0.13

Government Consumption (GCG)

Total Sample:

GCG (1970s) = 0.44GCG(1960s) + 4.00
(1.69) (2.21)

r^2 = 0.093
F = 2.85

High Group:

GCG (1970s) = 0.81GCG(1960s) + 2.01
(3.32) (1.11)

r^2 = 0.441
F = 11.03

Low Group:

GCG (1970s) = -0.47GCG(1960s) + 8.86
(-0.92) (2.68)

r^2 = 0.061
F = 0.84

Industrial Growth (INDG)

Total Sample:

INGD (1970s) = 0.25INDG(1960s) + 2.56
(1.00) (1.13)

r^2 = 0.03
F = 0.99

High Group:

INDG(1970s) = 0.54INDG(1960s) + 0.84
(2.06) (0.33)

r^2 = 0.233
F = 4.25

(continued)

Table 5.11. (continued)

Industrial Growth (continued)

Low Group:
$$INDG(1970s) = \underset{(-1.29)}{0.59}INDG(1960s) + \underset{(2.15)}{8.09}$$
$r^2 = 0.14$
$F = 1.66$

Manufacturing Growth (MANG)

Total Sample:
$$MANG(1970s) = \underset{(1.48)}{0.44}MANG(1960s) + \underset{(0.48)}{1.29}$$
$r^2 = 0.137$
$F = 1.24$

High Group:
$$MANG(1970s) = \underset{(2.29)}{0.67}MANG(1960s) + \underset{(0.35)}{0.98}$$
$r^2 = 0.273$
$F = 5.25$

Low Group:
$$MANG(1970s) = \underset{(-0.04)}{-0.02}MANG(1960s) + \underset{(0.43)}{2.96}$$
$r^2 = 0.001$
$F = 0.00$

Agricultural Growth (AGG)

Total Sample:
$$AGG(1970s) = \underset{(1.34)}{0.52}AGG(1960s) + \underset{(0.07)}{0.09}$$
$r^2 = 0.060$
$F = 1.80$

High Group:
$$AGG(1970s) = \underset{(2.89)}{0.57}AGG(1960s) + \underset{(0.79)}{0.63}$$
$r^2 = 0.373$
$F = 8.34$

Low Group:
$$AGG(1970s) = \underset{(-0.37)}{-0.14}AGG(1960s) + \underset{(1.15)}{2.56}$$
$r^2 = 0.04$
$F = 0.01$

MECHANISMS OF GROWTH AND MOMENTUM

In attempting to provide an explanation for the role of momentum in the growth process, Nugent drew on the theory of disequilibrium arguing essentially that many of the stabilizing and growth equalizing mechanisms assumed for the developed countries were inappropriate for the developing ones, i.e., cumulative movements toward expansion became cumulative while stagnation did not elicit forces capable of alleviating the condition.(17)

Three factors utilized by Nugent and drawn up to explain why disequilibrium tends to be more prevalent in developing countries are:(18) (1) the nature of technological selection and change in less developed countries; (2) the process of capital formation in the economy, and (3) the way in which human capital and income distribution tend to vary with growth in these economies. All three of these will be examined in detail in later chapters to determine the extent to which they may have influenced Iran's growth performance in the mid to late 1970s.

CONCLUSIONS

Based on the results of the cluster analysis, it is only suggested here that, whereas the factors suggested by Nugent may have possibly aided Iran's economic expansion in the late 1960s and early 1970s, they may have become self-terminating or even a detriment to that growth by the mid-1970s. Iran's position in the high savings-investment and the high export-import clusters indicates that there was a high probability that the country's growth should have been an ongoing process. That the country faced stagnation by 1978 suggests: (1) extenuating political factors may have predominated, (2) political uncertainity and erratic government policy toward the economy may have undermined savings and investment to the extent that old patterns and relationships no longer could be counted on to sustain growth, or (3) the mechanisms suggested by Nugent may have been altered by factors such as the leveling off of oil exports even though in absolute amounts they were still very substantial. Obviously this list is highly simplified but still adequate to identify areas in which further empirical analysis may be fruitful.

Neither Nugent's analysis nor the cluster analysis used here explicitly takes into account the manner by which oil exports may possibly differ in their impact on the domestic economy from that associated with a more diversified export sector, integrated to a greater extent than oil with the indigenous economy. An analysis of the manner in which the oil sector impacts on the economy is therefore the next step in determining the nature of the economic forces at work in the mid to late 1970s.

6 Economic Dynamics of Oil Revenues

INTRODUCTION

The role played by the export sector in Iran is both straightforward and complex. It is straightforward in that any casual examination of the historical record easily shows that oil exports were by far the largest and most dynamic individual item in the country's export sector (table 6.1). Similarly, revenues from oil dominated the government's fiscal resources. Generalizations about the sector's impact on the overall economy are much harder to make, however. Many links that may have existed between the oil sector and the rest of the economy are not nearly as apparent. Further, the precise magnitude of their strength has been a matter of controversy in the literature for some time.(1)

Quantification of the nature and degree of the petroleum sector's impact on the economy should provide some help toward an understanding of the mechanisms underlying Iranian growth during this period. In addition, an empirical estimate of the oil sector's impact during the 1959-73 period versus that for the 1959-77 period should provide insights as to the areas of the economy which were the chief beneficiaries of the 1973 oil price increase and those that were affected to a lesser extent.

OIL-GROWTH MECHANISMS

The mechanisms by which Iran's oil exports would have acted as a leading sector and the determinants of the overall impact of an increase in exports has been discussed in general terms

Table 6.1. Significance of Oil Exports in Selected Middle East Countries (1976)

Country	Oil Exports as % of Total Commodity Exports	Oil Exports as % of Total Exports of Goods and Services	Oil Exports as % of GDP	Oil Exports per capita (U.S. dollars)
Iran	97.5	88.4	34.9	$ 682
Algeria	89.2	83.6	30.6	275
Iraq	98.3	93.2	55.4	792
Kuwait	91.0	89.8	71.2	8,445
Libya	99.9	86.7	49.6	3,333
Saudi Arabia	99.9	98.9	82.7	3,935

Source: IMF, International Financial Statistics.

in the literature.(2) Oil exports contributed to the country's economic growth directly (through direct contributions to gross domestic product) and indirectly (through indirect linkages or spread effects) over time. The indirect impact can be considered broadly as a sequence or multiplier-accelerator mechanism, continuing perhaps for a number of years.

From an operational point of view, an assessment of the impact of oil revenues on the country's economy may be pursued from at least two perspectives: (1) the production function or "stable" theory approach which focuses analysis not so much on the oil industry itself as on the effects of petroleum production on the rest of the economy, and (2) an environmental approach where exports lead to development only if the social milieu and policy environment are supportive.

A consideration of the production function for oil is important because of the secondary and tertiary industries that could possibly develop around the petroleum sector through such external effects as: inputs demanded, outputs supplied, consumer markets created, and education provided or stimulated by the export industry.(3)

An appraisal of the existence of strength and reliability of the various linkage effects for the petroleum sector is, therefore, one way of understanding the country's growth dynamics. In this regard, the major conclusions drawn from studies of other oil producing developing countries are of interest. First, most studies in which the staple theory was expanded to the petroleum sector suggest that, unlike other historical staples, the petroleum industry has been relatively deficient in spread effects associated with its production and consumption linkages.(4) Obviously, failure of petroleum to generate production linkages was a direct result of its highly capital and skill intensive technology. Hence, in developing countries, for instance, its input requirements were highly divergent from domestic factor supplies. On the other hand, the failure of consumption linkages to arise could be due to the low labor demand created by petroleum technology.

The second conclusion concerning an examination of linkages in petroleum is that fiscal linkages in export-oriented economies are by far the most important medium through which developments in the petroleum sector are transmitted to the indigenous economy.

The third conclusion is that the difference between production and consumption linkages on the one hand and fiscal linkages on the other is critical in understanding the unique problems the sector has in transmitting its growth to the rest of the economy. Production and consumption linkages work themselves out through the market, but the success of the fiscal linkage depends on the willingness and ability of the government to tax or otherwise participate in the incomes originating from petroleum. More importantly, the ability to tax must be combined with an ability to invest productively. Lack of automaticity has probably been the major weakness of fiscal linkages for the OPEC countries.

Thus, an assessment of export-led growth in petroleum economies judged from the perspective of the staple theory approach suggests that Iran had to rely primarily on fiscal linkages.(5) The dominance of the fiscal linkage together with its lack of automaticity in generating potential spread effects necessarily meant that the government had to play the leading role in initiating development. While this role could have been direct (through active state participation) or indirect (through fiscal and/or financial channels), in actuality the country wound up combining certain aspects of each.

The evolutionary approach toward assessing the oil sector's impact stresses the fact that, historically, exports of raw materials have led to development only when social milieu and policy environment was supportive.(6) In particular, it is argued that history suggests that oil could never cause growth to be ongoing but, instead, would only be capable of facilitating growth through improving the efficiency and mobility of domestic factors of production.

What conclusions emerge from the literature on export growth that have relevance for the Iranian situation?(7)

- Successful export-led growth has in large measure hinged upon the creation of production and consumption linkages with the rest of the economy.
- Although the petroleum sector has relatively few production and consumption linkages, their existence is not a necessary condition for export-led development. In principle, fiscal linkages which tend to predominate with oil provide an alternative route to growth.
- Neither production and consumption linkages on the one hand nor the fiscal linkage on the other are sufficient conditions for export led growth; internal factors (the quality and mobility of factors of production), the policy environment, and the ability to invest fiscal proceeds productively must all be present.
- No single raw material industry can be expected to lead a country all the way through diversification and industrialization. The production and consumption linkages of a series of vigorous raw materials are required before the capacity to absorb is great enough to avoid the instabilities of an export economy, and the fiscal linkage of a single raw material in general is not large enough to foster the transformation of the entire economy.

It is a moot point, of course, to argue whether the level of revenues after 1973 created a fiscal linkage large enough to permit the country's transformation just on the basis of oil. If, in fact, this had occurred, it would have set a historical precedent. The implications of these conjectures for the study of the economy are:

1. Since export-led development depended primarily on the magnitude of the fiscal linkage rather than on production and consumption linkages, maximizing the fiscal linkage was a critical problem for the government.
2. Since successful export-led growth based on the fiscal linkage rested in large part on the ability of the government to productively invest its fiscal proceeds, the investment priorities of the country were of utmost significance.
3. Since export-led development was particularly responsive to the policy environment in which economic decision making occurred, mismanagement in the latter could easily have prevented the transformation of the economy and the attainment of its growth, distribution, and employment objectives.

IMPACT OF OIL REVENUES

Several issues of importance in understanding the 1978 economic-political crises are associated with the oil sector's fiscal linkage. The first centers around the implementation response on the part of the government: Was the country's bureaucratic decision-making process responsive and adaptable enough to control its expenditures in line with oil revenues or did expenditure changes follow shifts in oil revenues with a considerable lag?

The second issue refers to the ability of oil exports (through government expenditures) to stimulate economic activity on a broad scale: Did oil-induced growth operate within a narrow base with little impact on the indigenous economy or was the overall impact broad based affecting technology, the propensity to import, the creation of investment opportunities which, in turn, were responded to by the private sector? Provided that investment opportunities generated by the growth of the export sector were taken advantage of, the staple model of growth predicts that the country's growth would have evolved through industrial diversification around the petroleum sector.

GOVERNMENT REACTION FUNCTIONS

In terms of the first issue above, it is clear that by the mid-1970s the bulk of investment in Iran was being undertaken by the government (the sole recipient of oil revenues). Higher oil revenues had not only permitted greater public investment and consumption outlays but, in addition, apparently resulted in considerable political pressure on each of the government's major ministries to increase its investment expenditures. An understanding of the response of government expenditures to changes in oil revenues, therefore, would seem to be critical in any explanation of government expenditure patterns.

The historical relationship between government expenditures and oil revenues can be examined through various econometric techniques. Availability of data on government allocations permitted a number of components to be examined: GIT = government investment; GCN = government consumption; GENAN = total government expenditures (GIT + GCN); GIM = government investment in machinery; GIC = government investment in construction.

As a first approximation, all of the various categories of government expenditure are assumed to be linear stochastic functions of the country's oil revenues. However, since oil revenues attained their mid-1970s levels as a result of the extremely large 1973-74 increase in oil prices, a significant structural change in the public sector's expenditure patterns might have occurred at that time. To test this hypothesis, the following general government investment function was fitted:

GE = b1OR + b2DOMXOR + a

where GE = government expenditure by type; OR = current oil revenues; DOMX = dummy variable assuming values of 0 and 1.

A possible a priori structural change associated with the oil price increases could have occurred in either 1973 or 1974. Hence, two sets of regressions were performed: the first with DOM1 = 0, 1959-1977; 1, 1974-1977; and the second with DOM2 = 0, 1959-74; 1, 1975-1977. With the estimated equation in this form, b2 can be interpreted as a potential indicator of whether the government's spending with respect to oil revenues had undergone any significant change following the oil price increases. A lagged form of the type

GE = b3ORL + b4DOMXORL + b

was also estimated, with its coefficients interpreted as above. The results (as shown in tables 6.2 and 6.3) indicate that:

1. The coefficients for OR are significant in all cases for both the current period and lagged versions confirming the hypothesis that oil revenues are a statistically significant variable explaining variations in public expenditures. High r^2 statistics indicate a large proportion of the variation in the various types of public expenditures may be attributed to fluctuations in oil revenues.

2. The relationship between government expenditures and oil revenues underwent a visible structural change beginning around 1975 for investment, but a bit earlier for consumption. The best statistical results for investment were obtained for the subperiods 1959-1974, 1975-1977; consumption, on the other hand, was best defined in the lagged version form for the periods 1959-1973 and 1974-1977.

3. The results indicate that only with the OR (or ORL) term can one get a biased (upward) view of government expenditures out of oil revenues for the pre-1975 period. More precisely, total investment is depicted by equations 1a and 1b recognizing two subperiods: 1959-1973 and 1974-1977 for equation 1a, and 1959-1974 and 1975-1977 for equation 1b. The coefficient of the dummy variable bx is, of course, relevant to the second subperiod only. For example, equation 1b in table 6.2 indicates that total government investment expenditure increased considerably as a proportion of oil revenues in 1975. A change in government investment associated with a change in oil revenues was 0.26 in 1959-1974 as opposed to 0.57 in the

Table 6.2. Test for Structural Change in Government Expenditure-Revenue Pattern

Equation	Dependent Variable	OR	ORD1	ORD2	Intercept	r^2	F
1	GIT	0.52 (8.71)			25.75 (0.63)	0.854	75.90
1a	GIT	0.71 (1.48)	-0.18 (-0.40)		8.20 (0.13).	0.856	35.57
1b	GIT	0.26 (3.30)		0.31 (4.01)	53.34 (1.86)	0.937	89.88
2	GCN	0.64 (16.41)			65.09 (2.47)	0.954	269.19
2a	GCN	1.05 (3.70)	-0.40 (-1.49)		26.03 (0.71)	0.961	148.21
2b	GCN	0.26 (3.42)		0.40 (4.83)	69.74 (1.56)	0.981	307.84
3	GENAN	1.15 (12.15)			90.84 (1.39)	0.919	147.65
3a	GENAN	1.77 (2.37)	-0.57 (-0.83)		34.22 (0.36)	0.923	72.37
3b	GENAN	0.74 (5.90)		0.49 (3.90)	134.09 (2.90)	0.964	161.94
4b	GIC	0.17 (3.22)		0.25 (4.55)	38.80 (1.95)	0.944	101.22
5b	GIM	0.08 (3.44)		0.07 (2.76)	14.55 (1.62)	0.915	64.61

Note: See text for description of symbols.

Table 6.3. Test for Structural Change in Government Expenditure-Revenue Pattern - Lagged Version

Equation	Dependent Variable	ORL	ORD1L	ORD2L	Intercept	r^2	F
1	GIT	0.63 (10.29)			44.41 (1.38)	0.902	119.46
1a	GIT	1.06 (2.96)	-0.41 (-1.23)		7.33 (0.17)	0.913	62.78
1b	GIT	0.44 (6.58)		0.27 (3.66)	61.36 (2.61)	0.954	123.27
2	GCN	0.72 (11.75)			99.29 (2.87)		
2a	GCN	1.96 (10.33)	-1.17 (-6.59)		-6.43 (-0.28)	0.981	361.51
2b	GCN	0.66 (6.53)		0.09 (0.83)	105.12 (2.94)	0.919	67.72
3	GENAN	3.02 (5.59)	-1.58 (-3.13)		0.90 (0.01)	0.956	131.70
3a	GENAN	1.09 (6.88)		0.36 (2.05)	166.48 (2.95)	0.941	96.33
3b	GIC	0.46 (11.74)			29.34 (1.32)	0.914	138.03
4b	GIC	0.72 (2.93)	-0.25 (-1.07)		6.70 (0.22)	0.922	70.43
4c	GIC	0.33 (7.37)		0.19 (3.79)	41.17 (2.60)	0.961	141.17
5a	GIM	0.33 (3.02)	-0.16 (-1.55)		-0.20 (-0.16)	0.885	46.04
5b	GIM	0.11 (4.80)		0.08 (3.29)	20.19 (2.56)	0.927	76.57

Note: See text for description of symbols.

1975-1977 period. Note that this value is close to the value of 0.52 for the period as a whole. Looking at equation 1 alone, however, would mask the structural change and thus conceal the true evolution of the relationship between government investment and oil revenues.

3. Structural change by expenditure type was not of equal magnitude. Differences in response to the oil price increases can be obtained using equations 1 and 2 and by examining the ratio of absorption coefficients b1/(b1+b2). The higher the ratio, the smaller the shift in government expenditure. Based on the current period regressions (table 6.4), the greatest shift after the oil revenue increase took place in construction investment followed by investment in machinery with government consumption last. These patterns were repeated in the lagged formulation. What one sees, therefore, is a year or so passing after the oil revenue increase of 1973-74 before the government fundamentally altered its expenditure patterns. When it did adjust, the major incremental increases were in investment, especially in the area of construction.

The empirical results clearly indicate that, after an initial period of adjustment, government expenditures not only began increasing more rapidly than before (which can easily be explained by much greater volume of revenues) but their increase vis a vis an increase in oil revenues was also much greater, suggesting that previous constraints on expenditures were suddenly removed. These patterns are quite consistent with the sequence of changes made involving the Fifth Year Plan.

THE REVISED FIFTH PLAN

The Fifth Plan began on March 21, 1973. As oil prices rose in the last quarter of that year, however, the Shah abandoned the plan and ordered a revised version, taking into consideration the increased oil income. The revised version was in essence the original Fifth Plan plus most of the projects rejected for the original plan as being uneconomical.

In addition to doubling and sometimes tripling funding for many existing programs, the government launched several new programs at this time in nuclear energy development, foreign aid to several Middle Eastern and African countries, and equity investment in major industrial countries. During the 1974-75 fiscal year, the government also announced several major investment and trade agreements including purchases of nuclear power reactors, arms from the United States and Britain, and its intention of investment in a number of firms in Europe and the United States.

Table 6.4. Government Expenditure Shifts 1959-1974, 1975-1977

Measure of Government Expenditure	b1	b1+b2	b1/b1+b2
Current period			
Investment total	0.26	0.57	0.46
Consumption	0.26	0.46	0.57
Investment in construction	0.17	0.42	0.40
Investment in machinery	0.08	0.15	0.53
Lagged version			
Total investment	0.44	0.71	0.62
Consumption	0.66	0.75	0.88
Investment in construction	0.33	0.52	0.63
Investment in machinery	0.11	0.19	0.58

By mid-1975, the government was beginning to anticipate a deficit in its 1975-76 budget. International reserves after rising 800 percent in less than a year stabilized at around $9 billion. Government leaders predicted that the public sector and some semi-public banks would have to borrow short-term funds in the international capital markets. In less than two years after the October 1973 Middle East war, Iran had spent, invested, or loaned most of its oil revenues. The major question was not whether the country could spend or absorb its new-found wealth, but how to do so efficiently. Some government members began to question the unrestrained growth goal, asking whether it was wise to continue to expand the economy in light of widespread shortages, double digit inflation, and port congestion - all of which were major problems in 1975.(8)

In effect, the revised Fifth Plan eliminated the planning process in Iran that had been gradually built up during the first four plans. Targets and allocations were now increased without much thought, and the current budget became far more important than the development budget. Planning authorities were reduced to macroeconomic model makers with no input into government policy. In their place, budgetary authorities began to control the expenditure process through yearly allocations with little or no account taken of the longer-run ramifications of the stepped up level of expenditures.

By late 1976, the revised Fifth Plan was, for all practical purposes, no longer followed. Worries of future problems led to an early preparation of the Sixth Development Plan (1978-79 to 1982-83). This time it was decided that planning should be undertaken not only by the plan and budget organization but also by the users of funds both within and without the government. Thus, over 100 specialized joint committees began producing expenditure proposals for the Sixth Plan. By late 1977, however, it had become clear that the decentralized approach to planning was not going to work. The total revenues of the plan were estimated at around $120 billion while demands for funds because of the shift upwards in expenditures were around $500 billion.(9) However, rather than giving the plan and budget organization authority to come up with the plan, the Shah decreed to do away with five year planning altogether. Instead, he called for 10 and 25-year guidelines in planning with one year current development budgets. By then, the planning process was effectively over and expenditures completely out of control.

No clear long-term economic strategy, therefore, emerged to respond to the increased oil revenues nor the major problems their expenditure caused. The merits of the Revised Fifth Plan were so publicized by the government that the two became closely tied. Thus, the government was committed to fund all publicized projects.

IMPACT OF OIL REVENUES ON THE ECONOMY

Economic theory has historically been of a somewhat limited use in terms of the second major question raised - the ability of oil exports to stimulate economic activity on a broad scale (through government expenditures).

Classical political economists from Adam Smith through Karl Marx regarded the state as an ultimately determinate, not determining socioeconomic category. A common thread among the classical writers was the view that the state depended on social classes and that it was not an agent of economic change. While this view has been modified over the years, no general and satisfactory theory is available for the oil exporting developing countries, nor do the major economic theories (other than in their reference to linkages and spread effects) seem to be all that applicable in explaining the mechanisms through which oil impacts on the economy.

Keynesian models, for example, have come under increased criticism for their recent poor performance in forecasting economic conditions in both the developing and the developed market economies. Further, Keynesian models are largely designed to describe short-run conditions, usually for the purpose of suggesting policies designed to synchronize the levels of aggregate demand and supply. If one argues, as is often done, that the major problems in development economics are longer term, centering around such issues as the factors that influence the productive capacity, then, given their short-run nature, Keynesian stabilization models provide few insights.(10) However, Iran is one of the few developing countries for which a modified Keynesian framework should be easily adaptable and capable of providing useful insights into the linkage between oil revenues-government expenditures and the various components of aggregate growth. One of the principal assumptions underlying Keynesian models is that the money supply is exogenous, that it responds to accommodate increased levels of real economic activity. Government expenditures and taxes are the main investments through which policy-directed changes in income take place.

It is fairly safe to assume that, given the country's official policy of spending a high proportion of the oil revenues on development activities, a large proportion of these revenues were passed on to other sectors of the economy. Growth in the non-petroleum sector should, therefore, have been largely influenced by the trend in the petroleum exports. This should have also been the case with respect to the pattern of employment in the domestic economy. These mechanisms do not seem to be fundamentally different from the standard Keynesian-deficit financed government multipliers used to analyze unemployment and income changes in the advanced countries.

The fixed value of the rial during this period, a key assumption in the Keynesian framework, supports its applicability to Iran. As seen above, an important set of linkages present at this time consisted of oil exports providing most of the country's total export receipts and that of government spending being largely financed by petroleum earnings.

The above considerations suggest a Keynesian model for Iran along the following lines:(11)

(1) $NOXN = fE$
(2) $E = S + Z$
(3) $\Delta Z = z\Delta NOXN$
(4) $\Delta S = s\Delta NOXN$
(5) $\Delta E = s\Delta Y + z\Delta Y$
(6) $\Delta NOXN/\Delta EXPTNA = 1/s+z$

where E = total value of exports; NOXN = non-oil income; Z = total imports; X = total savings; z = marginal propensity to imports; and s = the marginal propensity to save.

In this model government spending is totally determined by oil export receipts; income generated in the non-oil sector is wholly induced by oil expansion; value of the export multiplier is determined by the reciprocal of s+z; income increases induced by increases in exports will continue to expand; and the level of imports and savings will eventually increase to equal the initial increase in public spending. In Iran's case, expanding oil revenues and thus expanding government expenditures should have generated over time a commensurate growth in non-oil income and its sectoral components.

It is in this sense that Iranian exports are seen as acting as a leading sector of growth through their direct contributions to gross domestic product and indirect impact or spread effects. As noted earlier, the indirect contribution to growth would embrace the linkages first analyzed by Hirschman. Thus, within this framework, Iranian growth over time can be considered as resulting from a sequence of oil induced, Keynesian multiplier-accelerator mechanisms.

Theoretically, indirect contributions (or spread effects) could have continued to accrue long after an increase in exports such as in 1973-74 had occurred. Certainly, neither the exact pattern exhibited by nor the relative size of exports' direct and indirect contributions to growth needs to be fixed and could conceivably be varied over time.(12) If the private sector had been capable and willing to exploit the investment opportunities, Keynesian theory predicts that the country's growth would have a process of diversification about the oil-led export base.

The postulated relation between export growth and GDP over time is, therefore, central to the Keynesian framework. The model specifies that exports can contribute to the growth of GDP directly and indirectly through their spread effects (or carry over effects which occur over time). It is important to note that, apart from the basic premise that the growth of the export sector and GDP are related over time through the sequence of multiplier accelerator effects, the model says little or nothing about the precise length of time that might be actually involved.(13) This shortcoming is obviously not confined to Keynesian models and seems common to all economic theories utilizing some sort of adjustment sequence between variables. The determination of the time lags between export growth and economic growth, therefore, is essential in identifying the mechanisms responsible for Iran's economic expansion during this time.

With this purpose in mind, a dynamic (or lagged) regression relationship utilizing annual data was developed. While preliminary investigations suggested that oil revenues lagged one year might have had the strongest impact on the economy, a number of different formulations of the export-growth relationship were examined.

RESULTS

Regressions were run with the variables: (1) assuming their absolute values (i.e., the historical figures) and (2) depicted in terms of their percent change from one year to the next.

While in all cases equations specified in absolute values gave the highest r^2, the growth rate formulation is conceptually superior because, in addition to eliminating much of the time trend, proper specification should incorporate some concept of change to take into account spread and accelerator effects. Secondly, there is little reason to expect a constant impact on the economy over time of an export stimulus of given intensity (for instance, because of diversification of the economy, import substitution, and technological change). Simple linear relationships would seem to be inadequate, therefore, in incorporating these effects.

To suppress any bias introduced by inflation, the relationship between exports and income was examined in constant prices. Improvements in the terms of trade were taken into account by deflating exports by an index of import prices. This allowed the true gain to the country of increases in export prices relative to that of imports to be incorporated into the analysis (as EXW).

In terms of absolute values (table 6.5), the results indicate that real non-oil GDP (NOXNP) shows a close relationship to real exports (EXW), as do government expenditures (GENANP) and total investment (TINP). As might be expected, the relationship seems strongest (in terms of r^2) with government expenditures where current and lagged values for one and two years are all significant. Nearly 99 percent of the fluctuations in government expenditures is associated with exports over this three-year timeframe. Total investment is related more closely to lagged exports than values for the current period. Results similar to those for total investment were obtained for private expenditures, investment in machinery, and investment in construction, whereas imports followed a pattern similar to government expenditures.

Regressions formulated in rate of growth terms did not yield nearly as good results statistically, but undoubtedly depict more accurately the forces implied by the linkage model. Because of the close relationship between income and other macroeconomic variables, only those of non-oil GDP and total GDP are presented here.

Table 6.5. Impact of Exports on Macroeconomic Aggregates

Equation	Dependent Variable	EXW	EXWL	EXWL2	Intercept	r^2	F
(1)	NOXNP	0.56 (11.32)			312.65 (43.90)	0.901	128.05
(2)	NOXNP		0.60 (10.76)		339.89 (7.68)	0.892	115.79
(3)	NOXNP	0.31 (2.60)	0.29 (2.25)		312.91 (8.09)	0.929	85.11
(4)	NOXNP	0.27 (1.98)	0.21 (2.04)	0.17 (2.53)	304.97 (6.05)	0.941	51.47
(5)	GENANP	0.44 (14.11)			23.80 (0.86)	0.934	198.99
(6)	GENANP	0.20 (3.76)	0.27 (4.58)		24.04 (1.36)	0.974	251.91
(7)	GENANP	0.18 (4.37)	0.16 (2.72)	0.17 (3.18)	21.79 (1.60)	0.986	288.87
(8)	TINP	0.34 (9.07)			14.55 (33.37)	0.8545	82.25
(9)	TINP	0.04 (0.69)	0.35 (5.56)		14.86 (0.79)	0.957	144.58
(10)	TINP	0.01 (0.42)	0.19 (4.92)	0.24 (6.57)	11.74 (1.28)	0.991	423.2

Two time periods were tested: 1959-1977; and (2) 1959-1973. The results can be found in tables 6.6, 6.7, and 6.8. In general, current price regressions gave the best results. Because exports are directly a part of GDP, regressions with total income gave higher r^2 values than non-oil GDP. For the constant price case, exports and non-oil GDP were more closely related during 1959-73 than for the period as a whole while in the current price case, there is little overall difference between these two time periods. There was only a weak relationship between real exports and real non-oil GDP.

When the growth in exports was regressed on sectoral output growth, only manufacturing (table 6.9), transport and communications (table 6.10), and public services produced significant results. Overall, those for manufacturing were best statistically. Again, the 1959-73 period gives the better results with the growth of exports in the current period the most important determinant of manufacturing output. Transport and communications on the other hand were best explained by export growth lagged one and two years (table 6.9).

A basic problem remains in resolving the apparent conflict between the results derived by the Koyck procedure(14) with that obtained from a direct regression on exports (current, and those lagged one and two years). The Koyck procedure gives a general picture of fairly strong spread effects over time and weak effects generated by current period exports. The opposite result was obtained when direct regressions on current and past exports were performed. In these regressions current period exports nearly always provide better statistical results, with only a few cases where exports lagged up to two years (or even one in some cases) were statistically significant.

The contradictory picture obtained from the two models may be due to the presence of strong trend elements in the data. As noted, there are several theoretical reasons for accepting the results of the estimates specified in growth terms over those in absolute values.

Specifying the Koyck formulation in growth terms produced results that were statistically insignificant for all equations. The same patterns were also examined using the Koyck distributed lag framework (table 6.11). Several patterns stand out.

1. In general, current period exports are usually not significant in explaining sectoral output patterns; they are significant only for manufacturing (MANP), construction (CONP), and banking (BP).
2. The short-run elasticity is low for all sectors and is roughly the same magnitude for each.
3. As is expected, the long-run elasticity is always higher than the short-run elasticity, but is fairly large only for manufacturing (MANP) and public services (PUBP).

Table 6.6. Impact of Exports on Gross Domestic Product (Growth Rates, Current Prices)

Equation	Dependent Variable	EXPORTS GEX	GEXL	GEXL2	Intercept	r^2	F
1959–77							
1	GGDPN	0.44 (6.07)			8.45 (4.74)	0.739	36.79
2	GGDPN	0.39 (5.69)	0.14 (1.99)		6.77 (3.73)	0.804	24.53
3	GGDPN	0.38 (5.58)	0.11 (1.55)	0.09 (1.26)	5.97 (3.17)	0.828	17.69
4	GGDPN		0.27 (2.22)		11.08 (3.63)	0.274	4.91
5	GGDPN		0.22 (1.69)	0.14 (1.11)	9.56 (2.88)	0.341	5.11
1959–73							
6	GGDPN	0.39 (5.44)			7.11 (4.40)	0.767	29.54
7	GGDPN	0.32 (4.35)	0.18 (1.70)		5.91 (3.62)	0.828	19.31
8	GGDPN	0.24 (3.26)	0.15 (1.62)	0.23 (2.09)	5.11 (3.64)	0.894	19.71
9	GGDPN		0.41 (2.56)		8.38 (3.16)	0.422	
10	GGDPN		0.24 (1.88)	0.41 (3.05)	5.84 (2.08)	0.733	10.99

Note: See text for identification of symbols.

Table 6.7. Impact of Exports on Real Non-Oil Gross Domestic Product (Growth Rates, Constant Prices)

Equation	Dependent Variable	GEXW	GEXWL	GEXWL2	Intercept	r^2	F
1959-77							
1	GNOXNP	0.07 (1.34)			0.09 (8.06)	0.113	1.79
2	GNOXNP	0.07 (1.27)	0.02 (0.38)		0.09 (6.34)	0.123	0.91
3	GNOXNP	0.05 (0.98)	0.01 (0.20)	0.13 (2.59)	0.08 (6.21)	0.436	3.10
4	GNOXNP		0.03 (0.45)		0.09	0.273	2.97
5	GNOXNP		0.01 (0.25)	0.14 (2.83)	0.08 (7.00)	0.391	4.18
1959-73							
1	GNOXNP	0.08 (1.40)			0.82 (7.32)	0.179	1.96
2	GNOXNP	0.06 (1.07)	0.11 (0.08)		0.07 (6.14)	0.348	2.13
3	GNOXNP	0.07 (0.95)	0.11 (1.36)	-0.01 (-0.14)	0.07 (5.53)	0.349	1.26
4	GNOXNP		0.13 (1.75)		0.08 (7.41)	0.225	3.07
5	GNOXNP		0.12 (1.57)	0.03 (0.34)	0.08 (6.01)	0.266	1.45

Note: See text for definition of symbols.

Table 6.8. Impact of Exports on Non-Oil Income (Growth Rates, Current Prices)

Equation	Dependent Variable	GEX	GEXL	GEXL2	GEXL3	Intercept	r^2	F
1959-77								
1	GNOXN	0.16 (1.92)				12.19 (5.93)	0.222	3.70
2	GNOXN		0.19 (2.35)			11.57 (5.78)	0.229	5.54
3	GNOXN	0.13 (1.71)	0.17 (2.20)			9.81 (5.08)	0.500	6.00
4	GNOXN	0.09 (1.23)	0.10 (1.35)	0.15 (2.05)		8.97 (4.45)	0.561	4.68
5	GNOXN		0.13 (1.71)	0.17 (2.20)	(5.08)	9.81 0.500	0.600	
6	GNOXN		0.11 (2.03)	0.10 (1.67)	0.19 (3.43)	8.02 (5.36)	0.758	11.51
1959-73								
1	GNOXN	0.19 (2.77)				8.95 (1.60)	0.460	7.66
2	GNOXN		0.30 (3.11)			8.49 (5.40)	0.518	9.66
3	GNOXN	0.12 (1.78)	0.21 (2.13)			7.56 (5.02)	0.655	7.59
4	GNOXN	0.07 (0.91)	0.19 (1.94)	0.14 (1.19)		7.09 (4.68)	0.713	5.80
5	GNOXN		0.22 (2.37)	0.19 (2.01)		7.30 (4.93)	0.679	8.48
6	GNOXN		0.22 (2.19)	0.19 (1.77)	0.02 (0.18)	7.18 (4.16)	0.681	4.98

Note: See text for definition of symbols.

Table 6.9. Impact of Exports on Manufacturing Sector (Growth Rates, Current Prices)

Equation	Dependent Variable	EXPORTS GEX	GEXL	GEXL2	Intercept	r^2	F
1959-73							
1	GMAN	0.25 (4.39)			10.15 (7.77)	0.682	19.30
2	GMAN	0.22 (3.33)	0.09 (0.91)		9.57 (6.53)	0.712	9.88
3	GMAN	0.19 (2.32)	0.07 (0.73)	0.09 (0.80)	9.25 (5.97)	0.736	6.51
4	GMAN		0.24 (2.02)		11.26 5.62	0.313	4.10
5	GMAN		0.14 (1.24)	0.24 (1.94)	9.78 5.13	0.533	4.57
1959-77							
1	GMAN	0.20 (2.91)			3.26 (1.57)	0.401	6.02
2	GMAN	0.17 (2.39)	0.10 (1.35)		1.55 (0.77)	0.594	5.84
3	GMAN	0.15 (2.27)	0.06 (0.90)	0.10 (1.47)	0.72 (0.38)	0.718	5.94
4	GMAN		0.15 (1.94)		2.59 (1.28)	0.483	8.40
5	GMAN		0.11 (1.34)	0.12 (1.56)	12.45 (6.14)	0.355	3.30

Note: GMAN = average annual growth of manufacturing; GEX = growth of exports current prices.

Table 6.10. Impact of Exports on Transportation and Communication Sector (Growth Rates, Current Prices)

Equation	Dependent Variable	EXPORTS GEX	GEXL	GEXL2	Intercept	r^2	F
1959-73							
1	GTC	0.22 (2.45)			3.26 (1.57)	0.401	6.02
2	GTC	0.13 (1.48)	0.26 (1.95)		1.55 (0.77)	0.594	5.84
3	GTC	0.04 (0.46)	0.22 (1.83)	0.24 (1.76)	0.72 (0.38)	0.718	5.94
4	GTC		0.35 (2.90)		2.59 1.28	0.483	8.40
5	GTC		0.24 (2.20)	0.28 (2.50)	0.85 (0.49)	0.709	9.77
1959-77							
1	GTC	0.07 0.75			6.97 2.84	0.041	0.56
2	GTC	-0.01 (-0.03)	0.24 (2.71)		4.10 (1.81)	0.405	4.09
3	GTC	-0.03 (-0.49)	0.17 (2.45)	0.22 3.18	2.15 (1.18)	0.690	8.17
4	GTC		0.23 (2.98)		4.07 (2.05)	0.405	8.86
5	GTC		0.16 (2.49)	0.21 (3.24)	1.85 (1.11)	0.683	12.94

Note: GTC = average growth of transport communications gdp; GEX = average annual growth exports, GEXL = average annual growth exports lagged one year, GEXL2 = average

4. Both non-oil GDP and GDP show higher long-term and short-term elasticities than is characteristic of any of the sectors (except the long-run elasticity for manufacturing).

The Koyck results seem to suggest that the oil revenues eventually used for investment tended to be concentrated in activities whose output did not depend much on the growth in exports (for example, investment in infrastructure and in certain services and import substitution industries for which demand was readily available). Moreover, some of the investment that was undertaken in the mid-1970s may have had a long gestation period. Another explanation for the observed pattern is the possibility that some of the imported capital goods may not have been fully utilized due to the small size of the domestic market or infrastructural bottlenecks (for example, due to shortages of electrical generating capacity).

The fact that both GDP and non-oil GDP have significant coefficients for not only current exports but also their lagged values (with the lagged values representing lagged exports via the Koyck geometrically declining weight assumption) might be interpreted as indicating the general strength of the spread effect in the country.

The analysis of the aggregates (table 6.11) indicates, however, that the long-run elasticity of exports tended to be quite low for private investment in machinery (PIMP); government investment in machinery (GIMP); total private investment (PITP); capital account balance of payments (CAPEP); current account balance of payments (CUREP); and private investment in construction (PICP). While it was relatively high for government investment in construction (GICP); total government investment (GITP); and imports (ZNP); and quite high for domestic absorption (DANP).

From this we might conclude that, in general, oil revenues were utilized more efficiently for consumption (a large part of domestic absorption) than investment purposes and that their impact on private sector investment spending was minimal compared to that of the government. The results produced much lower correlations, as evidenced by the lower r^2 term and the lower "t" statistic. In all cases for all variables, the impact of exports on the economy was statistically insignificant. The results suggest that, when both the trend and inflationary effects are excluded, there is no evidence of spread effects of oil exports to the rest of the economy.

With regard to the sectoral patterns, the most important result seems to be that manufacturing output experienced only marginal spread effects at best, indicating that the domestic economy was far from integrated from the export sector. The statistically significant intercept term for manufacturing (as with the other sectors) indicates that a good part of the coun-

Table 6.11. Measure of Export Elasticities

Equation	Dependent Variable	EXW	Lagged Dependent Variable	Short-run Elasticity	Long-run Elasticity	r^2	F
(1)	CAPEP	0.056 (2.48)	0.857 (5.14)	0.056	0.392	0.961	133.80
(2)	CUREP	0.185 (8.30)	0.382 (4.34)	0.185	0.299	0.989	480.49
(3)	DANP	0.227 (4.18)	0.874 (12.27)	0.227	1.802	0.994	917.76
(4)	PIMP	0.053 (2.45)	0.380 (1.48)	0.053	0.085	0.823	25.64
(5)	GIMP	0.020 (4.17)	0.797 (7.24)	0.020	0.099	0.976	225.87
(6)	PICP	0.016 (2.49)	1.071 (9.10)	0.016	-	0.973	200.83
(7)	GTCP	0.041 (3.01)	0.919 (8.14)	0.041	0.506	0.977	233.47
(8)	PITP	0.064 (2.37)	0.696 (3.54)	0.064	0.211	0.913	57.90
(9)	GITP	0.058 (3.94)	0.915 (10.36)	0.058	0.682	0.986	386.23
(10)	ZNP	0.095 (3.63)	0.803 (7.48)	0.095	0.482	0.983	309.62

(continued)

Table 6.11. Measure of Export Elasticities (continued)

Equation	Dependent Variable	EXW	Lagged Dependent Variable	Short-run Elasticity	Long-run Elasticity	r^2	F
(11)	AGP	0.014 (1.46)	0.638 (3.05)	0.014	0.039	0.786	23.88
(12)	MANP	0.015 (1.93)	0.997 (14.52)	0.015	5.000	0.9944	1163.05
(13)	CONP	0.012 (2.12)	0.572 (2.45)	0.012	0.028	0.815	26.68
(14)	TCP	0.012 (1.89)	0.854 (5.27)	0.012	0.082	0.973	236.02
(15)	BP	0.023 (3.51)	0.792 (7.83)	0.023	0.112	0.991	697.77
(16)	TP	0.012 (1.72)	0.828 (5.09)	0.012	0.070		
(17)	ODP	0.005 (1.15)	0.860 (4.60)	0.005	0.036	0.951	124.88
(18)	PUBP	0.015 (1.27)	0.974 (7.51)	0.015	0.577	0.978	288.36
(19)	PRIUP	0.008 (1.60)	0.864 (5.59)	0.008	0.059	0.964	174.86
(20)	NOXNP	0.086 (2.18)	0.986 (12.04)	0.086	6.143	0.993	782.81
(21)	GDPNP	0.028 (0.33)	0.980 (6.88)	0.028	1.400		

try's output grew independently of the expansion in exports. One explanation is that most manufacturing growth was through the import substitution process, i.e., in products for which there was already a demand. The results also could imply that the expansion in oil exports and the investment opportunities thereby generated were not fully taken advantage of by the private sector, perhaps due to market limitations. Aggregated and disaggregated investment analysis clearly suggests that public sector gross capital formation was extremely sensitive to growth in oil exports while that of the private sector was not, especially in the case of the private investment in machinery.

Thus, the combined analysis of output and investment suggests that, while the government's investment efforts were responding in a significant way to the growth in oil exports, the private sector preferred to invest in construction and that the growth in real (sectoral) output was largely independent of that of the export sector.

CONCLUSIONS

The major findings of this chapter are:

1. Government expenditures were highly dependent on oil revenues.
2. A major structural change in government expenditures took place in 1975, with public sector expenditures not only increasing but increasing significantly with respect to oil revenues.
3. While there was a major impact of oil revenues on the government's expenditure patterns, the private sector does not seem to have been affected to a great extent (directly or indirectly).
4. Of the private sector activities, investment in construction was the most influenced by changes in exports.
5. It is safe to say that whatever spread effects were present were quite minimal - the non-oil sectors did not respond dramatically to changes in oil exports.
6. The evidence indicates that investment opportunities generated by the export sector were, in general, not fully exploited and that output of most of the non-oil sectors was not responsive to changes in the rate of change in exports.

APPENDIX TO CHAPTER 6

It may be argued that Iran's oil exports and the income of the OECD or oil consuming countries were interrelated simultaneously, i.e., that an increase in exports resulted in an increase in Iranian income and imports which, in turn, increased the incomes of those countries that were major exporters of goods and services to Iran (and the other OPEC countries). Increased incomes in the rest of the world, thus, would further stimulate demand for oil and thereby stimulate an additional increase in Iranian exports (and, of course, those of the other OPEC countries).

Technically, therefore, the relationship between the country's exports and its income over time should be examined in the context of a simultaneous equation model that explicitly takes the interaction between exports, imports, and incomes into account.

In the simultaneous equation model estimated below, all variables are specified as growth rates. The first equation examines the relationship between income (GNOXNP and GGDPNP) and exports (GEXW) in a manner similar to that in the ordinary least squares estimates in Chapter 6.

The second equation tests the relationship between exports (GEXW) and imports (GZNP). A significant feedback effect would result in the coefficients for GZNP and GZNPL being statistically significant, i.e., increasing Iranian imports would expand the purchasing power of the exporting countries to the extent that further Iranian oil exports would be possible. The demand for imports in the third equation is set as a function of income in current (NOXNP) and past periods (NOXNPL).

In general, the following conclusions can be drawn from the results (table A.1).

1. The export-income relationships in the simultaneous model give a picture similar to those obtained in the ordinary least squares estimates. The coefficients of both the current and lagged export variable (which represents the spread effects) are significant in the real non-oil GDP equation.
2. Current and past changes in imports do not seem to be important factors in determining current changes in exports. Changes in export prices may play a role in determining current changes in exports but, again, the "t" value of the coefficient of the price term is low.
3. Current changes in income are more important determinants of changes in imports than past income.

It is clear from these results that the general conclusions as to the limited impact of the oil sector on the economy are

Table A.1. Exports and National Income, Simultaneous Equation Results

Levels

Two Stage Estimation

$$NOXNP = 0.13\ EXW + 0.92\ NOXNPL + 34.58$$
(2.19) (8.16) (1.08)
$r^2 = 0.993$
$F = 961.00$

$$GDPNP = 0.03\ EXW + 1.09\ GDPNPL + 20.39$$
(-0.23) 6.59
$r^2 = 0.981$
$F = 368.21$

$$EXW = 4.76\ ZNP - 2.40\ ZNPL + 3.28\ EUVP - 145.10$$
(3.07) (-1.40) (1.35) (-1.21)
$r^2 = 0.931$
$F = 58.68$

$$ZNP = 0.36\ NOXNP + 0.15\ NOXNPL - 122.78$$
(1.25) (0.44) (-6.35)
$r^2 = 0.9679$
$F = 210.81$

$$ZNP = 0.81\ ZNPL - 0.17GDPNP + 0.32\ GDPNPL - 44.50$$
(6.14) (-1.26) (2.07) (2.14)
$r^2 = 0.979$
$F = 204.43$

Limited Information Maximum Likelihood Estimates

$$NOXNP = 0.39\ EXW + 0.44\ NOXNPL + 150.77$$
(0.39) (0.44) (1.19)
$K = 1.55052$
$r^2 = 0.9617$
$F = 175.63$

$$GDPNP = 5.58\ EXW + 9.17\ GDPNPL - 2719.64$$
(-0.17) (0.19) (-0.17)
$K = 1.75216$
$r^2 = 0.112$
$F = 0.88$

$$EXW = 4.77\ ZNP - 2.41\ ZNPL + 3.27\ EWP$$
(3.07) (-1.40) (1.34)
$K = 1.04759$
$r^2 = 0.9312$
$F = 58.67$

$$ZNP = 17.29\ NOXNP - 19.50\ NOXNPL + 283.15$$
(0.15) (-0.15) (0.10)
$K = 6.33731$
$r^2 = 0.15$
$F = 0.71$

$$ZNP = 0.27\ ZNPL - 0.33\ GDPNP + 0.51\ GDPNPL - 42.61$$
(5.38) (-2.06) (2.70) (-1.88)
$K = 4.50273$
$r^2 = 0.976$
$F = 173.55$

(continued)

Table A.1. Exports and National Income, Simultaneous Equation Results (continued)

Rates of Growth

Two Stage Estimation

```
GNOXNP = 0.0076GEXW + 0.376 NOXNPL + 0.06
         (0.09)       (1.67)         (2.78)          r^2 = 0.189
                                                     F   = 1.52

GGDPNP = 0.06 GEXW - 0.20 GGDPNPL + 0.10
         (0.58)      (-0.61)        (3.33)           r^2 = 0.048
                                                     F   = 0.26

GEXW = -0.96 GZNP + 0.39 GZNPL + 0.002 EUVG + 0.14
       (-0.86)      (0.78)       (1.96)       (1.56) r^2 = 0.326
                                                     F   = 1.93

GZNP = 2.01 GNOXNP + 0.776 GNOXNPL - 0.14
       (1.04)        (0.69)          (-0.94)         r^2 = 0.233
                                                     F   = 1.24

GZNP = 0.44 GZNPL - 2.26 GDPNP + 0.41 GGDPNPL + 0.24
       (1.21)       (-0.84)      (0.20)         (0.78) r^2 = 0.135
                                                       F   = 1.57
```

Limited Information Maximum Likelihood Estimates

```
GGDPNP = 0.01 GEXW - 0.12 GGDPNPL + 0.10
         (-0.07)     (-0.31)        (3.01)           r^2 = 0.01
                     K = 1.31074                     F   = 1.62

GNOXNP = 0.44 GXUXNPL - 0.09 GEXW + 0.07
         (1.56)         (-0.67)     (2.41)           r^2 = 0.159
                        K = 1.45117                  F   = 1.23

GEXW = -2.56 GGZNP + 0.98 GZWPL + 0.004 EUVG + 0.24
       (-0.61)       (0.59)       (0.94)       (0.83) r^2 = 0.113
                     K = 1.07235                      F   = 0.51

GZNP = 2.47 GNOXNP + 0.62 NOXNPL - 0.17
       (1.04)        (0.49)        (-0.97)           r^2 = 0.233
                     K = 1.16293                     F   = 1.98

GZNP = 0.50 GZNPL - 3.55 GGDPNP + 0.18 GGDPNPL + 0.37
       (1.12)       (-0.92)       (0.09)         (0.87) r^2 = 0.1339
                    K = 1.07444                         F   = 0.02
```

still valid. It is also evident that feedback effects from the industrial countries were insignificant. This is not surprising given the fact that total Iranian imports amounted to less than 1 percent of total world exports (and only a slightly higher level of the total industrialized countries' exports during the period under consideration).

7 Absorptive Capacity

INTRODUCTION

The impact of oil revenues on the economy during a given time period can be broken down into several independent elements. The first, the response of the government to changes in oil revenues from the administrative side of identifying and implementing areas for expenditure, was examined in the previous chapter. The second involves the production inducing effect of these expenditures through linkage and spread effects. A third aspect concerns the production of government oil-derived expenditures as measured by the country's ability or absorptive capacity to utilize them effectively. Because economic development was the principal vehicle for converting oil resources into a continuing stream of real benefits to the country, the estimation of realistic spending levels or the absorptive capacity for oil revenues was undoubtedly the most important decision undertaken by the government.

It is important to remember the context of the problem. By the 1970s, the government was, to a large extent, controlling the rate at which oil was produced (subject to technical constraints) and the price charged for its export. All of the revenues from the export oil accrued to the government in the form of foreign exchange. Production from the petroleum reserves was desirable only to the extent that benefits, either monetary or nonmonetary, occurred and were valued by the government. Since the reserves were fixed, production and pricing decisions by the government determined a stream of benefits or revenues over a finite period of time. Increased production in the near term implied a decision to forego some oil revenues in the future.

Analysis of the country's absorptive capacity and the government's role in attempting to alter it throws additional light on several important factors leading up to the economic crisis that preceded the revolution.

CONCEPTUAL ISSUES

Absorptive capacity has been characterized as an ill-defined concept.(1) To this extent it is like the concept of economic development in that there have been a wide range of definitions. It is, however, possible to compose a definition that is broad enough to accommodate most of the interpretations that have been given to the concept: Iran's absorptive capacity was the ability of the domestic economy to absorb resources at an acceptable rate of return within a given period. In applying this concept, therefore, two issues must be addressed: (1) the nature of resources to be absorbed, and (2) what constitutes an acceptable rate of return.

In the first case, a distinction is often made between investable funds or savings and total financial resources in the economy, between supply of financial resources and its translation into physical goods, between foreign exchange components and the total financial resources, and so on. Ultimately, given such a variety of alternative definitions of financial resources, the choice of which one to use for analysis must depend on the use to which one wants to put the concept of absorptive capacity.(2)

In terms of the second issue, absorptive capacity must ultimately be defined in terms of the magnitude of oil revenues that would yield a minimum acceptable rate of return to the country, i.e., both economic and social returns would be included in the definition.(3) In Iran's case, there was a finite limit on the total magnitude of investment during any period that yielded a positive rate of return. This limit was set by the decline in the return on investment and reflected the scarcity of projects with high expected rates of return.

The scarcity of high return projects during any finite time period was due, in turn, to limitations on the supply of domestic resources to combine with the oil revenues, including the availability of labor with the needed skills, knowledge of available natural resources and technology, management and entrepreneurial experience, adequate financial and planning institutions to initiate and implement projects, and the absence of social or cultural constraints on development. The existence of such limitations restricted the country's level of absorptive capacity.

In this regard it must be stressed that, to be useful, the concept of absorptive capacity must explicitly take time into account. The factors hindering improvements in efficient capital utilization do not generally lend themselves to quick changes. In Iran's case, shortages of skilled manpower would have required that the educational system be extensively reformed. Changing sociocultural attitudes and building new growth-oriented political institutions was also a necessary element but one that, if approached correctly, would have been a protracted process involving practically every significant aspect of society. Thus, the abandoning of a controlled spending policy in favor of the immediate spending of oil revenues as they accrued appears to have been a major mistake on the part of the government.(4)

In more specific terms, during 1974, oil revenues increased to $20 billion from just $5 billion a year earlier. The government faced two alternatives: either spend these revenues as they accrued (the one they chose), or pace its spending in line with the economy's ability to efficiently utilize the funds. The latter approach obviously was superior because it would have permitted a smooth intertemporal allocation of oil resources in step with the needs of the economy. Thus, initial inflationary pressures would have been relieved as well as the balance of payments difficulties in later years.(5)

The novel condition of an elastic supply of financial resources dictated that planners changed their perspective. As Vakil noted:(6)

> Indeed these [oil] revenues are on the one hand, like the blood of the economy, carrying badly needed investment resources to particular areas for purposes of expanding productive capacity; and on the other hand, they are capable of producing an excessive liquidity situation, if capital resources become suddenly out of line with other complementary factors of production (such as skilled labor, technology, organizational skills, natural resources or general infrastructure services). This duality renders the planning task all the more difficult under conditions of financial surplus, since it requires a shift of emphasis in the planning circles from an allocation of resources according to the new abundant factor to an allocation of resources according to the real scarce factor.

It follows that absorptive capacity concepts should have been utilized by the government in implementing the country's development strategy. The best definition of absorptive capacity from a conceptual point of view, then, is the maximum level of spending of foreign exchange by the government that yielded positive returns, given constraints on factors prerequisite and complementary to such spending.(7) Unfortunately, it is difficult to make this definition operational because the process of evaluating the present value of both monetary and nonmonetary returns from all possible domestic spending opportunities for oil revenues over time in Iran would be exceedingly complex if not impossible. In view of this fact, it would have been best for the government to have chosen an indirect and more macroeconomic approach.

In terms of the factors associated with the Iranian revolution, it would seem that financial resources were neither allocated exclusively to economic projects nor were they spent efficiently when economic projects were involved. The abundance of financial capital contributed to extravagance, waste, and inefficiency. In this context, the best operational definition of absorptive capacity is one that explicitly takes into account the productivity of government expenditures in contributing to real non-oil gross domestic product. This approach would allow, from an operational perspective, not only the productivity of expenditures to be monitored but also facilitate rational discussions as to possible limits to be placed on real non-oil GDP growth irrespective of productivity trends. For instance, the revenues from oil after 1973-74 temporarily transformed Iran into a capital-surplus, skilled-labor-deficient, unskilled-labor-abundant country with skilled labor undoubtedly acting as the growth inhibiting factor. To alleviate this constraint and expand absorptive capacity, the government resorted to importing a large number of foreign technicians. The efficiency of such measures ultimately depended on what skills were transferred to the Iranian population and at what social cost.(8) Although this problem requires thorough research and analysis, the picture that has emerged so far is mixed at best. Reports of friction, discord, and distrust, as well as some violence between the Iranians and foreign nationals have been documented.(9) A cursory analysis seems to confirm Griffin's observation that large-scale participation in an economy by foreigners is likely to frustrate the growth of an entrepreneurial class, disrupt national cohesion, and delay the appearance of a development ideology.(10)

The analysis presented below is concerned with estimating the absorptive capacity of Iran as it related to the country's domestic constraints on efficient investment. Emphasizing the impact on domestic income has the advantage of avoiding the calculation of separate estimates for the trade account. The approach assumes that, if oil revenues were insufficient to meet the government's desired level of expenditure, the country would be able to easily raise the shortfall in the international financial markets.(11)

THE INCREMENTAL CAPITAL OUTPUT RATIO

All things considered, the incremental capital output ratio (ICOR) appears to be the best measure of the country's absorptive capacity.(12) This approach assumes that increases in national output are a fairly stable function of increments in real capital stock. The numerator of the ratio comprises the value increase in stock of all produced means of production (including working capital). The denominator represents the increment in real non-oil GDP. Because the precise time lag between initiation of the investment process and the eventual increase in output is not known (and in any case probably varies from year to year), two formulations of the ICOR were examined. The first one sets both the numerator and denominator to cover the same increment of time - the change in output and investment during a given year. The second measure assumes that incremental output is related to prior investment, i.e., that there is a one year lag between the implementation of the investment decision and the time at which output is forthcoming.

Investment of non-oil GDP ratios are calculated for a number of measures of investments in order to derive a number of specific policy conclusions. The ICORs examined included:

ICOR = total investment (t)/non-oil GDP(t)
ICORL = total investment (t-1)/non-oil GDP(t)

Similarly,

ICORPM = ICOR for private investment in machinery
ICORPC = ICOR for private investment in construction
ICORGM = ICOR for government investment in machinery
ICORC = ICOR for total (government plus private) investment in construction
ICORM = ICOR for total investment in machinery
ICORGC = ICOR for government investment in construction
ICORPT = ICOR for total private investment (construction plus machinery)
ICORGT = ICOR for total government investment

In each case, an L at the end of the symbol refers to the previous year's investment divided by the increment in this year's non-oil GDP. All variables are in real terms.

Historically, the ICORs have been relatively stable by international standards (table 7.1). They do, however, show

Table 7.1. Capital Output Measures

	ICOR	ICORL	ICORPM	ICORPML	ICORPL	ICORPCL	ICORGM	ICORGML	ICORL
1960	0.347	0.183	1.15	1.04	1.28	1.02	0.26	0.34	1.40
1961	1.656	0.195	3.99	5.69	6.54	6.38	1.81	1.28	5.81
1962	0.408	0.180	0.89	1.04	1.51	1.71	0.28	0.47	1.17
1963	0.273	0.159	0.60	0.60	1.05	1.01	0.13	0.19	0.73
1964	0.263	0.149	0.67	0.49	1.01	0.86	0.17	0.11	0.84
1965	0.230	0.158	0.44	0.45	0.77	0.68	0.26	0.11	0.71
1966	0.226	0.189	0.51	0.41	0.76	0.71	0.30	0.24	0.81
1967	0.284	0.184	0.71	0.48	0.70	0.72	0.41	0.29	1.12
1968	0.178	0.210	0.34	0.38	0.45	0.42	0.33	0.22	0.67
1969	0.427	0.225	0.68	0.74	1.00	0.96	0.89	0.70	1.58
1970	0.278	0.230	0.49	0.43	0.62	0.63	0.55	0.56	1.03
1971	0.292	0.217	0.59	0.42	0.66	0.53	0.52	0.47	1.11
1972	0.211	0.229	0.51	0.34	0.49	0.38	0.26	0.30	0.83
1973	0.217	0.249	0.50	0.52	0.46	0.44	0.34	0.23	0.84
1974	0.271	0.249	0.54	0.47	0.55	0.44	0.52	0.32	1.06
1975	0.408	0.289	1.27	0.46	0.73	0.47	0.50	0.45	1.78
1976	0.289	0.415	0.69	0.71	0.60	0.41	0.43	0.28	1.13
1977	0.687	0.488	1.32	1.56	1.59	1.35	1.06	0.90	2.40

(continued)

Table 7.1. Capital Output Measures (continued)

	ICORCL	ICORM	ICORML	ICORGC	ICORPT	ICORPTL	ICORGT	ICORTL
1960	1.38	2.62	2.03	0.93	2.43	2.06	1.19	1.35
1961	6.97	10.88	13.01	4.33	10.54	12.08	6.15	5.91
1962	1.52	2.58	2.84	1.08	2.39	2.75	1.36	1.61
1963	0.79	2.00	1.73	0.95	1.65	1.60	1.08	0.91
1964	0.60	1.78	1.64	0.77	1.69	1.35	0.94	0.89
1965	0.57	1.60	1.20	0.83	1.23	1.13	1.09	0.63
1966	0.65	1.45	1.47	0.69	1.26	1.13	0.99	1.00
1967	0.77	1.72	1.37	0.96	1.47	1.20	1.37	0.94
1968	0.62	1.11	0.95	0.67	0.79	0.81	0.99	0.76
1969	1.43	2.69	2.39	1.70	1.68	1.69	2.59	2.13
1970	0.99	1.75	1.69	1.13	1.11	1.05	1.67	1.62
1971	0.89	1.81	1.50	1.15	1.25	0.95	1.66	1.44
1972	0.64	1.28	1.04	0.80	1.05	0.72	1.05	0.96
1973	0.75	1.34	1.16	0.87	0.96	0.96	1.21	0.95
1974	0.79	1.64	1.26	1.10	1.09	0.90	1.62	1.14
1975	0.91	2.34	1.41	1.57	2.00	0.93	2.08	1.39
1976	0.99	1.77	1.30	1.17	1.30	1.11	1.60	1.16
1977	2.53	4.47	3.97	2.88	2.91	2.91	3.95	1.37

Note: ICOR = TINP/ΔNOXNP, ICORL = TINPL/ΔNOXNP, ICORPM = PIMP/ΔNOXND, ICORPML = PIMP/ΔNOXNP, ICORPCP = PICP/ΔNOXNP, ICORPCL = PICPL/ΔNOXNP, ICORGM = GIMP/ΔNOXNP, ICORGML = GIMPL/ΔNOXNP, ICORC = CITP/ΔNOXNP, ICORCL = CITPL/ΔNOXNPL, ICORM = MITP/ΔNOXNP, ICORML = MITPL/ΔNOXNP.

Where TINP = total real investment, TINP = total real investment in previous period, PIMP = real private investment in machinery with D and L versus same as with TINP. PICPL = private investment in construction; GIMP = government investment in machinery, and CITP = total investment in construction; ICORGC = GICP/ΔNOXNP, ICORGCL = GICPL/ΔNOXNP, ICORPT = PITP/ΔNOXNP, ICORPTL = PITPL/ΔNOXNP, ICORGT = GITP/ΔNOXNP, ICORGTL = GITPL/ΔNOXNPL.

GITLP = total government investment in construction (real), PITP = total private real investment; GITP = total real government investment.

Source: Computed from data in Bank Markazi Iran Annual Report, various issues.

several distinctive patterns. Relatively high ICORs were obtained in the early 1960s, undoubtedly a reflection of excess capacity resulting from the government's stabilization program. In general, ICORs declined until the late 1960s, then began to increase reaching very high values in 1977. These conclusions hold for all of the various ICOR measures.

While admittedly a very crude measure, one advantage of the capital output ratio in the present context is that its movements provide some substantiation for several hypotheses that would seem to explain movements in private sector investment in the 1960s. Given the lack of relevant data, these hypotheses would be pure conjecture in the absence of something like a capital output ratio.

Most importantly, the incremental capital output ratio lends itself to econometric analysis, thus providing a method whereby the impact of government expenditures, the rate of economic growth, can be determined.

CAPITAL OUTPUT PATTERNS

Capital output patterns suggest a number of possible forces at work during this period. Several mechanisms can be outlined that are consistent with the observed trends and also in agreement with events taking place at the time. This discussion is a prelude to and provides the rationale for the econometric analysis that follows. In terms of the revolution, the underlying causes of the rising capital output ratio in the mid to latter 1970s should be the main focus of attention. The events during this period suggest several causes for the observed fall in investment productivity: diminishing returns on investment stemming from high rates of growth; infrastructural bottlenecks; presence of easy profits, promoting waste; problems in implementing aspects of agrarian reform; and destructive effects of inflation and price control on labor motivation.

Decreasing Returns on Investment

The returns on capital apparently decreased in the 1970s as financial resources were applied in greater quantities during a given period of time. As noted, this pattern could have resulted from the fact that other factor inputs such as labor could not increase as rapidly as investment. It could also be a reflection of the fact that, as growth accelerated during the boom period, the most productive technologies and investments were undoubtedly chosen initially and inferior technologies (because of their availability) and marginal projects weighed heavier in total investment over time.

It seems safe to postulate, therefore, a negative correlation between the productivity of capital (as measured by the capital output ratio) and the rate of gross domestic capital formation. That is, investment opportunities with high returns are limited during any period of time and, from a certain point onward, further capital formation was only possible if companies and the government were willing to undertake projects with a lower prospective return.

A more formal explanation for the observed patterns of change in the various capital output ratios is that sometime in the late 1960s to early 1970s increases in the quantity of combined factors of production started generating a smaller output increment due to the pattern of supply of the factors themselves.(13) Most economic entities can be identified as having one or more required production factors in relatively fixed supply. From a certain level onward, additional output will be possible only if other economic resources are combined in ever greater quantities with the scarce factor. This generally amounts to a rise of input costs and a tantamount reduction in productivity and the rate of return.

Along somewhat different lines, it is now a well established fact that the investment process involves an important element of learning. The high capital output ratios after 1973 might be attributed, at least in part, to the relatively low rate of prior investment. The relationship between the past rate of investment and prospective rates is intricate and complex because a higher historical rate not only implies greater familiarity with and practice in the investment field, but also a larger economic system, which would be able to utilize considerably greater amounts of capital.

Finally, recent theories of economic growth have increasingly emphasized that the structure of capital formation is as relevant as its volume.(14) This hints at a final causative factor. It may be that the number of indirectly productive investments (infrastructure, educational facilities, residential housing, etc.) increased in the 1970s with the overall volume of capital formation. Since this type of investment has a relatively long gestation period, an increase in its importance could account for the rise in the overall ICOR. Unfortunately, reliable estimates for the indirectly productive investments in Iran as distinguished from directly productive capital formation are very difficult to distinguish and any arbitrary allocation would be quite hazardous.

Clearly, both decreasing and increasing returns are logically possible. Acceptance of the decreasing returns hypothesis for the 1970s does not imply that instances of increasing returns were not also forthcoming. These hypotheses need not necessarily be incompatible.(15)

The possibility of increasing returns may have been the real rationale for the government's development strategy. As derived from microeconomic analysis, productivity increases can take place because as the market increases the greater the differentiation and specialization of labor that is possible. The argument that may have been most convincing to the government was Arrow's contention that (in general), the faster the rate of growth of investment and output, the faster the rate of growth of productivity owing to the process of learning by doing.(16)

To sum up both the observed patterns of the ICORs in Iran and economic theory suggests that, at any time, there are certain forces working to increase the productivity of capital and at other times causing it to fall. Based on the available evidence, it is impossible to say that diminishing returns was a major contributing factor to the decline in productivity during the period.

Bottlenecks

The problem of infrastructure bottlenecks - ports, power, transportation - has been noted at length in the popular press. On a general level, shortages in these areas can be thought of as developing simply as a result of a sudden increase in demand together with a relatively long period required for the construction of additional facilities. Bottlenecks appear in the production chain so that firms relying on inputs such as electric power are forced to operate at less than full capacity as overall growth accelerates. This occurred at times after 1973 in Tehran, due to the fact that the area's power generating capacity was not sufficient to supply all users simultaneously. The result was a series of scheduled brownouts and an average complete loss of power of up to four working hours a day.

The fairly dramatic fall in productivity probably required more than limited supplies of service, however. A reading of accounts at the time(17) indicates that the manner in which the government allowed excess demand in these areas to develop contributed in large measure to the reduction in productivity.(18)

As will be discussed in detail in the following chapter, the government's response to the inflationary pressures that built up after 1973-74 was a comprehensive price control schedule.

Difficulties in the power industry are of particular interest since they were dramatic demonstrations of the failures of the government's price control schemes. Unlike many of the government's other mistakes, power failures could not be hidden behind a bureaucratic curtain of silence, and hence it is instructive to examine the problems of this sector in some detail.

The problem of an "empty" economy can be directly attributable to the workings of excess demand induced by price controls. In general, when price controls are in effect but no attempt is made to force demand and supply to balance at a fairly realistic price (as was the case in many instances between 1975-77), resources will be rapidly drawn out of the industrial stream into final output and final consumption. The result will be to threaten the continuity and efficiency of production and distribution. In fact, by the middle of 1977, an acute countrywide energy shortage was the most pressing concern for the government. Power blackouts, power failures, and insufficient generating capacity disrupted production schedules in industry and business as well as complicated the everyday lives of urban workers.

The problem was not a new one in Iran, but in the summer of 1977 the combination of factors associated with the lack of proper price signals to stimulate both public and private investment together with low rainfall, contractual difficulties, and poor planning exacerbated the situation.

One of the most devastating effects of the power shortage was documented in a report from the Imperial Commission's Committee on Industry, a watchdog responsible directly to the Shah. According to the commission's findings, the country's sole aluminum plant, Arak Aluminum, had experienced interruptions in its supply of electricity 760 times for a total of 33,000 minutes between March 1976 and March 1977.(19) The plant (whose main factor input was electricity) had access to a maximum 35 MW instead of the promised 115 MW. As a result, production had declined by 43 percent during the industrial boom year of 1974 - a year when the demand for aluminum was increasing at an unprecedented place. The company had not only lost millions but had disrupted the production schedules of its major buyers. During the same period, the report found that power failures were the major cause of a 45 percent fall in output at the country's principal machine tools factory, also located at Arak.

The problems at Arak were not isolated instances. Rather, they reflected a generalized situation throughout the country - especially where firms had believed official assurances that power could always be supplied at low rates from the national power grid and, therefore, did not go ahead with construction of their own private generators.

It is clear that, if power prices had been allowed to increase somewhat during the post-1973-74 period, not only would total demand (much of it for nonessential uses) have been much lower but a number of firms would have found it profitable to install their own systems, thus releasing public resources for other projects.

The government blamed most of the country's power difficulties on the failure of foreign firms to complete on schedule work on the 750 MW generating plant at Reza Shah Dam in Khuzestan. The project was originally supposed to be operational in 1977, but indications were that it might be some time before any electricity would be generated from the project. The government blamed the American contractors and the French suppliers of the turbines for their alleged failure to carry out their obligations. But the story appears much more complex, involving problems over the site of the dam, tremendous pressure for quick completion of preliminary studies, and finally delay in implementation that left the turbines on site for a year before their installation.

These are the kinds of inevitable problems that appeared everywhere in the economy as projects were initiated in a hurry responding to, but not in anticipation of, scarcities and shortages. In short, though the failure of the Reza Shah Dam to come onstream was clearly a contributing factor to the country's power shortages, it was not the real reason. The basic cause was largely one of miscalculation of the degree to which industrial and domestic consumption of electricity were increasing under the revised Fifth Five Year Plan. Even if the Reza Shah project had been fully operational, electricity demand would still have fallen short of supply.

Consumption was increasing at a rate of between 18 and 20 percent a year. By 1977, official figures placed the country short by 600 MW of power. Foreign specialists connected with the power business, however, believed the country's shortfall was nearer to 1,000 MW, perhaps beyond, given the tremendous expansion of electrification throughout the country and growing industrialization.

In addition to the wisdom of importing nuclear technology, the program was extremely ill-conceived from the start. There were serious questions about the risk involved since many of the nuclear plants were to be situated in earthquake prone western areas of the country. Costly long distance transmission of power would be necessary since local use was minimal. The country was also incurring massive expenses - several billion dollars alone for several West German nuclear power plants at Bushehr.

In terms of planning failures, one could criticize the government's whole approach to power. About 71 percent of the country's total energy generated in the mid-1970s was derived from petroleum, 18 percent from gas, with 5 percent coming from hydroelectricity and the rest from coal and noncommercial sources. The basic strategy evolved in 1974 was that alternative sources of energy must be developed to replace both oil and gas (being regarded as too important to waste), especially as production of oil was expected to begin to decline in the mid-1980s. Gas, too, was regarded as more important to conserve for use in secondary recovery industrial use (steel, direct reduction, and aluminum) and as a feedstock for the petrochemical industry, despite the fact that in 1976 Iran's proven gas reserves were the second largest in the world.

Many of the issues raised by such considerations were never answered convincingly, leading one observer to comment that Iran had no energy policy at all but, rather, a number of contending bureaucracies.(20)

Waste

Rising capital output ratios also suggest inefficient use of expenditures. While documentation is difficult to obtain, one recent study of Iranian import patterns reveals several startling facts about the extent of mismanagement taking place during this period. An examination of imports from 1972 to 1974 found that overpayments (in terms of the lowest potential price which could have been paid at the time) amounted to $539 million or 37.8 percent.(21) This sample represented about 60 percent of Iran's total imports. For 1973 and 1974, the overall results are similar but with one interesting difference. Following the oil price increases, overpayments increased to 49.4 percent in 1973 and were 46.2 percent in 1974.(22)

A number of reasons not related to overpayments have been suggested for this loss of exchange earnings.

1. There may have been variations in unit export prices for an exporter due to qualitative differences, price discrimination between purchasers, and tariffs. Also, the overvalued rial could have led to fake invoices (and thus to apparent variations in export unit values).
2. Imports may have been purchased by buyers with insufficient information. In reality, imports were likely to have been contracted for by many companies or individuals with fragmentary knowledge of world markets.
3. Existing trade patterns were, in large part, determined by historical ties and may not have accurately reflected current prices.
4. Some current trade was based on past contracts and thus sale prices differed from the spot figures.
5. Contracts were made in many currencies and thus fluctuations in exchange rates could have affected the dollar price from one source to another.
6. Quality differences could have been reflected in the price.
7. Quick delivery may have required a higher price.
8. A large part of imports were from multiproduct firms that placed restrictions on their importing agents. Major importers in the country contracted to multinational firms were committed to import all the products of that firm, and

could not import a competitive product from a lower cost producer.

9. Differential credit terms or contract or transport costs could contribute to variations in import prices.

A detailed analysis of each of these factors revealed that none, or even combinations of them, could come close to accounting for the calculated degree of overpayment.

Overpayments on imports were only one dimension of the economic waste that resulted from the oil price increases of 1973-74. In addition, industrialization proceeded with little or no consideration given to comparative advantage and domestic factor endowments. The structure of tariffs was not based on rational economic factors. The result was factories without workers, output produced in many instances at more than twice the world price, and negative value added in several industries.

Inefficiency in Agriculture

One of the objectives in the government's antiinflation program (because of their excessive profits) was to eliminate the middlemen between the farmer and retailer. Presumably, this would leave more profits for the farmers. In eliminating many of the traders and bazaar merchants from the system, however, the authorities did not replace them with a viable network. A large number of cold storage plants were being established as a key element of the Fifth Five Year Plan, but construction was far behind schedule. Plans were also made for the government to spend around $475 million to construct 27 silos in urban areas. But this program was also considerably behind schedule as a result of the acute nationwide shortage of cement in addition to the usual bureaucratic delays. But, in any case, given its other commitments, the country's trucking fleet could not come close to handling the scheduled 2 million ton capacity planned.(23)

As a result of distribution problems of the type outlined above and despite the price controls and subsidies, such as imports at stable prices, rice cost the consumer about twice as much in Iran as in Western Europe.

By 1977 realities, the main complaint seemed to be that shortages of many food items were becoming commonplace. Many complaints were made by distributors that the government's procurement agency was often late or negligent in meeting orders.

What was clearly antagonizing the agricultural sector was the low profitability of investment in farming activities, and the government's pricing policies were particularly troubling for the farming community. In particular, the contrast between the price for home goods and imported commodities was a major source of irritation in rural areas. For example, in late 1976, farmers received around 10 rials a kilogram for wheat. This was widely regarded as barely adequate to cover the costs of cultivation, let alone provide a reasonable living. At the same time, the government was paying 18 rials a kilogram for imported wheat. Policies of this type were apparently the source of so much anger that they drove tea farmers in some parts of the country to burn their crops while forcing a number of poultry farms to close their businesses. It was clear that the farming community could continue to carry their burdens only at the cost of lower productivity. Quality began slipping noticeably in the fruit and vegetable markets, and an increasing number of farmers began to vocally criticize what they considered to be outrageous government pricing programs.

In part, one of the government's major problems was its haste; the country's planners were moving too fast for the majority of the farmers who were largely illiterate. Many potentially proficient plans failed simply because the Agricultural Ministry lacked the qualified personnel to explain them adequately. As a result, some "impact programs had no impact at all."(24)

Disincentives for Labor

Under repressed inflation, the value of money depends on what is available for purchase opportunities. Whether the purchase of substitute goods will give the consumer as much satisfaction as the goods made artificially scarce by price controls becomes the crucial issue. If they do, the marginal utility of money income will be maintained. If they do not, then it is simply a matter of time until workers will refuse to accept money in exchange for additional effort. Clearly, the price controls imposed by the government after 1973-74 did increase social investment. However, to assure the success of the tremendous public investment expansion, it was soon apparent that controls alone were not enough due to such factors as skilled labor shortages. Successful implementation of the government's investment program meant a further restraint of consumption by workers; i.e., for increasing amounts of savings were taken out of wage income.

The government's strategy to increase its investment while avoiding inflation therefore depended on the willingness of individuals to accept substitute goods, the presence of a plentiful supply of such goods, and the belief that the government's action was the only possible solution and that the solution was in the hands of just and capable men.

The theory was that, if money had value and thrift was honored by the community, then savings would be viewed with respect by most individuals. Labor effort would not be withheld from the market and producers would be able to obtain the necessary labor force and reach their optimum levels of output.

It is difficult to speculate as to the precise timing, but it is clear that by 1975 Iranian producers were encountering absenteeism and there were difficulties in getting labor to shift to geographic areas and industrial sectors where it was most urgently needed.

Inasmuch as, under repressed inflation, high wages mean little more than larger amounts of savings, nonmonetary advantages such as living in a large city with its many amenities or the chance to work at a position higher on the social scale began to assume importance. Under the repressed inflation, labor was becoming inelastic with respect to money but elastic with respect to nonmonetary advantages. Where employers tried to impose wage restraints, they frequently found a well organized labor force capable of slowdowns and/or strikes (even though illegal) which by and large succeeded in further wage increases. Most employers recognized that, despite these increases, workers still had problems in meeting their basic needs. Rentals and land prices had risen so rapidly that by 1976 as much as 60 percent and more of take-home-pay went for housing. Labor problems also had the effect of frightening potential investors away from labor-intensive projects. This tended to reduce the productivity of capital as capital was substituted for labor.

In sum, the fall in productivity or the absorptive capacity in the mid-1970s was brought on by a number of government expenditure policy actions which resulted in the increasing reluctance of labor to offer effort in exchange for savings (reducing labor's productivity and increasing rigidities in the economy), the declining productivity of investment due to skilled labor shortages, the appearance of bottlenecks because of capital shortages, the presence of huge profits which promoted waste, and the continuation of the high cost of marginal producers in production (because of tariffs and price controls which form an umbrella of protection under which high cost producers can continue to operate).

EMPIRICAL RESULTS

Based on the previous discussion, a number of macroeconomic variables were selected as independent variables to be regressed on the various measures of the incremental output ratio. For the increasing economies of scale effect:

(1) GNOXNP = the growth of real non-oil GDP;
(2) GNOXNPL = the growth of real non-oil GDP lagged one year;
(3) GGDPNP = the growth of real domestic product;
(4) GGDPNPL = the growth of real domestic product lagged one year;
(5) GNOXNPL2 or GGDPNPL2 = the growth of aggregate income measures lagged two years.

Presumably, the greater these rates of growth the more productive capital would be. It should be noted that a bias occurs in the current period figures since the higher the growth of the income variable the larger the denominator ((DNOXNP) in the ICOR. This is not a problem in the lagged formulations.

The government impact is depicted by:

(6) GENANP = the level of real government expenditures;
(7) GGP = the growth of real government expenditures;
(8) GPRAT = the ratio of total real government to total real private expenditures;
(9) GPRATL = GPRAT lagged one year.

Presumably, the greater the value of these variables, the more they divert scarce labor-management from private sector activities and thus reduce the productivity of investment.

There is no a priori presumption as to the sign these values will take. Government investment in economic overhead capital reduces the costs of private production or the government's expenditures could divert scarce resources away from the private sector. The net effect could go in either direction.

The diminishing return effect is measured by:

(10) GTINP = the growth of total real investment;
(11) GTINPL = the growth of total real investment lagged one year;
(12) GTINPL2 = the growth of total real investment lagged two years;
(13) ICORL = the respective incremental capital output ratio lagged one year.

The expected sign is negative; the faster investment occurs, the greater the chance capital will outpace the suppliers of complementary factors of production.

The ICORs selected were: total investment (ICOR); private sector investment in machinery (ICORPM); private sector investment in construction (ICORPC); government investment in machinery (ICORGM); total (government plus private sector) investment in construction (ICORC); and total investment in machinery (ICORM). The most complete analysis was made on ICOR (total investment capital output ratio) and ICORL (lagged total investment capital output ratio). Only selective analysis was attempted with the other capital output ratios.

It should be noted that the results were insensitive to the measure of the incremental capital used, hence only those for ICOR are presented here.

The results for 1959-77 for ICOR (table 7.2) indicate that government expenditures had a strong negative impact on the productivity of capital; no positive economies or cost reducing linkages were created by government expenditures. The negative signs for GNOXNP and GNOXNPL must be interpreted as reflecting the output effect (ΔNOXNP) in light of the strong positive signs for their lagged values. Hence it is unlikely that economies of scale were present.

The strong positive value for the ratio of government to private expenditure is another indication of the effect of the government's bidding away of resources from the productive private sector when the public sector expanded relatively rapidly. The positive sign for total investment (GTIMPL) indicates the effect of diminishing returns to investment. Of particular interest is the fact that when the regressions are run for the pre-oil boom (1959-1973), several different patterns emerge (table 7.3). Apparently, preemption of resources by the public sector was largely a post oil boom phenomena. Government expenditure (GENANP) was not statistically significant in any of the regressions for 1959-73.

Diminishing returns of increased investment do not appear to have been present with the growth in total investment not significant in the 1959-73 regressions, in contrast to those for 1959-77.

Table 7.2. Determinants of the Incremental Output Ratio, 1959-1973 (Current Period Formula)

Equation	Dependent Variable	Independent Variables GENANP	GGDPNP	GNOXNPL	GGP	GNOXNP	GPRAT	GTINPL	Intercept	r^2	F
(1)	ICOR	-0.0006 (-0.26)							2.71 (6.17)	0.007	0.06
(2)	ICOR		-5.62 (-0.59)						3.20 (3.17)	0.037	0.35
(3)	ICOR	0.0005 (0.16)	-6.97 (-0.52)						3.25 2.58	0.040	0.17
(4)	ICOR			5.84 (6.82)					2.12 (3.12)	0.07	0.67
(5)	ICOR	0.0006 (-0.24)			-1.25 (-0.33)				2.92 (3.80)	0.020	0.08
(6)	ICOR			12.91 (3.58)		-21.09 (-5.66)			3.48 (8.99)	0.814	17.49
(7)	ICOR	0.002 (1.81)		8.51 (2.12)		-25.75 (-6.16)			3.81 (9.84)	0.873	16.05
(8)	ICOR					-27.33 (-7.36)	4.79 (4.71)		3.44 (10.76)	0.872	27.14
(9)	ICOR			6.71 (2.08)		-26.49 (-8.42)	3.36 (3.07)		3.31 (11.95)	0.921	27.04
(10)	ICOR					-30.62 (-6.37)	4.81 (4.76)	1.29 (1.06)	3.59 (10.33)	0.889	18.77
(11)	ICOR					-19.51 (-2.41)		1.21 (0.52)	4.30 (7.08)	0.531	4.53

Note: See text for classification of symbols.

Table 7.3. Determinants of the Incremental Capital Output Ratio, 1959-1977

Equation	Dependent Variable	Independent Variables							Intercept	r^2	F
		GENANP	GGDPNP	GNOXNPL	GGP	GNOXNP	GPRAT	GTINPL			
(1)	ICOR	0.003 (8.99)							2.17 (5.23)	0.357	7.20
(2)	ICOR		-21.79 (-4.19)						5.01 (9.60)	0.575	12.60
(3)	ICOR	0.002 (2.06)	-17.84 (-3.54)						4.14 (6.56)	0.686	13.10
(4)	ICOR			22.30 (3.24)					0.80 (1.10)	0.448	10.53
(5)	ICOR	0.003 (3.04)			-6.19 (-2.19)				3.23 (5.34)	0.540	7.05
(6)	ICOR			27.39 (5.14)		-19.54 (-3.40)			2.29 (3.28)	0.718	15.30
(7)	ICOR	0.004 (6.19)		7.81 (1.90)		-30.37 (-9.11)			4.11 (9.09)	0.937	54.24
(8)	ICOR					-36.06 (-6.37)	6.85 (6.97)		3.52 (7.32)	0.821	27.57
(9)	ICOR			10.55 (1.61)		-5.52 (-32.22)	4.91 (3.23)		2.98 (5.28)	0.855	21.67
(10)	ICOR					-46.19 (-7.81)	6.08 (7.20)	4.77 (2.71)	4.18 (9.09)	0.893	30.52
(11)	ICOR					-35.76 (-2.73)		9.06 (2.38)	5.29 (5.33)	0.387	3.79

Note: See text for identification of symbols.

CONCLUSIONS

Whatever merit the government's programs in the post-1973 boom might have had, they clearly achieved limited impact due to the falling productivity of capital. Analysis of the pre-1973 period, however, indicates that many of these problems might easily have been overlooked or at least statistical analysis along the lines used here would not have forewarned the authorities as to this difficulty.

This should not be interpreted as condoning the government's strategy so much as simply pointing out the problems any government would face in an environment characterized by considerable structural change. On the other hand, the authorities should have realized that, even though oil revenues transformed the economy into a capital surplus position, this was only a temporary and transient state. The government received ample warning at the time that Iran was not a true capital surplus economy as perhaps Saudi Arabia was. Given the transient nature of capital inflow, it follows that the country should not have followed a growth strategy based on the premise that capital was relatively abundant using capital intensive techniques to increase the national product.

It appears that the post-1973 growth strategy was based on the premise of capital abundance, and therefore economized on labor by increasing the capital intensity investment projects. The strategy further was predicated on the notion that labor both in quantity and in quality would soon catch up so that, by the time capital inflows from the oil sector began to diminish, the process of capital generation would have become internalized and the country's growth momentum self-sustaining. As noted in chapter 5, there is little historical precedent or empirical evidence for accepting the momentum thesis. The economic solution would have instead been to base the strategy on long-term scarcities rather than short-term abundances, i.e., the government's strategy should have aimed at maximizing the long-run return per unit of capital.(25)

8 Inflation

INTRODUCTION

Inflation poses a grave threat to any political system. It does so because it succeeds in touching the lives of the ordinary citizen - not some, but all - in a way in which government development expenditures are rarely able. Whether it is hyperinflation or gradual increases in prices over time, the damage done to the individual and society is evident. By creating an atmosphere of insecurity and futility, by permitting wholesale economic injustice, and by giving rise to abject poverty, an environment is created which makes for irrationality in politics which deeply affects the nature and effectiveness of subsequent stabilization measures.(1)

In retrospect, the development of inflation in Iran together with the government's inability to stabilize the price level were undoubtedly the major economic causes of the revolution. Therefore, the nature of the Iranian inflation and the course of inflation-related variables merit considerable attention.

In the analysis below, particular emphasis is given to inflation in the 1970s, with an attempt made to identify the type and source of the inflation experienced. Three main questions are addressed: (1) What role did accelerated government expenditures (including defense expenditures) play in increasing inflationary pressures? (2) To what extent was the recent inflation imported rather than domestically induced? (3) Did the underlying mechanism of inflation change after 1973 so that the inflation experience in the mid-1970s was fundamentally different from that in prior periods? While the first two questions seem sufficiently well defined, the third question needs clarification.

Iranian inflationary periods could have differed for two reasons. Suppose the operation of the economy could be described by a system of equations with certain variables exogenous, such as the money supply, the wage rate, and the levels of import prices. First, from one inflationary episode to another, the mix of movements in the exogenous variables may have been different so that one inflation was, for instance, largely imported and another was largely the result of domestic budgetary policy.

The second source of difference is that the structural equations through which exogenous influences work may have altered. In particular, Iranians may have become more responsive to inflation in the sense that, because of adverse past experiences, they began to anticipate and offset the effects of inflation on their activities. Apart from this expectational aspect, the underlying inflationary mechanism may have been altered for a variety of other reasons; as, for example, changes in the composition of output, of activity, and in institutions caused shifts in the type of responsiveness to the markets that made up the economy.

These are complex issues and the empirical analysis that follows can do no more than indicate tentative answers.

INFLATIONARY PRESSURES - AN OVERVIEW

The Iranian economy enjoyed a prolonged period of price stability through the 1960s. Beginning in 1972, however, growing inflationary pressures developed and were present throughout the rest of the 1970s. During the Fourth Five Year Plan (1968-72), the annual rates of increase in the average level of consumer prices were low, ranging from 1 to 6 percent (table 8.1). The corresponding rates of inflation for the Fifth Plan were, on the other hand, all in excess of 10 percent amounting to as much as 27 percent in 1977.

A comparison of the rate of increase in the money supply (table 8.1) and that of the major inflation indices confirms the conclusion already reached that, in the post-1973 period, the Iranian economy had advanced beyond its absorptive capacity in the sense of finding the complementary factors of production (such as human skills, natural resources, and infrastructure) to be put to work alongside the rapid increase in financial resources. Apparently, injections of oil revenues beyond a certain level - that level being the annual absorptive capacity - only led to higher inflationary pressures with little or no corresponding increase in output resulting from this expenditure.

The evidence for Iran during the post-1972 period suggests a tendency of trying to do too much in too short a

Table 8.1. Growth of Monetary Aggregates: Measures of Inflation (Average Annual Rate)

	M1	M2	M3	M4	CPI	WPI	GDPDF
1960	11.50	-	-	-	10.04	3.15	3.04
1961	-16.73	-	-	-	3.17	1.28	2.14
1962	22.72	24.94	-	-	0.72	1.27	-0.26
1963	12.96	16.22	-	-	0.17	0.18	0.79
1964	10.98	13.81	-	-	4.11	4.64	1.83
1965	12.87	13.01	13.30	13.09	2.06	3.33	-2.31
1966	10.07	12.48	13.83	11.19	-0.34	-1.18	-0.52
1967	14.92	16.07	16.48	16.35	1.52	0.17	-0.79
1968	7.86	13.43	12.09	14.89	0.67	0.66	0.53
1969	6.07	15.07	14.76	17.94	3.64	2.61	0.52
1970	12.78	15.23	16.36	19.06	1.59	2.84	0.52
1971	17.17	19.36	19.82	18.33	4.24	5.79	7.27
1972	27.71	26.07	26.89	21.28	6.49	5.46	6.78
1973	22.93	23.25	24.93	25.35	9.76	10.11	31.79
1974	27.09	29.97	36.11	37.27	14.30	14.47	55.67
1975	16.76	25.79	21.59	25.09	12.74	7.40	10.38
1976	44.25	44.88	42.53	42.34	11.29	8.26	16.90
1977	-23.01	-26.09	-25.77	-25.70	27.31	14.65	19.50

Source: Computed from: Bank Markazi Iran, Annual Report, various issues; International Monetary Fund, International Financial Statistics, various issues.

time.(2) The problem was aggravated by the jump in international inflation rates during 1973-74. Yet, it would be a mistake to suggest that the observed rates of domestic inflation were due to purely international factors. On the contrary, most studies on the subject indicate that, in general, international price increases contributed no more than 25 percent to domestic inflation in developing countries, leaving a substantial portion to be accounted for by domestic factors.

Most domestic sources of inflationary pressures built up in the mid-1970s can be traced to the decision to revise the Fifth Five Year Plan following the oil price increases. At that time, total investment projected for the duration of the plan was doubled and vast amounts allocated to social welfare and subsidy programs. Within the framework of the Fifth Plan, the government's expenditures for 1974 were triple those in

1973. From the total government budget for 1974 (Rls 1,254 billion), only 28 percent went into fixed capital formation, whereas 58 percent was spent on current expenditures. The remaining 14 percent went for other payments which, for all practical purposes, were very similar to current expenditures.

This unprecedented expansion in government expenditures created a corresponding expansion of liquidity. The result was a rapid increase in effective demand. One net impact of the government's fiscal actions was the creation of an economic environment whereby producers were encouraged to make the utmost use of their means of production. Another consequence was that traders responded quickly to increase imports to balance supply with demand. As a result, the demand for means of production and for primary and intermediate goods increased while simultaneously the available infrastructural facilities were used at maximum capacity. However, due to the general shortage of skilled workers and infrastructure capacity in certain key areas, the supply of domestically produced goods could not increase at the same rate as the demand. Inflationary pressures, therefore, mounted while, at the same time, the feedback effect of the oil price increases - an acceleration in world inflation - resulted in increased import prices.

Initially, the greatest inflationary pressures were concentrated in the construction and housing sector. Both the rapid increase in incomes and the increasing migration from rural to urban areas played an important role in creating shortages of not only available living quarters but construction materials as well (which was already evident prior to the Fifth Development Plan). The result was a sharp escalation in the price of land, construction materials, and wages of construction workers. In turn, the acceleration of inflation in the construction and housing sector spilled over to other sectors, finally increasing inflationary pressures in all other activities of the economy.

As bottlenecks began to develop, the time lag in converting financial capital into productive capital lengthened, further impeding the adjustment of supply to demand, with increased shortages of materials and skilled labor. Many projects, both public and private, were not completed, despite the fact that in many cases the budgets for these projects were actually spent. At the same time, a considerable volume of goods ordered from abroad did not arrive on time. As a result of these factors, aggregate supply was never able to catch up with aggregate demand during the Fifth Plan, the adjustment between demand and supply taking place instead through price increases.

Needless to say, the overspending of financial resources not only represented a loss in real resources with intertemporal implications, but also set in motion a series of inflationary pressures that were difficult to halt without the eventual resort to fairly drastic restrictive measures. The amount of real resources lost - real in the sense that they represented an equivalent in exported barrels of oil - could have been used in the future to expand the country's productive capacity at a time when the relationship between the economy's annual financial inflow and annual absorptive capacity would permit. When used in the present, as was the case, these resources were simply dissipated in the form of higher prices.

THEORIES OF INFLATION

A number of other sources are logically possible and at least not inconsistent with the data on price changes that is available for this period. While few would argue in principle with the broad interpretation of Iranian inflation outlined above, its high level of generality makes it of somewhat limited use in evaluating the effectiveness of the government's antiinflation programs.

The increase in the rate of inflation in the first half of the 1970s together with the government's seeming inability to stabilize the price level dramatized the need for a deeper understanding of the country's inflationary process. Something of a debate concerning the precise cause of the rapidly accelerating price level transpired during this period. For convenience, two extreme views of the country's inflationary process can be distinguished: the monetarist interpretation and the structuralist explanation.

The Monetarist Position

The monetarist view on inflation in Iran can be gleaned from the various statements made over the years in the Bank Markazi Iran Annual Reports. Nearly every year after 1970, the bank made some statement to the effect that inflation in the country was a problem of excess monetary demand. Typical of the bank's approach was the implicit application of Fisher's version of the quantity theory of money.(3) In 1975 the bank noted that:

> During recent years, due to the very speedy growth of income the total demand increased at a higher rate than total supply of goods and services. This situation not only resulted in creating new difficulties for the economy, but also increased inflationary pressures. During recent years, especially in 1353 [1974], due to the expansionary financial activities

> of the Government and the speedy growth of credits extended by the private sector, the money supply and consequently the effective demand increased at a much higher rate than could be accommodated by domestic production.(4)

We find in their reports, therefore, that the bank accepted a model which usually implicitly but sometimes explicitly linked inflation with monetary factors. Furthermore, a careful reading of the bank's reports leads one to conclude that its senior economists tended to view the economy as one where aggregate demand was determined by factors associated with Fisher's version of the quantity theory of money. Specifically, in recommending policies designed to assure monetary stability, the bank implicitly assumed that the economy's prices and wages were, for the most part, flexible. Stabilization measures suggested by the bank at one time or another included restrictive monetary policies, restrictions on government expenditures (mainly government consumption expenditures), reduction of import controls, and lower wage and salary adjustments (presumably limited to less than the previous year's inflation rate).

Nowhere in the bank's analysis of the country's inflation is there any evidence that its officials felt the underlying structure of the economy prevented high and steady rates of economic growth with price stability, provided the proper monetary and fiscal policies were implemented.

The Structuralist Position

Structuralism was associated from the beginning with the more leftist writers and a number of the leading technocrats in the Plan Organization.(5) As developed in Iran, structuralism was concerned largely with the examination of potential and actual conflicts between growth, stabilization, and equity.

Structuralist stress was always in disequilibrium and the notion was that the country's inflation was inevitable once the government attempted rapid growth in the presence of structural bottlenecks or constraints. Their chief assumption was, therefore, that certain fundamental facets of the economic, institutional, and sociopolitical organization of the country in one way or another acted to inhibit economic expansion.

The structuralist analysis was concerned largely with the identification and examination of alleged structural constraints.(6) While not always spelled out, these could be taken to include the inelastic supply of foodstuffs, the infrastructure bottleneck, and the savings constraint. In their view, inflation could not be stopped if these structural limitations were not eliminated. The cumulative inflationary pressures were distortions generated by the inflationary process itself which were an increasing function of the rate of inflation. The main cumulative factors were distortions of the price system, mainly caused by the price control policies associated with inflation; and misallocation of resources, mainly investment funds.

One version of structuralist thought contended that the country's inflation was inevitable, given the country's phase of transition from an outward-oriented export-based economy to an inward-oriented domestic-market-based economy.(7) Such a transition, it was argued, required massive changes in the socioeconomic structure of the country that the price mechanisms, operating within very imperfect market structures and with limited resource mobility, were unable to achieve. That is, given the imperfection of the system, the result of attempting major structural change was simply shortages and disequilibrium on many fronts. For example, urbanization and rising incomes led to a rapidly rising demand for foodstuffs that could not be met by the agricultural sector. The supply response of the agricultural sector was low because of the structural constraints within that sector - the domination either by small firms operating at a near subsistence level and barely integrated into the larger market economy or larger foreign dominated business which as noted earlier had not been able to adapt to the Iranian conditions for one reason or another.

The basic position of the structuralists was, therefore, that agricultural production failures could not be attributed to market demand and/or price conditions but, instead, had to be the direct result of factors inherent in the institutional and economic organization of the agrarian sector itself.

In this context, the term "bottlenecks" and the relationship of bottlenecks to inflation must be clarified. Structuralist analysis has often been criticized as unsound because there is no reason, at least in theory, why an increase in the price of one commodity (i.e., a bottleneck) should raise the general price level and provoke an inflationary spiral.(8) In an open economy, an increase in imports can keep prices constant and in a closed economy, neoclassical theory would predict that a rise in the relative price of one type of good (for example, rice) should lead to a shift in demand to other goods and a reallocation of the factors of production leading to the restoration of an equilibrium position. But, if the prices of manufactured goods are inflexible downwards, a rise in food prices (with other prices constant) raises the average price level. In turn, if industrial wages are tied to consumer prices, they will rise leading to an upward movement in industrial prices. The change in relative prices may be insufficient to lead to a shift in demand and thus an inflationary spiral will develop.(9)

The Iranian inflation of the 1970s cannot be explained by structural factors alone. In addition, some sort of propagating mechanism had to be present to sustain price increases over such a long period of time. Here, the structuralists are not particularly explicit. Mention is made of a struggle among different economic groups to improve their shares in total income. This manifested itself, to a certain extent, in conflicts between wage earners and profit earners.(10) Secondly, and probably more important, was the struggle between the private and public sectors to increase their share of real resources. This worked through the expansion of oil-based expenditures and the competition with the private sector over skilled labor and managers.(11) Again, although a complete structuralist model has not previously been developed for Iran, one can easily construct one by incorporating a number of structural elements into a general Bruno-Chenery-Strout model.(12)

As an illustration, a structural inflationary process in the Iranian context could begin with a rapid expansion in economic activity stemming from oil-financed government investment in the industrial sector. Such an expansion should cut back underemployment generated over time by the static conditions in the agricultural sector and a moderately high population growth. In turn, increased incomes would create an expanded demand for food, thus generating pressures in the agricultural sector. Due to the low price elasticity of supply in agriculture (a structural problem), however, substantial increases in relative prices in favor of the sector would be necessary to clear the market. Food shortages (at relatively stable prices) were aggravated by the fact that oil-financed imports were already straining the country's port facilities and transport system. The result was that imports of food and consumer products, while capable of being financed out of oil revenues, could not increase rapidly enough to augment domestic supplies, thus maintaining a relatively stable price level.

If unemployed resources could have been productively moved to the industrial sector and if industrial prices had been flexible downward, a change in relative prices without inflation might have taken place. However, because of the low mobility of most domestic resources and the inflexibility of industrial prices (due to monopolistic positions encouraged by the import substitution-industrial strategy), monetary expansion was required to generate prices high enough for the change in relative prices.

In short, a structuralist interpretation of Iran's inflation would contend that domestic price increases stemmed largely from the inability of supply to adapt to a changing and growing level of demand. In the 1970s, this problem was characterized by inelasticity and instability in agricultural output together with insufficient infrastructure facilities which precluded imports from aiding in adjustment to equilibrium at relatively stable prices. With these mechanisms in mind, a structuralist two-gap model can be hypothesized for Iran as follows. If the Iranian authorities wanted to increase the rate of growth of real non-oil income from the historic rate of 12 percent, the economy would generate a foreign trade gap due to the inelasticity of import demand (a structural problem) together with fixed export revenues. Imports must increase because additional amounts of raw materials and capital goods would be required by the industrial sector. The country's extremely underdeveloped tax system would not be capable of absorbing the excess liquidity from the expanding consumer sector. The result (given most individual's low propensity to save) would be a gap between total domestic savings and investment greater than that between exports and imports. In these circumstances, inflation would most likely be the only mechanism capable of facilitating an equilibrium adjustment between the domestic (savings-investment) and external (export-import) gaps; i.e., inflation would result in savings increasing up to the point (through pricing individuals out of certain product markets) where the domestic (savings-investment) gap equaled the external gap.

Structuralists, therefore, view inflation as emerging in the process of making the two gaps equal ex post. The actual adjustment process is achieved through two struggles for the available consumer goods: (1) that between wage earners and profit earners, and (2) that between the private sector and the public sector. The ultimate distribution of income will be determined by the relative strength of these groups.

QUANTITATIVE ASSESSMENT OF INFLATIONARY MECHANISMS

The structuralist approach is largely of interest because it provides a useful framework for developing an integrated view of the country's inflationary process. Realistically, however, because it relies on such concepts as relative inelasticity (how inelastic does something have to be before it is relatively inelastic?), the theory is not directly amenable to empirical testing. Several indirect tests are possible, however, and are undertaken below.

A discussion and quantitative assessment of the importance of cost factors is much more straightforward. This analysis is undertaken in the sections that follow. Because of its theoretical link with the country's balance of payments, the monetary theory of inflation is reserved for testing in the following chapter.

It should be noted, however, that any analysis of Iranian inflation will suffer from: (1) the limited availability of data, and (2) the existing data's limitations. There is no consistent time series for wages, nor is there an import prices series. Further, the GDP deflator is so weighted by oil that it is of little value in analyzing the possible determinants of domestic price increases. There is a cost of living index and a wholesale price index, but both of these measures are subject to serious defects. The cost of living index is based on a limited sample of goods and services purchased in the major urban areas and is, therefore, unrepresentative of the consumption patterns of the majority of the rural population, while the wholesale price index is heavily weighted with imports.

Given the data, two cost factors are examined: (1) world prices and (2) wages; and two structuralist elements examined: (1) the presence of bottlenecks and (2) the effects of deviations from the trend in real non-oil GDP on prices.

Movements in World Prices

Given its size, it is safe to assume that Iran's purchases and sales of non-oil goods in the world market had no effect on the prices of these goods. For all practical purposes, the prices of the country's non-oil exports and imports were determined by global demand and supply conditions. For purposes of analysis, therefore, the U.S. dollar export and import prices of these goods can be taken as exogenous variables. Given these international prices, the export and import prices in rials were dependent on the officially determined rial/dollar rate.

There are two channels by which rising import prices might induce domestic inflation: (1) the direct effect due to rising prices in world markets, and (2) an indirect effect transmitted through the higher cost of domestic production of finished products stemming from increases in the prices of imported raw materials. In terms of the second channel, the degree to which Iranian producers had little or no way of substituting for imported materials meant that there were few real possibilities (at least in modern industries) of switching from expensive imported goods to cheaper domestic sources of supply.

The data on external sources of inflation for this period are somewhat limited. Nevertheless, several patterns seem fairly clear.

Expenditure for merchandise imports averaged from 12 to 15 percent of aggregate expenditure on GDP between 1970 and 1974; the proportion rose to nearly 20 percent in 1975. Nearly the same proportion was maintained in 1976. The great increase in imports in 1975 was undoubtedly a significant factor in dampening the inflationary pressures caused by excess demand. On the other hand, it is likely that the increase in import prices beginning in 1972 exerted its own inflationary impact through the cost structure of firms.

Import induced cost-push pressures are a real possibility since, prior to 1975 and 1976, intermediate goods accounted for more than 60 percent of total imports (table 8.2). By far, the greatest proportion of intermediate imports were for manufacturing; another 20 to 30 percent of imports were capital goods. The remaining 12 to 13 percent (rising to about 17 percent in 1975 and 1976) were consumer goods. Clearly, a great potential existed for increases in import prices to have significantly affected the domestic price structure and level. Of course, increased prices of consumer goods imports acted directly on the consumer price level (depending upon the relative importance of imported food and other consumption items in total consumption).

Table 8.2. Composition of Imports (% Total Inputs)

Year	Intermediate Goods	Capital Goods	Consumer Goods
1959	49.15	20.60	30.25
1960	47.16	24.28	28.56
1961	53.50	21.05	25.44
1962	57.20	20.98	21.82
1963	55.52	20.33	24.15
1964	54.96	21.88	23.16
1965	57.68	24.82	17.49
1966	57.92	27.05	15.03
1967	59.73	27.67	12.60
1968	61.65	27.09	11.26
1969	63.99	25.10	10.90
1970	63.73	23.32	12.95
1971	64.84	23.43	11.73
1972	62.09	25.00	12.90
1973	60.84	24.16	14.92
1974	64.50	20.12	15.38
1975	53.11	29.83	17.06
1976	52.59	29.79	17.62
1977	54.17	27.19	18.63

Source: Computed from data in Bank Markazi Iran, Annual Report, various issues.

During this period, a number of important food items such as cereals, sugar, and meat experienced exceptionally large domestic price increases resulting in dramatic increases in their importation. Sugar imports, for example, rose from a small proportion of the total supply in the early 1970s to nearly one-third by 1975. Imports of cereals varied considerably from crop to crop and from year to year, depending on the harvest. Rice and wheat imports averaged about one-third of total supply each, while imports of barley and maize accounted for about one-eighth and four-fifths, respectively, of total supplies. Clearly (except for meat) the size of these import shares indicates that increased world prices would have had a significant effect upon domestic prices. By 1974 or 1975, meat imports had grown to the point where increases in the world price were also likely to have a significant impact on domestic prices.

Consumers were buffeted somewhat from world price increases for cereals, meat, dairy products, sugar, and fruit through an extensive government subsidy program. Government subsidies for these products rose to $1,000 million annually from 1974 to 1976, thus significantly aiding in reducing the rate of consumer price increases for these products to levels considerably below those in international markets. The subsidy program makes any general assessment of world price increases on Iranian prices extremely difficult. It is possible to arrive at several tentative conclusions, however, through examining the trend in wholesale prices for imported goods and those for domestic goods. It appears that import prices had their greatest impact on the domestic price level in 1972 and 1973, the years in which import prices clearly led the rise in general wholesale prices. The introduction of the subsidy programs in 1974 and the decline in international prices of food and raw materials in 1975 makes further conclusions quite difficult.

Also, given available data, it is very difficult to make any clear distinction between external and internal sources of inflationary pressure for intermediate inputs into manufacturing and construction. Certainly there is a relationship between the import price of building materials, the rise in domestic wholesale prices, and the increase in the cost of housing and housing rentals. A similar pattern between import and domestic prices can be observed for textiles. For all of these items, it is apparent that both domestic and foreign sources of price increases contributed to the rise in Iranian wholesale and consumer prices. The domestic component of inflationary pressures corresponded generally in its timing to the expansion of consumer incomes, and for building materials on the rapid expansion of expenditures in the construction sector.

In general, one can conclude that, because Iran's terms of trade improved dramatically, especially relative to many developing countries, and because of the rapid rise in domestic prices after the oil price increases, it was only logical for the authorities to promote increased imports as a means of reducing inflationary pressures.

In fact, recent empirical work on a large sample of countries suggests that there may be a possible relationship between the degree of national integration into the world economic system and inflation; the more open countries have experienced less price inflation.(13) Presumably, openness serves as a kind of safety valve; domestic inflationary pressure spills over into the balance of payments in the open economy, thus necessitating less price inflation.

One way of testing for the effect of openness on domestic inflation is to test various formulations of a price equation with measures reflecting the degree of contact with the world economy included as independent variables. Logical candidates in this regard are: (1) the country's import-income ratio, (2) the rate of change in Iran's import-income rate, (3) the country's terms of trade (ratio of import prices to export prices), (4) the rate of growth of the Iranian money supply, and (5) the rate of growth of Iran's real non-oil GDP.

Iyoha, the originator of this test, used imports/GDP as an independent variable hypothesizing that a negative correlation between these two variables could be interpreted as evidence in support of the hypothesis that, in an open economy, domestic inflationary pressures spill over into the balance of payments, thus resulting in less domestic inflation than would have otherwise been the case.(14)

It has been argued that this mechanism is not a very accurate depiction of the mechanisms at work in most developing countries where foreign exchange shortages pose a severe limit to the possibility of absorbing potential inflationary pressures through increasing import surplus.(15) The typical developing country, therefore, may not really have a choice between its rate of domestic inflation and its magnitude of balance of payments deficit; the rate of inflation may, in part, be determined by the foreign exchange constraint. Iran's oil revenues and borrowing capacity would seem to rule out this problem for most of the period under consideration.

Since there is no real consensus in the literature as to the best way of measuring "openness," several formulations were tried. All use the symbol Z and are ratios to some measure of domestic production. Hence:

(1) Z = nominal imports (from the national income accounts) divided by real non-oil income (or ZN/NOXNP)

(2) ZX = nominal imports from the national income accounts divided by nominal non-oil GDP (or ZN/NOXN)

(3) ZZ = ZN/DOMEST, where DOMEST = nominal agriculture + manufacturing value added
(4) ZAG = agricultural imports/NOXN
(5) ACON = consumer imports/NOXN

Terms with "L" at the end indicate the value lagged one year (tables 8.3 and 8.4).

Other independent variables included in the analysis were the deviation of real non-oil GDP from its historical trends (DTNOXPL), the rate of change in the export price index of industrialized countries (WINF), the growth of M2 money (GM2), the growth in real non-oil GDP (GNOXNP), and the terms of trade (TTC).

A number of different combinations were tried with the best results occurring when the various measures of openness were regressed simultaneously with some measure of excess demand such as DTNOXP or GM1, GM2; and the rate of import price increases (WINF). Regressions on the consumer price increase gave consistently better but quite similar results to those of the wholesale price index. Hence, only the results obtained from the regressions with the rate of change in consumer prices are presented in tables 8.3 and 8.4.

In all cases, the value of Z (and L) is significant and has the expected negative sign. Caution should be observed in attributing a great deal of significance to the results, however. In several cases, the t-statistic for the Z measure is only slightly significant at the 95 percent level. Also, it should be noted that when only Z (equation 1, table 8.3) was regressed on inflation (INFC), its sign was positive. The change in signs may simply be a problem related to correlation between the independent variables.

A plausible explanation of the positive relationship between Z and the rate of inflation is that a substantial portion of imports during this period were required for industrialization; they did not represent a spillover effect "proper" from the domestic inflation. This type of import may have increased over time independent of changes in domestic prices. When world prices (WINF) together with a capacity constraint (DTNOXND) were added to the regressions to take part of this effect into account, the Z term always became strongly negative. A possible explanation for this result is that, on the margin, additional imports represented spillover imports to an extent great enough to overcome the positive effect of the price inelastic imports.

This issue, while interesting and of some significance for policy design, was not pursued at length simply because several alternative (and somewhat competing) theories of the inflationary process in Iran were found to be sound from both a statistical and theoretical point of view.

Table 8.3. Test of Openness and Inflation

Equation	Dependent Variable	Independent Variables											
		Z	GMTL	ZL	GM2	GNOXNPL	DTNOXPL	WINFL2	WINF	TTC	Intercept	r^2	F
(1)	INFC	21.28 (6.05)										0.769	36.60
(2)	INFC	10.22 (2.96)	0.44 (4.19)									0.916	54.61
(3)	INFC	22.41 (2.06)		-2.51 (-0.21)							-2.00 (-1.05)	0.753	16.78
(4)	INFC	20.30 (7.79)			-0.16 (-3.00)						0.79 (0.47)	0.864	34.82
(5)	INFC	12.90 (2.93)				0.89 (2.23)					-7.96 (-2.58)	0.829	26.82
(6)	INFC			-21.70 (-4.28)			0.07 (8.98)				9.38 (6.71)	0.959	128.39
(7)	INFC			-32.58 (-5.06)			0.08 (10.62)	0.35 (2.28)			11.11 (7.87)	0.973	119.92
(8)	INFC	-10.14 (-2.17)					0.05 (6.60)		0.35 (3.95)		5.12 (3.58)	0.957	75.92
								0.42 (2.27)	-0.009 (-5.09)			0.787	18.55

Note: See text for identification of symbols.

Table 8.4. Openness and Inflation in Iran

Equation	Dependent Variable	DTNOXPL	WINF	GM21	Z	WINFL2	ZL	INFCL	ZX	ZZ	ZAGL	Intercept	r^2	F
(1)	INFC	0.036	0.31									1.90		
		(11.88)	(3.38)									(2.42)	0.949	94.06
(2)	INFC	0.023	0.23	0.31								-2.61		
		(2.32)	(2.16)	(1.48)								(-0.83)	0.959	70.94
(3)	INFC	0.050	0.36		-8.59							4.37		
		(6.25)	(4.11)		(-1.79)							(2.81)	0.963	77.51
(4)	INFC	0.078				0.35	-33.32					11.36		
		(10.06)				(2.21)	(-4.84)					(7.27)	0.973	109.15
(5)	INFC	0.047	0.42					-0.52				3.09		
		(10.73)	(5.27)					(-2.88)				(4.25)	0.974	111.11
(6)	INFC	0.072					-22.2					9.57		
		(8.47)					(-4.02)					(6.08)	0.959	116.29
(7)	INFC	0.044	0.38						-15.49			5.29		
		(8.69)	(4.10)						(-1.76)			(2.57)	0.962	76.88
(8)	INFC	0.045	0.37							-5.39		4.93		
		(7.00)	(4.20)							(-1.87)		(2.79)	0.964	79.43
(9)	INFC	0.062	0.22				-17.11					6.98		
		(10.39)	(3.86)				(-4.50)					(5.73)	0.985	190.25
(10)	INFC	0.042									-64.34	8.07		
		(12.43)									(-2.80)	(4.70)	0.940	77.65
(11)	INFC	0.039	0.22								-35.59	4.85		
		(11.73)	(2.10)								(-1.48)	(2.21)	0.959	70.81

Note: See text for identification of symbols.

Wage Increases

A second potential source of cost pressures during this period came from wage increases reflective of manpower shortages. Manpower shortages emerged as one of the most critical long-term problems confronting the government's development aspirations. In fact, in 1976, the Ministry of Labor estimated that the country's manpower shortage for that year was roughly 600,000. Previous estimates made in 1975 projected shortages of 3,740 engineers, 1,820 doctors, 6,500 skilled technicians, and 84,000 skilled and semiskilled workers. At this time, the ministry suggested that up to 700,000 foreign workers might have to be recruited if the Fifth Plan targets were to be met.(16)

Instead, it appears a much more selective foreign labor program was adopted. Foreign workers were concentrated in several areas with, for example, a substantial number of foreign technicians (mainly Americans) recruited to keep the country's armed forces operational. Doctors from India were actively sought because of their willingness to work for lower wages than their Iranian counterparts and in parts of the country that Iranians would not practice because of the climate or the lack of amenities. As with Saudi Arabia, a substantial number of South Koreans, Pakistanis, and other Asians were recruited for construction work. While a larger number of foreigners were recruited by the government, there seems to have been much less willingness than in Saudi Arabia's case to resort to the mass importation of foreign workers as a means of overcoming labor shortages. All in all, however, at the peak of labor immigration, only around 35,000 foreign workers were in the country. This was forecast to increase to 55,000 by the late 1970s. Also present in 1975-76 were 15,000 to 20,000 temporary foreign consultants.(17)

For industry, one of the more obvious effects of labor shortages was the fast increase in wages as companies competed for the higher skilled workers. Official figures list average wage increases of around 35 percent for 1977. For that year, construction wage increases were officially placed at 48 percent. However, numerous accounts in the business-financial press support the argument that increases in the 60 to 70 percent range were quite common.(18)

The rapid expansion of the Iranian economy during this period was accompanied by generally expanding employment in manufacturing and construction (although the slackening of activity in 1975 brought relatively minor decreases in employment in manufacturing and mining and in construction activities). The overall rate of expansion in employment exceeded 3 percent per year (again, except for 1975), increased levels of investment, and expanding output levels resulted in significant increases in real output per worker.(19)

It is easy to see how the combination of rapid increases in employment, increasing real output per head, labor shortages, and, especially from 1973, rapid rates of inflation would be conducive to increases in wages and earnings certainly in nominal terms, and possibly in real terms as well. Given the relatively free market system for most sectors of the Iranian economy at this time, one would predict that the most rapid increases in wages and earnings would occur in the sectors and industries in which employment was expanding most rapidly. Similarly, jobs requiring relatively higher levels of skill, given the relative shortage of trained manpower, should also have led in obtaining wage increases. Impressionistic evidence suggests that these were indeed the patterns predominating the country's labor markets where numerous accounts exist attesting to the hindrance to growth posed by shortages of skilled labor.(20)

Although the data for selected, large-scale manufacturing industries are generally compatible with the overall sectoral figures (table 8.5), it would appear that employment in the former group expanded rather more rapidly than the latter. Moreover, employment for the selected industries (which accounted for about 7 percent of total employment in manufacturing and mining) did not decline in 1975. These patterns suggest that wages and earnings in the selected manufacturing industries were likely to be higher and to have increased more rapidly than those in smaller-scale enterprises and the informal or craft establishments.

In general, the expansion of wages and earnings in construction and selected manufacturing industries exceeded the increase in the consumer price index throughout this period, resulting in subsequent increases in the real wage or earnings indices. This was especially the case in 1975 when the rate of inflation slackened appreciably. These patterns are easy to explain given the supply-demand conditions in the country's labor markets.

A more difficult pattern to account for is the apparent coincidence during 1975 in both manufacturing and the construction sectors of high rates of increase in nominal wages and earnings occurring simultaneously with: (1) the reduction in the level of employment in both sectors (though not the selected manufacturing industries), and (2) the decline in the rate of inflation in consumer prices. Most logical is a mechanism of delayed wage adjustments under increased government pressure. The Ministry of Labor began compelling firms to pay between two and three month's bonus at the end of each year irrespective of productivity increases.(21) Greater insight into the functioning of labor markets is required to explain the apparent decline in the skill differential in successive years, while construction employment first expanded in 1974 at an unprecedented rate and then declined in 1975.(22)

Table 8.5. Employment, Earnings and Labor Cost in Manufacturing and Construction (1970 = 100.0)

	1971	1972	1973	1974	1975	1976	1977	1978
Manufacturing and Mining								
Value added (constant prices)	116.8	138.7	162.1	191.7	224.2			
Employment	105.2	111.1	118.8	127.6	125.3			
Value added per employee (1 3)	111.1	124.0	136.5	150.2	179.0			
Selected Manufacturing Industries								
Production	117.3	140.0	165.9	196.3	228.1	261.9	291.9	245.9
Employment	104.5	112.3	122.0	131.2	139.3	144.8	147.6	149.7
Labor Productivity	112.1	124.7	136.0	149.6	163.8	180.9	197.8	147.7
Labor Cost	98.6	102.2	110.4	124.2	152.4	177.1	221.4	274.6
Industrial Raw Materials Wholesale Price Index	117.3	128.6	148.5	164.2	158.9	202.9		
Average Annual Earnings	110.6	127.5	150.1	185.8	249.6	320.6		
Cost of Living Index	104.9	111.5	123.9	143.1	157.3	183.4		
Real Earnings Index	105.4	114.3	121.1	128.9	158.7	174.8		
Construction								
Value Added at Constant Prices	107.0	117.2	130.4	174.7	239.6			
Employment	108.3	118.3	128.3	153.2	147.2			
Value Added per Employee	98.8	99.1	101.6	114.1	162.8			
Wage Index	102.6	120.6	146.7	189.0	278.1	387.7	520.9	613.1
Labor Cost	103.8	121.7	144.4	165.6	170.8			
Construction Materials Wholesale Price Index	98.6	105.5	128.4	164.9	173.4	198.8	249.4	257.3
Real Wage Index	97.8	108.2	118.4	132.1	176.8	211.4		
Skill Differential	1.026	1.025	1.110	1.065	1.022	1.071		

Source: Plan and Budget Organization, Economic Trends of Iran (Tehran, March 1977); Bank Markazi Iran, Annual Report, various issues.

Despite these unexplained patterns, it is fairly safe to tentatively conclude that wage cost-push pressures did not dominate the inflationary process at this time (despite the increasing labor cost indices). Indeed, wage increases contributed to the general rise in production costs, but other costs were rising equally or more rapidly. In the context of this period, it is apparent that considerable reserves of unskilled labor existed both in the agricultural sector and as urban unemployment at the beginning of the period.(23) It is hard to see, therefore, how increased labor costs could have been anything but one aspect of the heavy demands oil financed expenditures placed on all productive resources. There is little evidence to support the singling out of labor as a significant contributor to cost-push forces, not least because of the absence of strong labor unions.

In sum, while a case could perhaps be made for the existence of a wage-cost push mechanism in the manufacturing and construction sectors, it is difficult to see how as an empirical matter this effect could have dominated the inflationary process in these sectors, let alone the economy as a whole.

Infrastructural Bottlenecks

As noted, a source of structural inflation was created by the lack of excess capacity and the generally low levels of efficiency present in most of the country's basic infrastructure at the beginning of the boom period.(24)

As a result, the acceleration of output which occurred in both the oil and non-oil sectors created an immediate shortage of available capacity, particularly in the areas of ports, domestic transportation, and electrical power.

The country's obsolete and inadequate port facilities and slow customs clearance procedures resulting in low productivity were the most publicized bottlenecks with inadequacies in the transportation system another major impediment to increased imports. As an illustration of the magnitude of port congestion, the recorded rate of utilization of nominal cargo handling capacity increased from 132 percent in 1973 to 185 percent in 1974. In that year, Iran was forced to pay over $1 billion in demurage charges (amounting to more than 15 percent of the value of merchandise imports).(25)

Similarly, electricity generating capacity fell far short of the new requirements placed on it. By the end of 1974, power failures had become common in large cities and industrial areas. Consequently, many companies failed to achieve anticipated levels of production. Moreover, implementation of the development plan for electrical power fell way behind schedule with less than two-thirds of the Fifth Plan targets met. By way of comparison with other countries of a comparable level of per capita GNP, Iran's 1975 per capita electrical production ranked as one of the world's lowest (at 460 KW per annum versus a median value of 1,140 KW per annum).(26)

Largely because of shortages linked to the underdevelopment of the nation's infrastructure, Iranian industry was working at about 60 percent of capacity in May 1977 (61 percent for textiles, 46 percent in bricks, 96 percent in cement, 90 percent in sugar, 51 percent in automobiles, and 32 percent for tractors). Blackouts, inadequate transport facilities, and shortage of building materials (particularly cement) all contributed to this situation.(27)

DEVIATIONS FROM THE TREND AS A MEASURE OF INFLATIONARY PRESSURE

A proxy measure of the general level of bottlenecks, strains, and ultimately structural inflationary forces is some measure of the deviation of production from its long-run trend. This approach assumes that:(28)

1. Short-run deviations of output from its long-term trend are an adequate measure of the inflationary pressure.
2. The monetary authorities either cannot or do not neutralize the impact of changes in holdings of foreign exchange on the money supply.

As later analyses will show, the second assumption is open to some question. For now, however, several formulations of the general type

$$INF = D + WINF + EXP$$

were estimated. Here, INF is a measure of domestic inflation (usually consumer goods); D is a measure of the deviation of real production from its long-run trend; WINF is the rate of increase in world prices, and EXP a measure of price-induced expectations.

In direct contrast to a quantity of money-type price equation (which takes Y as given in the short run), this formulation incorporates a growing body of literature contending that (at least in the short run) the level of real output in developing countries is subject to the influence of domestic policy measures (such as money supply changes).(29) Whereas in a quantity of money equation at a given level of income, money supply changes are the measure of excess demand, the above formulation implies that shifts in money supply will affect prices only if they cause output to rise above its long-term trend.

Obviously, the major empirical issue surrounding this approach is the ability of D to serve as an effective measure of excess demand. If D does not properly account for this factor, and because the various determinants of inflation tend to some degree to rise together, an undue share of the variation of the prices of home goods may be attributed to import prices and the lagged price changes used in the expectations variable.

With these caveats in mind, a number of regressions of the above general form were run. As with the test of the openness inflation theory, regressions on the rate of increase in the consumer price index gave somewhat better (but again similar) results compared with the wholesale price index.

Again, because the literature is not precise as to the best aggregate income measure to use in deviations from the trend analysis, several different income series were tested. Two time periods were also used for computing the trend: 1959-1977 and 1959-1972. Logarithmic forms were estimated along with the regular formulation. Measures of D were real non-oil GDP, logarithmic form (DDLNOXNP); real domestic absorption (DTDNANP); real non-oil GDP (DTNOXNP); and real gross domestic product (DTGDPNP). Lagged values end with an L.

As might be expected, deviations from the 1959-1972 trend (extrapolated to 1977) gave better results than those from the 1959-77 trend. By itself, the best measure of the deviation from the trend was real non-oil GDP (DTNOXNP), with its current period value accounting for over 81 percent of the fluctuation in the consumer price index, and its lagged value accounting for nearly 85 percent of the fluctuation (table 8.6).

Using the lagged value of deviations from the trend (1959-72), real non-oil GDP gave excellent results with r^2 values all above 0.90 percent, and one form with openness and world inflation (equation 12, table 8.7) accounting for nearly 98 percent of the fluctuation in the rate of consumer price inflation (INFC).

As noted in the discussion of openness and inflation, all measures of openness were quite significant when regressed with DTNOXPL and hence for comparison purposes only two of these are given here (equations 5, 10, and 11, table 8.7). Again, the rate of world inflation (WINF) is significant when regressed with DTNOXPL as is the growth in M2 and M1 measures of money (especially GM1L and GM2L, equations 6 and 7, table 8.7). While these results seem quite satisfactory, several conceptual difficulties detract somewhat from their acceptance as an accurate depiction of the inflationary process in Iran during this period.

In general, at least three characteristics of the Iranian economy might limit the effectiveness of DTNOXPL as a measure of excess demand: (1) the high proportion of agricultural

Table 8.6. Deviations from Trend as a Measure of Inflationary Pressures (Consumer Price Inflation)

Dependent Variable	Coefficient	Intercept	r^2	F
DTLNOXNP	0.03 (6.90)	6.07 (6.42)	0.798	47.63
DTDANP	0.02 (6.62)	3.19 (2.82)	0.785	43.83
DTNOXNP	0.03 (7.22)	3.19 (3.03)	0.813	52.07
DTNOXNPL	0.04 (8.23)	7.40 (9.15)	0.849	67.82
DTGDPNP	0.02 (5.44)	-0.85 (-0.46)	0.712	29.62
DTGDPNPL	0.02 (7.89)	-0.59 (-0.46)	0.838	62.24
DTDANPL	0.02 (6.75)	3.91 (3.67)	0.792	45.62

Note: See text for identification of symbols.

products in both non-oil production and consumption, (2) a fairly high rate of inflation, and (3) an uneven growth of productive capacity.

Implicit in the use of DTNOXPL as a measure of excess demand in the inflation equations is the notion that, when the growth of output rose above its long-run trend, the country's domestic productive capacity was being strained and prices had to rise if output was to be increased any further. Clearly, this assumption is predicated on the existence of an upward sloping supply curve of output, whereby increasing prices stimulate further production. This situation is undoubtedly better suited for conditions present in the more advanced economies where gross domestic product has a much higher proportion of industrial products. In general, there should be more scope for expanding the output of manufacturing and services in the short run than would be the case for agricultural products, particularly in Iran where most products were

Table 8.7. Deviations from the Trend and Consumer Price Inflation (1959-77)

Equation	Dependent Variable	Independent Variables											Intercept	r^2	F
		DTNOXPL	GM2	WINF	GM2L	INFCL	Z	GM2C2	GMTL	TTCL	WINFL2	ZL			
(1)	INFC	0.038 (9.37)	-0.05 (-1.09)										4.76 (4.01)	0.901	50.10
(2)	INFC	0.036 (11.88)		0.31 (3.38)									1.90 (2.42)	0.950	94.06
(3)	INFC	0.033 (12.40)	-0.08 (-2.71)	0.33 (4.21)									3.71 (4.71)	0.964	90.22
(4)	INFC	0.048 (10.29)		0.41 (4.83)		-0.57 (-3.00)							3.54 (5.04)	0.968	99.18
(5)	INFC	0.052 (6.60)		0.35 (3.95)			-10.14 (-2.17)						5.12 (3.58)	0.958	75.92
(6)	INFC	0.015 (1.27)		0.17 (1.59)	0.42 (1.93)			0.10 (0.67)					-5.59 (-1.19)	0.956	49.21
(7)	INFC	0.024 (4.50)							0.32 (3.32)				-0.51 (-0.36)	0.945	95.03
(8)	INFC	0.039 (9.53)											3.62 (4.43)	0.892	90.86
(9)	INFC	0.047 (8.61)								0.0036 (1.91)			-13.19 (-1.48)	0.918	61.31
(10)	INFC			0.60 (1.88)			-10.14 (-2.16)						3.44 (1.20)	0.237	3.41
(11)	INFC	0.077 (10.62)									0.35 (2.27)	-32.58 (-5.06)	11.11 (7.87)	0.973	119.92
(12)	INFC	0.022 (2.32)		0.023 (2.16)	0.31 (1.48)								0.02 (2.32)	0.959	70.94

Note: See text for identification of symbols.

subject to a crop cycle or weather conditions. Even though import substitution industrialization was proceeding rapidly, Iran's non-oil GDP was still heavily concentrated on agricultural products in the early 1970s. Given the rapid expansion in the consumption of food during this period, agriculture's output was probably more subject to fluctuations in domestic supply than in domestic demand. Conceivably, short-run deviations of agricultural production above its trend could result in lower rather than higher prices and vice versa, thus distorting the measure of excess demand the overall deviation from the trend figure was attempting to capture.

A second limitation on the usefulness of DTNOXPL as a measure of excess demand is its implicit assumption that productive capacity grows at a fairly constant rate. While investment fluctuates from year to year in most advanced countries, Iran's investment in both construction and machinery seems to have been especially volatile by any standards (table 8.8). Whether these fluctuations in capacity are high enough to invalidate the DTNOXPL measure of excess demand is difficult to assess. They do, however, cast serious doubts on the procedure.

Finally, applicability of DTNOXPL as an accurate measure of demand pressure in Iran is also questioned because of the country's high rates of inflation and money supply growth, particularly in the 1970s. Within a limited range, changes in short-run demand pressure could have resulted partially in higher industrial output and partially in price increases. Nevertheless, a point may have been realized in the early 1970s beyond which an increase in demand resulted in higher prices only. The high rates of money supply growth combined with a high proportion of output in agriculture may have been sufficient to have significantly reduced the economy's short-run supply elasticity.

Table 8.8. Growth in Investment
(Constant Prices)

	Private Sector			Government Investment		Total Investment		
	Machinery	Construction	Total	Machinery	Construction	Machinery	Construction	Total
1960	9.2	20.4	15.1	-30.1	-8.1	22.4	1.8	7.2
1961	-42.6	2.5	-14.6	29.6	-7.0	-19.6	-20.1	-4.1
1962	-17.6	-13.5	-15.0	-66.0	-5.0	-10.0	-29.3	-6.2
1963	0.7	3.9	2.7	-44.3	23.9	13.4	-7.4	0.1
1964	26.9	14.9	19.7	36.1	-1.5	7.8	28.7	14.6
1965	-1.6	11.4	7.9	56.7	37.7	25.0	20.2	23.5
1966	19.7	6.7	10.8	19.3	-10.3	-1.4	19.5	6.1
1967	31.8	5.2	18.0	29.7	31.9	20.2	31.0	24.4
1968	-14.1	5.8	-2.8	31.1	20.2	14.5	8.0	12.0
1969	-8.0	4.3	-0.7	21.5	15.5	11.4	8.7	10.4
1970	12.5	-0.9	4.9	-2.6	5.7	3.3	4.5	3.8
1971	28.8	19.2	23.7	9.3	15.4	16.8	19.7	18.1
1972	40.4	21.8	31.8	-15.4	16.8	18.7	22.9	20.2
1973	-4.0	4.5	0.1	31.3	17.5	13.0	10.4	12.0
1974	13.3	20.1	16.7	38.7	25.2	23.6	25.8	24.4
1975	63.4	35.7	53.4	11.8	40.1	35.6	48.7	43.0
1976	-1.7	32.6	14.2	33.8	24.8	26.4	11.8	21.4
1977	-17.9	14.9	0.0	16.5	9.1	11.2	-5.2	5.8

Source: Computed from Bank Markazi Iran, Annual Report, various issues.

CONCLUSION

Taken in their entirety, the empirical results presented above cast doubt on the role of pure cost-push factors as a significant contributing factor to the Iranian inflation of the 1970s. Admittedly, these may have been present in certain industries and at certain times, but their overall impact seems to have been minimal. The structuralist interpretation of inflation would seem to be on much sounder ground. In fact, it might even be argued that, in the medium term, the development of Iranian industry through the country's import substitution strategy further added to domestic inflationary pressures. High levels of protection afforded new industries from world competitors turned the domestic terms of trade sharply against agriculture in the 1970s, thus reducing the rate of growth of agricultural output below what it would otherwise have been. (The lack of investment in agriculture further exacerbated this problem.) It is also likely that the industrialization that did take place aggravated or even created a number of rigidities that began to characterize the economy in the 1970s, i.e., the inadequacy of infrastructure created by the sudden demand placed on power and transport by the new industries. Similarly, the short-term inadequacy of labor - both skilled labor and industrial entrepreneurs - was created by excessive industrial growth. Finally, increased pressures on the commercial banks to extend credit to industry were made by the Bank Markazi.

Ultimately, the issue comes down to the fact that the tests outlined above using proxies for structural factors, while statistically satisfactory, suffer from conceptual difficulties. Specifically, many of the underlying assumptions critical for the validity of the deviation from the trend measure may not have been present in Iran during the time examined. The real issue is whether or not, given the limitations of these theories, the quantity of money approach (or a version of it), given the availability of direct data for its testing, might not give a better idea of the relative inflationary impact of external versus domestic factors.

Monetary elements also warrant more attention simply because, in tests with structural factors (equation 6, table 8.7), the growth in money supply was statistically significant while the structural proxy (DTNOXPL) was not.

The importance of this fact lies in the fact that, in responding to inflation, the government appears to have implicitly accepted the argument that its underlying causes were cost related and not of monetary origins.

In order to curb the price rises, instead of reducing public sector expenditures and restricting the expansion of private sector credits, the regime embarked upon an antiprofiteering campaign which sowed the seeds of distrust and resentment of the government by the bazaar and at the same time received and harbored the historical alliance of the ulma and the bazaar.

9 A Monetarist Framework

INTRODUCTION

The monetarist theory of inflation differs essentially from those just discussed in the basic assumptions from which it starts.(1) Instead of assuming, for example, that wage changes provoke price changes and conversely through institutionally given (and, therefore, arbitrary) reaction coefficients, it assumes that, in an inflation, the economy would become accustomed to the expectation of continued inflation, so that the processes of determining wages and prices are fundamentally real processes and not arbitrary processes determined exogenously.

As will be shown in more vigorous fashion below, this approach is a logical one to use in examining Iran's price movements. First, the economy is relatively small in the sense that prices of goods and capital are determined in world markets, and Iran has little control. Second even though Iran is considered a less developed country, it did have a relatively advanced financial sector, headed by a central bank which, over most of the period under examination, was responsible for influencing the external balance (the balance of payments) as well as domestic credit conditions. Thus, Iran provides not only the conditions necessary for testing a monetary model but also provides some interesting insights into the model's policy implications, especially with regard to the nature and causes of inflation experienced by the country.

THE ROLE OF MONEY

The role of money and monetary policy has been one of the often debated issues in development economics for a long time. Despite Schumpeter's dramatization of money and credit as a "phenomenon of development,"(2) the nature of monetary policy remained indistinct and ill-defined in Iran for two reasons. For one thing, monetary policy was viewed in a narrow perspective as influencing aggregate spending via the regulation of interest rates, credit availability, and credit allocation. For another, views on the role of money and monetary policy were dominated by the then prevailing perception by the government of the growth process itself, which had not assigned a meaningful function to money but, rather, emphasized the role of physical capital accumulation.

The lack of interest in monetary aggregates and monetary control largely stemmed the excessive preoccupation of economic policymakers with techniques of monetary management, reflecting an emphasis on cyclical rather than long-term objectives, and on the deficiencies of these techniques for Iran.(3) For instance, it was not considered effective for the central bank to manipulate bank discount rates as an instrument of policy because there were no market instruments or traditions among banks to react to bank rate changes in a definite and predictable fashion. Open market operations were not thought to be feasible because there were insufficient government bonds that the Bank Markazi could buy and sell on a fairly large scale.(4)

As noted in the previous chapter, the issue of whether Iran's inflation was the consequence of the upward push of costs or the upward pull of demand on prices is important largely from the difference between the recommendations for antiinflationary policy. The demand pull explanation leads to the recommendation of monetary restraint and controlled levels of government expenditure, while the cost-push explanation leads to the rejection of macroeconomic measures of this sort in favor of policies directed at the process of price formation and wage determination.

The difference in policy recommendations was not entirely a difference between right wing conservative and liberal technocratic solutions. Nevertheless, the two schools of thought did differ fundamentally over policy: one school (the monetarist) recommending measures involving a higher volume of unemployment in order to stop inflation,(5) the other (the government) preferring repressive measures that sought to restrain inflation without sacrificing growth or increasing unemployment. (Both schools were united in their belief that inflation should be stopped, a conviction that became increasingly strong by 1977.)

As in many instances in Iran, the economic issues surrounding the control of inflation became so closely bound up with political issues that, for some writers at least, it is difficult to determine whether the economic analyses preceded the policy recommendations or vice versa. Rather than survey the writings of each position, therefore, the key aspects of both will be referred to selectively in the discussion that follows.

Suffice it to say that, in terms of numbers, those who thought that attempts to control the money supply were a useful and productive endeavor were quite in the minority. The predominant view among most officials in the country was that the scope for demand management was severely limited for several reasons. The nonpolicy disturbances to which monetary policy must respond invariably originated in the supply side (bad weather, poor crops, etc.) or abroad (changes in oil revenues) so that policy efforts to change domestic demand were of little or no consequence for their net effect on output and employment. Instead, the conventional wisdom in Iran was that the country's employment and growth were more closely related to the pace and nature of economic development, particularly the composition of the development budget contained in the five year plans. The state of aggregate demand was given little recognition in this regard. It was also felt that coordinating supply and demand (equating savings and investment, etc.) is the central task of markets. The more complex an economy becomes (i.e., the more indirect are the economic relationships between members of a society), the more difficult this coordinating task is and the more sensitive these relationships are to disturbances. Here, the conventional wisdom maintained that, as the economy was by its very nature relatively uncomplex in this sense (still with a high degree of barter), the coordination of supply and demand was without meaning; "fine tuning" types of demand management by the authorities would be of little avail.

THE MODEL AND ITS ASSUMPTIONS

As noted above, the monetary model simply assumes that, if a small open economy such as Iran's wishes to maintain a fixed exchange rate, then the balance of payments through its effect on the quantity of money will be the main channel for attaining and maintaining monetary equilibrium. When the domestic money supply exceeds the demand for money, people must readjust their portfolios by purchasing in the goods or assets markets in order to achieve portfolio equilibrium. In Iran's case, a part of this process took place (usually with a fixed exchange rate) as residents purchased foreign exchange from the Bank Markazi to make payments to foreigners. This resulted in a gradual lowering of the domestic money supply until monetary equilibrium was finally achieved. In this sense, the country's balance of payments is assumed to have been a monetary phenomenon.(6)

The fundamental element in the monetary theory of the balance of payments is the existence of a stable demand for money function. Usually this demand is considered to be a function of the level of real income and the opportunity cost of holding money. If each of these determinants remains constant, the monetary approach can be regarded as a theory of the rate of inflation whereby the price level will adjust to ensure that, whatever the stock of nominal money, the level of money in real terms will be equal to the amount of money demanded, i.e., the nominal money supply determines the price level.(7)

These assumptions imply a three equation model which includes: (1) the demand for money, (2) the supply of money, and (3) money market equilibrium conditions.

$$(1)\quad Md = kPy^{a1}e^{v}.u^{a2}$$
$$(2)\quad Ms = a(R+D)$$
$$(3)\quad Md = Ms$$

Differentiating equations (1) and (3) logarithmically with respect to time yields:

$$(4)\quad gM = gP + a1gy - a2gi + v$$

for the money demand equation and

$$(5)\quad (\frac{R}{B})gR = gP + a1gy - a2gi - ga - (\frac{D}{B})gD + u$$

for the reserve flow equation. The coefficient a1 is the income inelasticity of demand for nominal money. Based on studies in other countries and for theoretical reasons, a value of around 1.0 would be expected.(8)

For a given interest rate, price level money multiplier (a) and domestic credit (D) growth in income (gy) should be associated with reserve inflows just sufficient to result in a1 percent increase in the nominal and real stock of money.

Increases in the interest rate should result in reserve outflows. Other things equal, a given increase in the interest rate would depress the demand for money creating an excess demand for it and, consequently, would result in reserve outflows. Again, work in other developing countries suggests that a2, the interest elasticity of demand for money, should be a positive number.

Interest rates in the United States and the Euromarkets were used in the empirical testing, since figures on Iranian rates are not available. Clearly, however, if changes in the actual Iranian rate during this time was dominated by changes relative to the rest of the world, estimates of a2 could very well be positive, i.e., increases in the rest-of-world rates relative to Iranian rates should attract capital and generate reserve inflows (and vice versa). If no money illusion existed during this period, the price coefficient should be around 1.0. Similarly, the theory predicts the coefficients of ga and $(\frac{D}{B})$gD should each be -1.0.

Finally, the money multiplier (ga) and the domestic credit creation $(\frac{D}{B})$gD were both policy variables of the central bank during this period. An increase in either or both would tend to increase the money supply and *ceteris paribus* should lead to an outflow of reserves sufficient to restore money to its previous level.

In summary, income and prices should be positively related to reserve flows while domestic credit, money multiplier, and the interest rate would be negatively related to reserve flows. Most of these implications are in disagreement with the Keynesian theory of the balance of payments; and, thus, at first sight, this theory might seem to have little relevance for Iran. Casual observation seems to indicate that the reserve flows of the country were determined almost exclusively by real variables (the price of oil, the volume of oil exports, etc.).(9) Thus, it is difficult to see where monetary factors could enter. This view stems from a narrow view of the balance of payments, however, where focus is on a particular component (or components) of the balance of payments account rather than taking a unified view of the entire account.

More precisely, it is clear that the immediate cause of the bulk of reserve flows into the country was, in fact, the increased oil revenue. Were there no demand for the money created by these reserve flows, however, a corresponding reserve outflow would have been necessary to balance the new level of supply and demand for money. The reason that this compensating outflow did not occur in the short run was that the government followed restrictive policies with respect to the domestic component of the money supply. The increase in the price of oil resulted in a substantial increase in the country's real income, but the resulting increase in the demand for money was not met by the inflow of foreign reserves.(10)

It is also clear that the Iranian authorities were in a position to considerably modify the impact of the reserve flows on the domestic money supply. Because the oil revenues accrued directly to the government, they did not affect the domestic money supply until the government decided to inject them into the domestic economy through its expenditures.(11) Therefore, the primary tool of monetary management became a byproduct of the government's budgetary decisions rather than the situation in most countries where it was an instrument of the central monetary authority.

In fact, as an accounting matter, one observes that net foreign assets were the major sources of reserve money (monetary base) while government deposits with the Bank Markazi arising from budgetary surpluses constituted the major contractive component of reserve money (table 9.1).

The implication of the above patterns is that the primary determinants of the monetary base in Iran were the accumulation of foreign assets and the budgetary decisions of the government. To the extent that oil revenues were retained by the government as deposits in the Bank Markazi, the inflow of foreign reserves was not permitted to affect the supply of money. This action however, did not, necessarily constitute a conscious attempt by the government at sterilization of reserve flows. Instead, it appears governmental budgetary decisions in Iran were made largely on the basis of perceived military needs and the requirements of the development plan.

EMPIRICAL RESULTS

The estimates of various formulations of the reserve flow equation yielded:

$$(R/B)gR = \underset{(2.97)}{1.00GNOXNP} - \underset{(26.49)}{0.97(D/B)gD} + \underset{(3.88)}{1.08INFWP} + \underset{(0.34)}{0.01}$$

$$r^2 = 0.992 \qquad F = 411.40$$

$$(R/B)gR = \underset{(5.24)}{1.49GGDPNP} - \underset{(35.93)}{1.01(D/B)gD} + \underset{(6.97)}{1.51INFCPI} - \underset{(-1.43)}{0.05}$$

$$r^2 = 0.994 \qquad F = 564.18$$

$$(R/B)gR = \underset{(2.85)}{1.39GNOXNP} - \underset{(22.91)}{1.05(D/B)gD} + \underset{(0.62)}{0.03}$$

$$r^2 = 0.979 \qquad F = 267.39$$

where INFWP and INFCPI are the wholesale and consumer price indices, respectively, representing the cost of holding money balances.

In first difference form, the estimates were:

Table 9.1. Factors Responsible for Changes in the Money Supply
(billions rials)

		1962	1963	1964	1965	1966	1967	1968	1969
Changes in									
1	Money (4+7+10+11)	3.9	5.2	4.9	6.4	6.5	10.3	10.8	2.5
2	Credits of banks to private sector	(10.8)	(11.4)	(15.2)	(14.1)	(19.0)	(21.1)	(24.9)	(31.4)
3	Quasi-money	(8.6)	(7.7)	(5.9)	(6.8)	(8.7)	(13.3)	(20.2)	(27.9)
4	Net debt of private sector (2-3)	2.2	3.7	9.3	7.3	10.3	7.8	4.7	3.5
5	Credits of banking system to public sector	(-2.0)	(6.3)	(6.3)	(6.0)	(6.0)	(19.7)	(16.8)	(27.2)
6	Deposits of public with banking system	(-0.6)	(5.4)	(14.1)	(-7.3)	(3.8)	(7.1)	(1.0)	(12.1)
7	Net debt of public sector	-1.4	0.9	-7.8	13.3	2.2	12.6	15.8	15.1
8	Foreign assets	(1.8)	(2.5)	(7.7)	(-3.8)	(-1.7)	(6.4)	(-4.6)	(3.8)
9	Foreign debts	(-1.2)	(-0.2)	(0.1)	(0.6)	(0.8)	(8.7)	(1.4)	(8.9)
10	Foreign assets (net)	3.0	2.7	7.6	-4.4	-2.5	-2.3	-6.0	-5.1
11	Other (net)	0.1	-2.1	-4.2	-9.8	-3.5	-7.8	-3.7	-11.0

(continued)

Table 9.1. Factors Responsible for Changes in the Money Supply (continued)
(billions rials)

	1970	1971	1972	1973	1974	1975	1976	1977
Changes in								
1 Money (4+7+10+11)	7.0	19.6	41.7	44.0	124.5	119.4	164.7	179.3
2 Credits of banks to private sector	(31.6)	(47.4)	(84.8)	(126.7)	(210.4)	(387.9)	(424.1)	(352.2)
3 Quasi-money	(23.0)	(41.0)	(61.4)	(72.4)	(169.8)	(216.1)	(283.3)	(324.2)
4 Net debt of private sector (2-3)	8.6	6.4	23.4	54.3	40.6	171.8	140.8	28.0
5 Credits of banking system to public sector	(31.7)	(29.4)	(45.0)	(77.0)	(147.5)	(178.9)	(335.4)	(78.6)
6 Deposits of public with banking system	(5.0)	(42.7)	(32.2)	(77.8)	(173.8)	(133.1)	(322.1)	(-139.2)
7 Net debt of public sector	26.7	-13.3	12.8	-0.8	-26.3	45.8	13.3	217.8
8 Foreign assets	(0.0)	(37.2)	(28.4)	(23.5)	(377.5)	(9.9)	(170.6)	(169.3)
9 Foreign debts	(20.9)	(0.4)	(-5.4)	(21.1)	(26.3)	(59.6)	(66.1)	(51.2)
10 Foreign assets (net)	-20.9	36.8	33.8	52.4	351.2	-49.9	104.8	118.1
11 Other (net)	-7.4	-10.3	-28.3	-61.9	-241.0	-48.3	-94.2	-184.6

Source: Computed from data in Bank Markazi Iran, Annual Report, various issues.

$$\Delta BMFA = 0.83\Delta BMDA + 0.09\Delta GDPN + 1.67\Delta CPI - 1.99$$
$$(-39.65) \quad (11.36) \quad (9.33) \quad (-0.68)$$
$$r^2 = 0.998$$
$$F = 1332$$

$$\Delta BMFA = -0.83\Delta BMDA + 0.14\Delta GDPN - 3.86\Delta EURO + 2.43$$
$$(-13.33) \quad (7.99) \quad (-1.25) \quad (0.29)$$
$$r^2 = 0.979$$
$$F = 155.89$$

$$\Delta BMFA = -0.97\Delta BMDA + 0.23\Delta NOXN - 2.66$$
$$(-58.90) \quad (30.45) \quad (-1.21)$$
$$r^2 = 0.997$$
$$F = 2580.07$$

where BMFA = the change in reserves (foreign assets held by the Bank Markazi); BMDA = the change in Bank Markazi domestic credit; GDPN = changes in GDP; and EURO = change in Euro-interest rate.

IMPLICATIONS OF THE RESULTS

The empirical results provide considerable confirmation of the monetary model as applied to Iran. First, it is clear from the results that foreign reserve flows did take place to restore equilibrium in the money market. In a sense, the massive reserve inflows could be seen as necessary to satisfy the increased demand for money arising from the oil price induced increases in real income.

Second, a further implication of the results is that, as long as the country's real income continued to rise at rates which were rapid relative to those in the rest of the world, the demand for money in the country would continue to rise relative to the demand for money in other countries. Assuming the government did not suddenly create a budget deficit, this demand for money had to come from additional reserve inflows.

If the government did move toward a budgetary deficit (perhaps as expenditures on development projects, military equipment, and social programs outstripped oil revenues), the resulting increase in the domestic component of the money supply would likely provide the needed domestic liquidity. Massive inflows would be curtailed and possibly reversed.

THE MONETARIST APPROACH TO INFLATION

The monetary approach to inflation in Iran is similar to that outlined above in connection with the balance of payments; i.e., it starts with the fundamental proposition that inflation is merely an interaction of market supply and demand for money. Put differently, price movements are viewed by this model as systematically dependent upon current and immediate past evolutions of the interaction between supply and demand conditions.

The starting point of this analysis is the basic monetarist model derived from the equation of exchange.(12) More specifically, assume a simple money demand function of the following form:

$$(1) \quad M/PY = Y^aC^b$$

where M is the exogenously determined nominal stock of money, P is the price, Y is a measure of real income, and C is the expected cost of holding real balances. Equation (1) is solved for P and expressed in terms of growth rates (or depicted by G prefixing the variable):

$$(2) \quad INF = RM - (1\text{-}a)GY - bGC$$

Equation (2) incorporates the basic elements of the monetarist approach to inflation: money, real income, and the expected cost of holding real balances. In addition, this formulation captures the basic methodological bias of the monetarist school; i.e., the equation has a limited number of variables, and the nature of relationships is clear and straightforward. The growth of money relative to output and cost of holding real balances will generate an increase in the rate of inflation. The growth of real income will cause decreases in the rate of inflation (via absorbing money in the increased demand for real balances). Similarly, the rate of inflation is assumed to be inversely related to the expected cost of holding real balances.

Equation (2) assumes instantaneous adjustment of monetary changes and no money illusion. Therefore, the tested form of the monetarist equation is:

$$INF = a + a1GM + a2GML + GML2 - GNOXNP + EXP$$

where GNOXNP is the growth of real non-oil income, GML is the growth of the money supply lagged one year, GML2 is the growth in the money supply lagged two years, and EXP is some measure of inflationary expectations.

The basic monetarist contention is that: (1) the causal relation runs from money to prices and output, (2) any persistent increase in money relative to output is a sufficient condition for inflation, (3) the magnitude and length of inflation is dependent on the magnitude and persistence of monetary growth, (4) the occurrence of inflation is independent of the level of employment in the economy, and (5) it is the increasing growth rate of money which yields inflationary pressures.

The results of the monetary regressions on the rate of increase in the consumer price index indicate that the monetarist model performs extremely well. The growth in both M1 and M2 was used, with M2 performing slightly better. M2 by itself, however, is not significant when lagged one year.

GM2L is highly significant, explaining nearly 93 percent of the observed rate of inflation (equation 7, table 9.2). When combined with other variables, GM2L is still significant, rising to over 97 percent explanation of the variance in INFX when combined with GM2L2, expected inflation (INFC, lagged one year), and world inflation (WINF). In general, the growth of world prices gives somewhat better results than world inflation lagged one year. The growth in non-oil GDP does not significantly contribute to the regression equation when introduced with lagged GM2 nor does the deviation from the trend of real non-oil income used in the previous chapter (equation 8).

Openness measures (ZLON) are significant and of the right sign when regressed with GM2L and GM2L2. They are right on the border of acceptability, however, but do improve r^2 somewhat further.

The negative sign on the inflationary expectation term (INFCL) as proxied by last year's rate of inflation is of interest and has certain implications for monetary policy. The negative sign indicates that, with increased inflation, individuals may have actually increased their holdings of money. An apparently irrational move since inflation was eroding the value of these holdings at the time. This, however, can be explained to some extent by the financial structure of the country, which can be characterized by:(13)

- greater reliance of firms on internal financing than on the issuance of new securities;
- only limited activity in the domestic stock exchange with new securities being mainly purchased by the financial institutions rather than the nonbank private sector; and
- deposits with the monetary system constituting the major portion of the public's claims on the financial intermediaries.

The lack of developed markets where borrowers and lenders could interact directly together with a lack of confidence in the stability of the country's financial markets and the inadequacy of government regulations for dealing with fraud in

Table 9.2. Monetary Determinants of Inflation, 1959-1972

Equation	Dependent Variable	Independent Variables								Intercept	r^2	F
		GM2L	GM2L2	INFCL	GNOXNP	WINF	GM2	ZAG	DINOXPL			
1	INFC	0.66 (2.19)								-7.01 (-1.62)	0.445	4.81
2	INFC	0.62 (2.79)	0.85 (2.46)							-19.00 (-3.28)	0.749	7.45
3	INFC	0.05 0.26	0.62 (3.39)				0.36 (3.94)			-13.21 (-4.03)	0.949	24.68
4	INFC	0.87 (4.02)	1.07 (3.62)	-0.61 (-1.99)						-24.64 (-4.57)	0.874	9.24
5	INFC		0.55 (1.32)		-0.47 (-1.92)		0.34 (2.50)			-6.77 (-2.30)	0.897	11.60
6	INFC	0.71 (3.62)	1.01 (4.23)	-0.81 (-3.04)		0.26 (1.82)				-21.70 (-4.73)	0.940	11.80
7	INFC	0.53 (2.14)	1.09 (3.20)			-0.04 (-0.23)		-64.39 (-1.93)		-17.00 (-2.88)	0.892	6.17
8	INFC	0.45 (1.48)	0.70 (2.16)	-0.41 (-1.49)					0.043 (1.73)	-12.42 (-1.49)	0.937	11.15
9	INFC						0.47 (4.88)			-4.63 (-3.08)	0.799	23.89
10	INFC		-0.80 (-0.26)				0.47 (3.00)			-3.94 (-1.25)	0.802	10.12
11	INFC	0.15 (0.58)	0.44 (1.41)						0.05 (2.27)	-4.89 (-0.64)	0.890	10.83

Note: See text for identification of symbols.

the stock markets apparently made broad money (M2) the most desirable asset to hold during this period. The reason for the desirability of money, despite the fact of rapidly rising prices at the time, must have been due to the fact that individuals perceived it a relatively riskless asset in the short run.(14)

When the results of 1959-72 (table 9.2) are compared with those for the period as a whole (table 9.3), several differences appear. In general, the monetary impact is not as strong (based on r^2 values). The monetary impact came sooner in the 1959-72 period with GM2 significant then, but not for the period as a whole. In general, the coefficient for money lagged one year was quite similar for both the periods (except when included in regressions with GM2).

Tentatively, there is no real evidence here that a fundamental structural shift occurred after 1972. Monetary variables seem to have played a predominate role in influencing the movement in the country's price level before and after the oil price increases.

CONCLUSIONS

Based on the above analysis of the impact of openness, deviations from the trend, and monetary movements, it is clear that any meaningful framework for the analysis of inflation in Iran must systematically take into account the role of money in the economy. The link between real expenditures and monetary increases would seem to be the key element. Real demand in the country is determined in part by factors that depend on aggregate supply and in part by factors that are determined independently of supply. An approach along these lines might assume that the factors that bring demand and supply into balance are ultimately responsible for the economy's domestic price changes. A model along these lines is developed after a discussion of the policies actually pursued by the Bank Markazi and the government's overall approach to inflation.

Table 9.3. Monetary Determinants of Inflation, 1959-1977

Equation	Dependent Variable	Independent Variables								Intercept	r^2	F
		GM2L	GM2L2	INFCL	GNOXNP	WINF	GM2	ZAG	DTNOXPL			
1	INFC	0.80								-9.19		
		(0.03)								(-6.09)	0.928	142.51
2	INFC	0.67	0.26							-11.42		
		(7.17)	(1.72)							(-6.01)	0.945	85.40
3	INFC	0.50	0.51				-0.09			-10.87		
		(3.67)	(2.48)				(-1.66)			(-6.09)	0.958	67.82
4	INFC	0.76	0.59	-0.57						-16.15		
		(8.39)	(2.91)	(-2.12)						(-5.83)	0.963	78.31
5	INFC		0.93		-0.63		0.12			-7.20		
			(10.16)		(-1.93)		(1.74)			(-3.30)	0.950	56.51
6	INFC	0.61	0.41		-0.41	0.10				-8.98		
		(7.57)	(2.96)		(-2.53)	(1.20)				(-5.05)	0.972	68.77
7	INFC	0.75	0.62	-0.67		0.14				-16.78		
		(9.06)	(3.34)	(-2.66)		(1.71)				(-6.61)	0.973	71.92
8	INFC	0.65	0.31			0.07		-40.88		-9.55		
		(7.49)	(2.19)			(0.70)		(-1.81)		(-4.83)	0.964	53.40
9	INFC	0.86	0.69	-0.62			-0.17		0.007	10.26		
		(-1.01)	(2.36)	(-2.09)			(-1.21)		(-0.51)	(3.20)	0.118	1.47
10	INFC	0.81					0.01			-9.47		
		(10.66)					(0.20)			(-4.54)	0.929	65.06
11	INFC	0.65	0.23						0.002	-10.62		
		(2.92)	(1.03)						(0.14)	(-1.74)	0.945	51.35

Note: See text for identification of symbols.

10 Monetary Policy

INTRODUCTION

Before 1973, stabilization was not a major concern of economic planning in Iran. The fundamental economic problem of the country was one of accelerating the rate of non-oil income. Price inflation was exceptionally moderate by world standards. The problems of both unemployment and disequilibrium in the balance of payments were of a structural rather than of a cyclical character. As in the early 1950s, disputes with the oil companies or from time to time adverse weather unsettled the economic system, but these shocks were only temporary and were dealt with by ad hoc measures.

There is no question that after 1973 stabilization became a central policy issue for the Bank Markazi as accelerated government expenditures and worldwide inflation began driving price increases into double digit figures.

At issue is the degree to which the bank could actually affect stability. The government's role in destabilizing the economy, especially the price level, through its excessive expenditures after 1973 is easy to document.(1) Much more difficult to focus on is the role played by the monetary authorities and the extent to which this goal was, in fact, pursued.

Of particular interest is examining the validity for Iran of the following general observation on oil exporting countries.

> The reaction of the leaders of these countries to the sudden increase in their revenues was predictable, they all embarked on lavish development plans, discarding all fiscal restraints. The end results of these programs were also predictable. None of the

developing economies were ready for the tremendous boost in consumer demand, which led to shortages, inefficiency, waste, immense bottlenecks, and high rates of inflation. Caught off-guard by their economic problems the leaders of the oil exporting countries turned to Western and Western-trained economists, both Keynesian and monetarist, for solutions. These economists developed stabilization policies based on the neoclassical foundations far removed from the existing realities of the developing countries.(2)

POLICY INSTRUMENTS

The principal instruments of monetary policy available to the Bank Markazi were interest rate and selective credit controls, reserve requirements, credit ceilings, refinancing facilities, in some instances open market operations, and exchange rate policies. For analytical purposes, it is useful to treat separately the consequences of the use of these instruments on the quantity of money and credit from their consequences on the price and allocation of credit.

Interest in the behavior of the money supply per se was a fairly recent phenomenon in Iran. Formulating policy in terms of the money stock required determination of: (1) the most appropriate definition of money given the country's economic and institutional setting; (2) the consequences of the behavior of money so defined for prices, output, development, etc.; (3) the process by which the stock of money was determined; and (4) the role played by the Bank Markazi's policy instruments in that process.

There were two main sources of change in the Iranian money supply during this period. One source was the purchase of the government's foreign exchange receipts from oil exports by the Bank Markazi, and the other was the expansion of domestic assets held by the banking system. The latter could originate from either the public or private sectors. Since oil revenues accrued to the government, the rise in foreign assets was exactly offset by an increase in government deposits. However, if the government injected the oil revenues into the economy by converting its foreign reserves into domestic currency and undertook a higher level of outlays or subsidies for goods and services, an increase in the money supply occurred automatically.

Changes in the money supply, therefore, came about in three ways:(3)

1. external transactions of the nongovernment sector;
2. changes in supply of credit to the nongovernmental sector by domestic banks; and
3. changes in the government's domestic budget.

The discussion of the factors determining money's behavior in the preceding chapter helps place the role of the traditional instruments of monetary control in their proper context. The Bank Markazi had to manipulate those factors in the base or the multiplier which it controlled in the light of the expected effect on money of those factors it did not control.

The evolution of the bank's monetary policy and the means by which it was implemented in the 1970s are outlined below.

EVOLUTION OF MONETARY POLICIES DURING THE 1970s

While the assignment of specific dates is somewhat controversial, most observers would have to argue that inflationary pressures in Iran began to build up before the oil price increases of late 1973. The lagged impact of the growth of money supply on price changes noted in the previous chapter indicates that the Bank Markazi's liberal financing of government deficits in the late 1960s and early 1970s was certainly a contributing factor to the acceleration of prices that was to come in the mid-1970s.

In addition, several new sources of inflationary pressure began to develop. First, the mobilization of quasi-money in 1968 and 1969 by the commercial banks providing them (by 1970) with the potential for expanding credit at a very rapid rate. Secondly, the private sector's demand for credit was beginning to accelerate in 1970.(4)

Monetary Policy in 1970

The Bank Markazi's policies in the late 1960s to early 1970s were predicated on the belief that the curtailment of credit to the public sector - especially that allocated to the Plan Organization - could jeopardize the country's economic development. Hence, most of the bank's actions at this time involved attempts at regulating the volume of credit allocated by the commercial banks to the private sector.

Placing its objective of high real economic growth first, the Bank Markazi did not subject the specialized banks (e.g., the agricultural bank) to the same credit ceilings it began to impose on the commercial banks. In addition, the Bank Markazi provided exporters with preferential treatment in obtaining credit while credit for imports and activities the bank considered as unproductive were checked. In addition to the credit ceiling imposed on the private sector during 1970, the Bank Markazi:

1. raised the legal reserve requirements for demand deposits from 20 to 23 percent;
2. maintained the legal reserve requirement for non-sight deposits at 15 percent and revoked the 5 percent which banks were allowed to hold in the form of government securities rather than cash;
3. required banks to hold 16 percent of their incremental deposits in 1970 as government securities; and
4. lowered the maximum interest rate payable on savings deposits from 5.5 percent to 4.5 percent, and lowered the maximum interest rate payable on time deposits by .5 percent for all maturities.

The expressed interest of these policies was to restrict the bank's overall lending activities.

As it turned out, the public sector's demand for funds in 1970 was much higher than its historical level, its previous demand, or what the banking system could easily accommodate. Because the Bank Markazi felt that the curtailment of government credit (especially to the Plan Organization) would jeopardize the country's economic development plans, the private sector was forced to feel the entire burden of the bank's credit policy. Few at the time faulted the bank's actions since their impact resulted in an enlargement of the banking system's net foreign liabilities. Further, the country achieved a very high rate of growth of GNP (10.3 percent) while incurring only a 1.7 percent increase in the GDP deflator.

Monetary Policy in 1973

By 1973, the bank was beginning to view inflation as the economy's major problem. In particular, the bank was concerned with the tendency of inflation-induced speculation to gradually divert the economy's resources from productive to nonproductive activities. At the time, the bank also expressed some concern that the interest ceilings it had imposed on the commercial banks were, because of increasing prices, undermining the willingness of individuals to place their funds in savings and time accounts. Along with its other antiinflationary measures, therefore, the bank also began to gradually increase the rate of interest that could be paid by the commercial banks.

Specifically, the Bank Markazi raised the rediscount rate for bills and promissory notes on commercial transactions from

7.5 to 9 percent per annum, and for bills (and notes based on industrial and agricultural transactions) from 7 to 8 percent. It also increased the maximum rates payable on savings deposits from 5.5 to 7 percent per annum, on time deposits of up to one year from 6.5 to 8 percent per annum; and on longer deposits from 7.5 to 9 percent per annum.

In determining the new rates of interest, the bank explicitly took into account the returns that could be obtained on government securities. The increase in interest rates on bank deposits, therefore, were not aimed so much at increasing savings per se as at expanding the sources of commercial bank credit. The Bank Markazi was, however, concerned that the banks' additional funds might result in a disproportionate credit expansion. Other measures were introduced to adjust the general level of credits and to ensure proper distribution of credits among the various sectors. These included the following:

1. Maximum increase authorized in aggregate loans and credits to the private sector during 1973 was to be 20 percent over aggregate loans and credits granted by the end of 1972.
2. Legal reserves were increased over the year from 23 to 30 percent.
3. While no changes were implemented in the ratio between legal reserves and time deposits at 15 percent, banks were instructed to purchase treasury bills or government bonds equivalent to 50 percent of all monthly increases in these deposits.
4. Recommendations were made that banks direct the increases in their deposits toward productive and import and export loans.
5. The banks were informed that Bank Markazi would respond to calls for rediscount in order to assist them in the implementation of its past and present regulations. This assistance was to be in the productive and international trade areas.
6. The Bank Markazi promised not only to undertake increased rediscounting, but would also extend loans to banks up to three years for productive undertakings in industry and agriculture.

In an official assessment of its performance for 1973, the Bank Markazi felt that its raising of the rate of interest proved effective in mobilizing savings. On the other hand, it argued that the higher ratio it had set for legal reserves combined with the obligatory purchases of government bonds had curbed bank liquidity. At the same time, it felt it had fulfilled its function in the regulation and proper distribution of credits through facilitating rediscount operations and the granting of loans and credits to priority areas.

Monetary Policy in 1974

By 1974, the bank saw its major objective as largely one of restricting the increase of loans and credits which were for inflationary use, while simultaneously encouraging the expansion of loans and credits for productive purposes and imports. At least in its official statements, the Bank Markazi did not give any inkling that there was an incompatibility in its objectives. It seemed to feel that all productive projects could be financed without an increase in inflationary pressures.

In addition to the obvious problem of deciding what a productive and nonproductive activity was, the bank seems to have subscribed to the controversial view often associated with the British Radcliffe Report. That approach contends that it is not the existing stock of money but, rather, the amount of credit which people think they can utilize that determines the expenditure level in the country. However, given the empirical results in the previous chapter linking inflation to changes in the money supply and also those demonstrating the stable demand for money, it would have been much wiser for the bank to concentrate on controlling the money supply rather than the level of credit.

In addition, the imposition of overall credit ceilings meant that what was essentially nonprice rationing of credit began to characterize bank lending practices. The result was that the more efficient and innovative commercial banks were able to increase their share of the market; the bank's policy was in effect a subsidy to the smaller less efficient banks.

Bank Markazi's policy in setting ceilings on the credit of banks was limited to commercial banks only. No constraints were placed upon the increase in loans and credits of specialized banks because of the capacity-increasing nature of their lending operations. Furthermore, the government provided these banks with considerable amounts of funds as loans, credits, and administered funds (in order to presumably strengthen their lending capabilities).

The net result of the bank's various credit policies, despite all of its talk of restraint, was an expansion of credit by 41 percent during 1974.

Monetary Policy in 1975

The volume of banking operations continued to expand in 1975 as the assets and liabilities of the banks increased by 34 percent. Expansion took place despite a decline of 11 percent in the banking system's net foreign assets. Expansion, therefore, resulted largely from the rapid growth in bank credits to both the private and public sectors. On the other hand, the growth in liabilities of the banking systems resulted mainly from the increase of money and quasi-money.

The Bank Markazi was apparently becoming more concerned with the rapid expansion in liquidity, and acted by increasing reserve requirements on savings and time deposits from 12 to 15 percent. It also increased the amount of government treasury bills the banks were required to purchase (from 30 to 45 percent of deposits). In addition, reserve requirements on the commercial banks' net foreign liabilities were increased from 15 to 30 percent. Credit ceilings remained in force, but, as in the past, no limits were applied to increased credits by the specialized banks. In fact, the expansion of credits by these banks was actually encouraged through financial assistance extended by the government and Bank Markazi in view of their effective role in expanding and mobilizing productive investments.

Monetary Policy in 1976

Inflationary pressures had become a major problem by 1976. The Bank Markazi now took the position that it was an excessively rapid increase in private sector liquidity, that was the chief cause of the price increases. However, the bank's response was not to attempt to control over-liquidity, but instead to continue its policy of restraining the increase of loans and credits.

In implementing its policy, the Bank Markazi undertook a number of studies designed to determine the credit ceiling for financing private sector investment at a level that would be the least inflationary. On the basis of studies, it set the commercial bank credit ceilings for 1976 at Rls 1,068.6 billion, implying a target expansion in commercial bank credit to the private sector of 30 percent in 1976.

In the case of the specialized banks, Bank Markazi felt that the capacity-increasing nature of their lending operations justified a higher credit ceiling. These banks were authorized to expand loans and credits to the private sector by 42 percent during the year.

Although the Bank Markazi had controlled interest rates for some time, it wasn't until 1976 that systematic studies were undertaken to determine the degree to which these rates either discouraged or encouraged the flow of funds into priority areas.

In one of its studies, the Bank Markazi found that returns of investments in productive sectors were considerably higher than the lending rates of the specialized banks. Furthermore, these rates were not as high as the cost incurred by these banks in obtaining funds. The specialized banks were, therefore, found to be overly dependent on financial assistance from the government.

In order to decrease this dependence and reduce the gap between lending rates of the specialized banks and interest rates prevailing in the capital market, the Bank Markazi raised the maximum lending rates of the specialized banks for industrial, mining, and construction projects from 8 to 9 percent. For large scale agricultural projects, the rate was increased from 6 to 8 percent to 7 to 9 percent.

Bank Markazi also increased its rediscount rate from 7 percent for industrial activities and 8 percent for commercial activities to 9 percent for either in order to maintain a balance in the interest rate system after the increase in the specialized banks' lending rates. As noted above, another reason for this increase was to reduce the difference between the maximum lending rates of the commercial banks and their cost of loanable funds.

These increases seem insignificant and more of a token effort considering that the consumer price index increased by an average of 16.6 percent and the wholesale price index by 13.5 percent during 1975. By the end of 1976, these rates had increased to 27.3 and 21.5 percent, respectively. During 1976, the economy's supply of goods and services rose by 12.5 percent (at constant prices), but overall monetary demand increased by 39.1 percent.

As always, the bank's efforts were too little and too late; the result was that neither an efficient allocation of investment nor price stability were anywhere near being met.

In addition, Bank Markazi's measures made it unattractive for the commercial banks to attract time deposits. On a year's fixed deposit, for example, banks had to pay 10 percent. But, of this sum deposited, the bank was obliged to place 15 percent with the Bank Markazi (at 1 percent) and purchase government bonds with a further 45 percent (bearing around 9 percent). Thus, they had only 40 percent of the initial deposit to invest while still guaranteeing the depositor 10 percent return on the whole amount. It was argued that these measures were necessary to control inflation. But it is hard to see how discouraging banks to accept savings accounts was consistent with this objective.

Admittedly, many of Bank Markazi's problems were caused by the relatively immature commercial banks. This manifested itself in many ways but, as far as credit was concerned, many of the commercial banks still managed to reach their credit ceilings in the early part of the year. This meant that credit became tighter toward the end of the year, and great pressures were then applied by the authorities to permit credit increases above the ceiling. For example, the authorities would have liked to have had around a 35 percent increase in credit to the private sector in 1976. It turned out to be nearer 40 percent simply due to the limited relief granted by the Bank Markazi when many of the commercial banks reached their ceilings by mid-year.

In general, at this time it appears that the monetary policies pursued in Iran were concerned almost exclusively with facilitating high rates of economic growth. When price stability finally became a major concern, the bank relied largely on the control of bank credit to the private sector rather than controlling the money supply directly. In general, it is safe to argue that undue attention was given to policies that would influence the composition of investment portfolios, encourage private savings, or further the development of financial intermediation and an efficient capital market.

Monetary Policy in 1977

By 1977, inflationary pressures were clearly out of control, reaching 30 percent (on an annual basis) during the first quarter of 1977. Again, prices continued to rise more rapidly in construction than in other activities. In addition, the growing disequilibrium between demand and supply for construction materials and services created a number of problems for related sectors.

Given the seriousness of the situation, the monetary authorities would seem to have had little choice but to attempt to curb the expansion in liquidity and thereby restore some sort of equilibrium to the economy. However, instead of simply attempting to control the overall increase in the money supply, the bank continued refining its ill-defined policy of attempting to divert loans and credits to productive investments in the agricultural and industrial sectors while, at the same time, preventing the concentration of bank credits in those activities that had limited possibility of expansion due to infrastructural bottlenecks. Given this objective, credit expansion targets during 1977 for the specialized banks were set as the amount of financing required for the private sector's fixed investment. The target for commercial banks to the private sector was set at 20 percent, down from the goal of 30 percent for the year before.

Along with these policies, the bank increased both its rediscount rate to the commercial banks and maximum interest rates payable and receivable by the banks. In general, the maximum lending rates of the commercial banks were increased by 1 percent, whereas their maximum lending rate for construction activities was increased by 3 percent. On the other hand, the maximum lending rate of the specialized banks for construction activities was increased by 1 percent but their maximum lending rates for other activities was not altered. Finally, the maximum interest rates that the commercial banks could offer on time and savings deposits was increased by 1 percent. In light of a 30 percent rate of inflation, this action hardly seems worth the effort. While these measures were being implemented, inflation continued unabated with the consumer price index up 25.1 percent by the end of the year.

Despite the enormous increase in liquidity that had been taking place since 1974, the Bank Markazi continued to argue that the main causes of inflation were the considerable increase in the costs of production, the reduction in the agricultural output, and the fall in the growth of industrial output.

Perhaps part of the bank's reluctance to significantly reduce the liquidity of the private sector in order to decelerate the growth in effective demand stemmed from the fact that, given the unprecedented increase in the price of housing, even the slight slowdown in liquidity that took place in 1977 resulted in a situation where the majority of Iranians were simply priced out of the housing market. The result was that a fall in the demand for houses occurred during most of 1977. In an effort to attain some sort of equilibrium in the construction and housing sectors, the government began to place some restrictions on issuing construction permits in early 1977. Limitations were also imposed on extension of loans for expensive and large housing units. The net result of all these measures was a slowdown of price increases in both construction materials and houses.

On the other hand, the cost of food, which was the second most important contributing factor to the rise in the consumer price index, continued its upward trend during 1977, finally reaching 27.4 percent by the end of 1977 (compared to 18 percent during the latter part of 1976). The average annual increase in consumer goods prices was 20.6 percent in 1977 with a decline in the production of some basic agricultural products aggravating the problem even further.

In sum, the reduction in the expansion of funds to the private sector in 1977 reflected a sharp switch away from the liberal credit policies of the previous two boom years, and a determined attempt by the monetary authorities both to limit credit to the private sector and to channel investments into productive sectors. This policy was continued through 1977 even though more funds from higher than anticipated oil revenues were available.

Finally, by 1977, most officials had accepted the fact that, though difficult to contain at the time, the massive increases in liquidity, particularly between 1974 and 1976, were the real cause of the country's inflationary problems.

In all fairness to the Bank Markazi, the scope for effective monetary policy was severely constrained all through the 1970s. The bank was caught between the government's highly over-expansive fiscal policy on one side and a fairly unsophisticated commercial banking system on the other.

The commercial banks themselves were dominated by the "Big Five"--Bank Melli, Bank Saderat, Bank Sepah, Bank Omrand, and Bank of Tehran. Together they accounted for 75 percent of total deposits and 70 percent of all loans. The remaining 20 commercial banks accounted for the rest. The big five banks all had numerous branches and, by 1977, accounted for almost 80 percent of the 7,367 branches in Iran.

One of the major complaints about the banking structure was that the managers of most branch banks were not well trained in lending operations. The net result was that the branch banks created a flow of funds from the provinces into the major cities (primarily Tehran) where demand was higher and management more adept. Provincial areas were thereby deprived of the use of their own funds. Tehran contained 25 percent of all bank branches but only 11 percent of the population.

With regard to commercial banking practices, a bazaar mentality that placed a premium on short-term gains was still prevalent even as late as 1977. This attitude was particularly evident in the property and construction sectors. Indeed, there was some concern by the Bank Markazi at the way a number of the banks exposed themselves in property. Apparently, it was common practice for branch managers to overvalue property to secure large credits for their friends.

In terms of markets, the more sophisticated bankers would have liked to see a more active promotion of an interbank market, but this was not as easy as it might seem. Because of its historical role as the government bank and effective position as central bank before the establishment of Bank Markazi, Bank Melli continued to dominate the financial markets, i.e., the bulk of government funds which were not handled directly by Bank Markazi were handled by Bank Melli. Thus, for practical purposes, the remaining commercial banks had to go to Bank Melli for funds. So the interbank market, such as it was, remained very lopsided. The result was that, despite penalties imposed by Bank Markazi, many of the commercial banks borrowed funds abroad, thus making the control of the money supply that more difficult.

Monetary Developments in 1978

By 1978, it was hard to call the bank's actions part of a rational stabilization policy. The whole financial system was coming apart at the seams, and the bank's actions appear as simply one of trying to prevent a total collapse of the economy.

However, despite the economic stagnation and the standstill in most productive activities, private sector liquidity still grew by 23 percent in 1978. The growth of liquidity for the first part of 1978 was actually somewhat similar to the pattern exhibited for the comparable period in 1977. However, beginning around August, the hoarding of money increased rapidly and at an unprecedented rate. Increased holdings of money were undoubtedly caused by political unrest and loss of confidence in the banking system. Most depositors withdrew their savings from the banking system and converted it to cash. Thus, in August 1978, a total of Rls 34 billion was cashed and, by the end of January 1979, the volume of notes and coins in circulation rose by Rls 413 billion.

The vast withdrawals of savings from banks and the very slow return of these funds to the system caused the banks to face an acute shortage of cash for financing their liabilities. In order to prevent complete bankruptcy and closures of the banking system, the Bank Markazi decided on September 22, 1978, to reduce the ratio of legal reserves and release part of the blocked reserves of the banking system. As a result, Rls 120 billion was made available to the banking system. These funds were not sufficient to handle the accelerating rate of withdrawals. Therefore, in November 1978, the Bank Markazi again reduced the legal deposits and the requirement of compulsory purchase of government bonds. The rediscount rate was also reduced by 1 percent. Additional facilities were arranged whereby banks could borrow from the Bank Markazi and use government bonds as collateral. Despite these drastic measures, the system remained paralyzed until the change of government in January 1979.

OVERALL ASSESSMENT

The economic crisis of 1978 had its monetary origins in the economic boom of the years immediately following the sharp increase in oil prices. The crisis began to manifest itself as economic stagnation of the economic sectors in 1977 and continued through 1978. After the unprecedented price increase of oil in 1974, the economic and social targets of the Fifth Development Plan were revised hastily and without proper coordination of the physical and financial structure of the country. Total planned investment was doubled without any appreciable change in the country's financial institutions or monetary policies.

The existing time lag in converting financial capital into productive capital and for coordinating supply with the demand, however, resulted in a number of projects never being completed despite the fact that the budget for these projects was spent. At the same time, a considerable amount of goods requisitioned from abroad did not arrive on time. Hence, aggregate supply fell far short of aggregate demand during the Fifth Development Plan period.

The execution of the plan had left sharp expansionary effects on the liquidity of the economy in a very short time span. Due to manpower and technological shortcomings, and import bottlenecks, aggregate supply could not meet the ever increasing demand. The resulting disequilibrium and build up of liquidity was too much for the banks to contend with. However, the response to these pressures by the Bank Markazi was not only too late but ill-conceived as well. Instead of attempting to control the money supply directly, it concentrated on credit and then only credit for certain uses. Given the tools at its disposal, the Bank Markazi could have done a much better job in stabilizing the economy.

AN ALTERNATIVE STRATEGY

The stated objectives of monetary policy in Iran were the standard ones for the developing countries: a steady non-inflationary expansion of the money supply and continued monetization of the economy. Iran fitted into the model of the "underintermediated" financial system sketched out by McKinnon(5) and Bruno(6). The public holds money but few other financial instruments. Credit was rationed by the Bank Markazi with low rates of interest on both advances and deposits. The money supply is greatly influenced by fiscal and balance of payments movements. Monetary restraint took the form of restrictions on the flow of credit to the private sector. This restriction may have led to sharp increases in the black market rate of interest, thus increasing the costs of manufacturing and thereby adding fuel to inflation rather than providing the intended damper.

It is useless to criticize the policies of the monetary authorities unless there is an alternative theory available which takes into account the special characteristics of the country's capital markets. For one thing, the Bank Markazi should have begun alleviating the fragmentation of the country's capital markets, and in its statements there is evidence that the bank recognized this would be necessary if it were to use monetary policy as an effective tool in stabilization policy.

In fact, the fragmentation of capital and financial markets in the country was ultimately one of the most important factors leading to the economy's retardation of growth and development. A major aim of monetary policy, therefore, should have been to promote the development of capital and financial markets rather than to focus on short-term credit allocations. This conclusion follows directly from the McKinnon assertion that money and capital are substitutes(7). Due to the limited availability of alternative financial assets in the economy, money was a major vehicle for the debt intermediation process arising from capital accumulation.

As a corollary to this argument, the Bank Markazi's monetary policy should have strived for high rates of interest on monetary assets in order to shift the portfolio of private savings from nonproductive physical goods to monetary assets. In this view, the bottleneck in the process of capital formation was the inadequate flow of monetary savings to financial investment projects, rather than the lack of profitable investment opportunities (which would call for a reduction in interest rates). Therefore, the major goal of the Bank Markazi should have been to promote the development of domestic capital markets so that savings of rural and urban households could have been attracted into the financial system. This result could have best been attained by providing alternative liquid assets with attractive real yields. In the McKinnon type framework, therefore, the overall role of the bank's short-term stabilization policy would have been rather limited, primarily because emphasis is on the longer-term development of the financial sector, a goal best achieved by providing a stable monetary situation conducive to the growth of capital markets.

Along these lines, it appears the authorities were too slow and too cautious in raising the interest rates (or allowing them to rise) so that the real return on financial assets became attractive in terms of the return on real investment. Such a policy would have been desirable, less as an inducement to save than as an incentive to channel what was saved more efficiently into financial assets and thus into the most productive uses.

The real yield on deposits can be raised by lowering the rate of inflation or by raising deposit rates. In Iran's case it might be argued that it might have been best to raise deposit rates first and, only then, gradually lowering the rate of inflation. This follows if we assume that: (1) the services of capital were utilized roughly in proportion to working capital (which in turn is closely linked to the real value of the money stock), and (2) there was unutilized capital (or what would normally be called an excess supply of capital).(8) It follows that, once inflation was under way and inflationary expectations had been built up, an initial and permanent increase in real balances would have occurred when the authorities raised deposit rates first and only subsequently reduced the rate of growth of the money supply. On the other hand, if they were to have reduced money growth and inflation first, real money balances would have declined. Given that output is assumed to be determined by the behavior of real money balances, the economy would have experienced a recession.(9)

As a practical matter, the short-run choice between raising deposit rates and lowering the rate of inflation would have had to concern itself with the impact on bank profits. A sharp increase in deposit rates could have been serious for those banks with longer-term assets due to the short-term nature of their liabilities. And these would have been the banks most likely to have been making productive loans, as opposed to trade financing, speculating on inventories, etc. An increase in deposit rates would raise the cost to banks on a major part of their funds almost immediately, while the resulting, spread preserving, increase in loan rates would increase the return of their assets only gradually as new loans at the higher rates replaced maturing older loans at lower rates. Given the government's financial resources, however, no doubt, a subsidy program of sorts could have been arranged for the seriously affected banks.

CONCLUSIONS

The traditional instruments of monetary policy available to the Bank Markazi tended to affect the supply of money through changing either the stock of reserve money or the money multiplier. Insofar as the components of reserve money are concerned, changes in foreign assets which are a reflection of the developments in the oil sector could not generally be considered as a policy instrument for changing the stock of reserve money. Nor could variations in credit from the bank to the government have been used by Bank Markazi as an active instrument to adjust reserve money, because this item was usually adjusted passively to the government's budgetary position. Thus, the authorities were largely confined to concentrating on changing the net claims on the private sector (principally the commercial banks) through which they could affect reserve money, and affecting changes in the multiplier itself, largely through altering the banks' reserves to deposit ratio.

In general, Bank Markazi's instruments of monetary policy can be classified depending on whether they operated to affect reserve money, or whether their major impact was through altering the public's and/or banks' preferences. Of course, certain instruments worked through both channels. As a practical matter, the main instruments of aggregate monetary policy were Bank Markazi bank credit to commercial banks, changes in reserve requirements, interest rate controls, limits on commercial bank credit, and moral suasion.

The credit to the commercial banks directly affected the stock of reserve money and, therefore, could be considered potentially the most potent in varying the supply of money and credit. Reserve requirement changes and interest rate regulations worked on the components of the money multiplier. On the other hand, ceilings on the supply of credit can be said to have ignored both reserve money and the money multipier by setting a limit directly on their product. Finally, moral suasion could have an effect on the stock of reserve money, or the multiplier, or both. In effect, moral suasion substituted for explicit regulatory action by Bank Markazi.

Monetary policy was closely linked to fiscal policy throughout this period, restricting the authorities' ability to carry out short-term stabilization policies. Given this environment, it would have been more appropriate for the monetary authorities to concentrate more on the medium-term goals of price stability and growth and to engage in short-term stabilization policy only when the shocks to the economy were severe and well defined.

The assumptions underlying this conclusion are: (1) that there was a complementary relationship between real money, money balances, and capital formation at this time in Iran; and (2) money is simply a vehicle through which real resources are made available for investment by savers. Under these circumstances, if the Iranian public could have been induced to hold more money through higher interest rates, in effect, it would have given up its command over capital labor which could then have been put to use somewhere else in the economy, thereby ensuring simultaneous growth of both savings and investment. Since money assets formed the largest proportion of savings in Iran, the higher the accumulation of liabilities by the financial intermediaries, the greater would have been the amount of investment. It is precisely these flows that, in the experience of other countries pursuing financial liberalization, increased in response to raising the rate of return on deposits. It is always debatable whether, given these tools the Bank Markazi, irrespective of the level of government expenditures, could have controlled the money supply at any rate of expansion it felt best for medium and long-term price stability. Evidence based on the bank's ability to sterilize foreign exchange flows would seem to indicate that the authorities had the power to control the money supply within a wide range.

Given that by 1977 most Iranian officials had accepted price and output stability as the appropriate stabilization goals of the country's monetary policy, what would have been the method best suited for the attainment of these objectives? Should the monetary authorities have used their intuition and judgment (discretion) in determining the behavior of the money supply most conducive to economic stability? On the other hand, did difficulties of international price movements, pressures for massive development spending, and limited knowledge of the economic forces at work in the country make such discretion ill-advised? The issue of rules versus authorities as the best approach to avoiding many of the monetary problems encountered by the Iranian economy during this period is examined in the following chapter.

11 Macroeconomic Adjustments

INTRODUCTION

In a long interview granted to Iran's daily newspaper Kayhan on October 27, 1976, the Shah said that, if the government continued to increase its involvement in the economic affairs of the state, "all Iranians will perish."(1) At that time, he announced that the policy of accelerating economic growth at all costs would end, and that belt tightening would begin. His interview was a clear admission of government policy failures and acknowledgment of the existence of grave problems. It was also designed to concentrate more on removing economic and social greviances. It is against this background that the government's frustrations with its post-1973 economic program in general and its antiinflation programs in particular can be best understood.

THE FIFTH FIVE YEAR PLAN

Briefly reviewing the situation, the Fifth Development Plan began in 1973 and ended in 1977. During this period, the economy grew at a rate much faster than that achieved during the Fourth Development Plan. In fact, the average annual growth of gross national product at constant prices (including the compensation for valuation of terms of trade) reached 17.2 percent. At the same time, vast amounts of foreign exchange were allocated to investment in various economic activities, especially in industry and construction. Many large projects were initiated at this time.

In fact, total investment projected for the duration of the plan was doubled soon after the oil price increases. Similar increases were allocated to social welfare and subsidy programs. Within the framework of the revised plan, government expenditure for 1974 was tripled over that of the previous year. From the total government budget for 1974 (Rls 1,254 billion), only 28 percent went into fixed capital formation, whereas 58 percent was spent on current expenditures. The remaining 14 percent went for other payments which, for all practical purposes, were very similar to current expenditures.

The outstanding increase in government expenditures resulted in an unprecedented expansionary effect on liquidity and effective demand. This situation encouraged producers to utilize their plants at full capacity, while importers responded rapidly with an increased volume of foreign goods in an attempt to balance supply and demand. As a result, the demand for the means of production and for primary and intermediate goods increased while available infrastructural facilities were used at maximum capacity. However, due to the shortage of skilled workers and to infrastructural bottlenecks, the supply of domestically produced goods could not increase at the same rate as the demand. Inflationary pressures, therefore, mounted along with the increase in the cost of imports and production.

The construction and housing sector was faced with the highest rate of inflation due to rapid increase in incomes and an increasing rate of migration from rural to urban areas. As a result, shortages of housing materials (which was already evident prior to the Fifth Development Plan) became more acute during this period. The result was a sharp escalation in the price of land, construction materials, and construction worker wages. The acceleration of inflation in the construction and housing sectors quickly spread to the rest of the economy.(2)

In sum, rapid acceleration of economic development after 1973 soon led to an unprecedented rate of inflation, preventing the completion of some of the development projects. A situation thus developed where various policies were needed to restore equilibrium to the economy.

CONSIDERATIONS IN STABILIZATION

In terms of designing an antiinflationary policy, it is useful to distinguish between one-shot events that led to a once and for all rise in the price level and those processes that are cumulative in the sense of possibly leading to continuing and perhaps accelerating rates inflation. The different types of inflations must be validated by monetary expansion, but the costs and possible success of particular antiinflationary monetary and fiscal policies will be different in each case. For example, since the inflation resulted primarily from excess demand, it could have been reduced more easily with the traditional tools of monetary and fiscal policy than if it had originated from shifts in supply.

The cost of reducing the demand component of inflation must be measured in terms of the resulting level of temporary unemployment and diminished rate of growth in real non-oil GDP.

Apparently the government felt the spectacular rise in prices after 1973 was a once-and-for-all phenomenon. If this were the case, one might easily argue that oil-financed government expenditures could not continue increasing at a rate sufficient to generate chronic inflationary pressures. Given the potential costs of stabilization policy, it is easy to understand the government's rationale against adopting an all-out, restrictive monetary-fiscal antiinflationary policy.

In this regard, it is obvious that, despite the number of unique aspects characterizing the Iranian economy during this period, a number of automatic stabilizing mechanisms existed to restore equilibrium just as in the more developed economies. The government's first inclination after inflationary pressures built up was to do nothing, thus relying on a self-regulating process of price deceleration.

Again in retrospect, the government's interpretation of the manner in which the economy functioned was incorrect. While it is true that the oil price increase could be looked upon as a once-and-for-all event, it does not follow that the economy was incapable over time of generating sufficient demand pressure to prevent the process of automatic stabilization from occurring.

Because inflationary forces did not self-terminate, it is of some interest to examine the mechanisms that countries usually rely upon to eliminate disequilibrium. Of particular interest here is the identification of the manner in which the automatic process of stabilization was circumvented during this period.

MACROECONOMIC ADJUSTMENT MECHANISMS: I-S EQUILIBRIUM

Ex post, the gross national product identity requires:

$$(1) \quad Y = C + I + X - M$$

where C = public and private consumption; I = gross domestic capital formation; X = exports (including factor income from abroad); and M = imports (including factors payments to foreigners). An equivalent statement of (1) is the I-S or investment-savings identity:

(2) $I = S + F$

where S = gross domestic savings defined by $S = Y - C$, and F = foreign capital flows as defined by $F = M - X = I - S$.

As an initial proposition, it is assumed that (1) and (2) hold not only as (actualized ex post) identities but also as equilibrium conditions.(3) The latter implies that the economy's commodity markets were cleared at equilibrium prices. But what would happen if the desired (ex ante) investment exceeded desired (ex ante) savings at prices that had prevailed in the preceding period? If international capital movements were elastic, the internal adjustment problem would be mitigated since any difference in S over I would simply be equal to F. However, because of uncertainty over political conditions in Iran and various restrictions (OPEC) on Iranian investments outside the country, it is possible that large components of these capital movements were exogenously determined and the economy could not rely completely on F as an equilibrating variable.

If output were flexible, so that it responded significantly to increases in demand, then I and S would have adjusted in the short run to establish the equilibrium level of income (Y). If this Keynesian channel of adjustment had been effective, the savings and investment functions would have responded to the change of GNP with movements that were not only of the right direction but also of the correct magnitude.

After 1973, when output was constrained with infrastructural limitations and not sufficiently responsive, price changes most likely had to assume the role of macroeconomic adjustment. In other words, the aggregate price level rose under the pressure of excess demand for goods which was represented by an excess of ex ante investment (in the sense that desired I was higher than that compatible with the economy's absorptive capacity) over ex ante savings plus capital flows (evaluated at the previously prevailing price level). Price inflation could have eliminated the aggregate demand-supply gap in this situation if the investment function and/or savings function had been able to shift in the appropriate direction in response to inflation.

There is no reason to question, after 1973, that mechanisms of this sort began to become more important than capital flows as the means through which commodity markets were cleared and convergence to macroeconomic equilibrium induced.

The price mechanism was strengthened by the fact that the Bank Markazi maintained relatively constant interest rates during most of this period, thus (inadvertently) precluding adjustment through movements in this variable. Due to political motives surrounding the control of interest rates in Iran, it was impossible for the variable to move sufficiently to clear the country's financial markets. Rather, the monetary authorities tended to create new credit more or less independently of domestic savings, often in response to governmental pressures.

Changes in the volume of real credit were, in turn, likely to have influenced the change in capital stock. In particular, investment in construction was dependent on credit for its financing all during this period.

Using two-stage estimation techniques in the context of the large-scale macroeconomic simulation model developed in the next chapter, real credit (PCP) was found to be significant in determining various facets of private investment. For private investment in construction (PICP):

$$\underset{}{PICP} = \underset{(9.19)}{0.16\Delta GENANP} + \underset{(7.14)}{0.52\Delta PCP} + \underset{(11.61)}{18.27}$$

$$r^2 = 0.965;\ F = 11.49$$

$$PICP = \underset{(2.84)}{0.06\Delta GENANP} + \underset{(8.55)}{0.14PCP} + \underset{(7.28)}{13.13}$$

$$r^2 = 0.975;\ F = 154.69$$

where GENANP = real government expenditures. For investment in machinery (MITP):

$$MITP = \underset{(3.71)}{0.12GENANP} + \underset{(2.81)}{0.17PCP} + \underset{(2.79)}{0.56CITP} + \underset{(6.69)}{12.07}$$

$$r^2 = 0.998;\ F = 1498.71$$

$$MITP = \underset{(9.37)}{0.49PCP} + \underset{(3.39)}{0.13EXRL} + \underset{(1.52)}{5.01}$$

$$r^2 = 0.991;\ F = 467.99$$

$$MITP = \underset{(7.06)}{0.19GENANP} + \underset{(3.51)}{0.23PCP} + \underset{(1.22)}{0.10\Delta NOXNP} + \underset{(5.07)}{11.98}$$

$$r^2 = 0.992;\ F = 379.46$$

where EXRL = real lagged exports; CITP = total construction investment (constant price).

Clearly, private credit and changes in private credit influence both machinery and construction investment decisions and hence the capital stock. Ultimately, therefore, private credit would affect the level and growth of real non-oil GDP.

More formally, in considering the influence of credit, price changes, and income changes on movements in savings and investment (and thus possible paths to macroeconomic equilibrium), the functions are specified as:

(3) $S = a_1\Delta Y + a_2INF + a_3SNL = a_0$

(4) $I = b_1\Delta Y + b_2INF + b_3\ PC + b_0$

where ΔY is the change in real income over the preceding period, INF is the rate of inflation, and ΔPC is the change in real volume of private credit over the preceding period. Both real non-oil GDP (NOXNP) and GDP (GDPNP) were used as income variables while the rate of change in both the consumer INFC and the wholesale price index (INFW) were tested as inflation terms.

The I-S equilibrium can now be obtained by substituting equations (3) and (4) into (1) and solving for the endogenous variables.

In terms of the signs of the coefficients, a_1 and a_3 [in equations (3) and (4) above] should be positive since saving in Iran was responsive to income changes. The lagged savings term SNL depicts the time lag in adjusting savings to the new level of income. The sign for a_2 could be either positive or negative (since public and private savings might respond differently to movements in inflation). Saving is likely to be positive, however, since an increase in inflation is likely to result in private forced savings, while the government savings (determined almost entirely by oil revenues) are not expected to be affected by price changes.

In terms of the investment equations, b_1 is likely to be positive, reflecting an acceleration effect. The term b_2 should also be positive, reflecting speculative investments, particularly those in urban housing and construction. Of course, increases in real private credit should stimulate investment (thus b_3 should be positive).

While the Bank Markazi could always determine the nominal supply of credit (PC) due to the usual situation of credit rationing at low interest rates, changes in real credit depend on the rate of inflation, or:

(5) $\Delta PCP = \Delta PC/PC - PCL(INF)$

The I-S equilibrium equation can be obtained by substituting (5) into (2) and solving for the endogenous variables:

(6) $(b_1-a_1)\Delta Y + (b_0-b_3)(PCL) - a_2(INF) = a_0 - b_o - b_3\Delta PC/PL + a_3(SL) + F$

If prices are constant, INF = 0, and (6) determines the change in real output.

In terms of adjustment to equilibrium and with fixed prices, it can be shown that stability requires $b_1 < a_1$ i.e., investment is less responsive to changes in income than is savings.

On the other hand, if we assume that the change in output is autonomously determined (e.g., by supply capacity), adjustment would be determined by price level changes and stability would require that $b_2 - b_3(CRL) < a_2$. That is, investment must be less responsive than savings to changes in price.

As noted above, changes in either aggregate output level or aggregate price (or both) would facilitate the adjustment process. During the post-1973 period, however, most of the burden for adjustment must have been placed on prices.

The equations were estimated for both measures of inflation (INFC and INFW) and changes in the consumer wholesale price indices (ΔCPI, ΔWPI). As might be expected, changes in non-oil real GDP produced much better results (in terms of statistical significance) than did changes in total GDP. The rate of change in the consumer price index was also more significant than in the wholesale price index. Alternative measures of investment (TINP), total investment in machinery (MITP), and total investment in construction yielded very similar results. In general, incorporating changes in price (ΔCPI and ΔWPI) gave better results than inflation in the investment equations.

Of interest is the fact that the parameters for the ΔY and the INF (the variables which the savings and investment functions have in common) are generally fairly similar. The close response of savings and investment to the same stimuli (ΔY) suggests that decisions to save and invest in Iran were undertaken interdependently by the same individuals, the banking system played a limited role in the country's financial intermediation process, and the public sector dominated the country's capital formation process.

In terms of the fixed price stability conditions, b_1 was less than a_1 so that the conditions for convergence to a stable equilibrium seem to be present.

On the other hand, the flexible price case is quite likely to yield unstable results since the critical values (using total investment) of $b_2 = 20.92$, $b_3 = 0.20$, and $a_2 = 16.38$ imply that $(b_2 - b_3)PCL\ a_2$, i.e., total investment is more responsive to price change than is savings. This situation was undoubtedly created by the heavy speculation in urban construction in the 1970s, whereas oil revenues, the chief factor responsible for savings (equations 8-10, table 11.1), were largely determined by exogenous factors.

This finding provides some insight into the problems faced by the government. Once price increases got out of hand, the inflationary process fed upon itself due to the fact that the demand-supply gap actually increased, as opposed to the nominal case where inflation tends to decelerate due to the expansion of savings.

Simply put, the results imply that, after 1973 when macroeconomic instability was created, pressures conducive to disequilibrium dominated those tending to restore price stability. Since Iran was generally considered to have a stable economy, the finding of a tendency toward destabilization comes as something of a surprise. Because instability was only present during periods of inflation, its occurrence after 1973 must have taken the government by complete surprise. For example, regressions over the period 1959-73 yielded:

$$\begin{array}{llll} \text{FTINP} = & 1.1\text{S}\Delta\text{NOXNP} & + 4.02\text{INFC} & + 0.64\Delta\text{PCP} \\ & (2.53) & (1.00) & (0.99) \end{array}$$

and

$$\begin{array}{llll} \text{SNP} = & -0.29\Delta\text{NOXNP} & + 6.86\text{INFC} & + 1.84\text{SNPL} \\ & (-0.21) & (0.84) & (1.88) \end{array}$$

These results show that, during the period of price stability prior to 1973, the response of savings to price had definitely been greater than that shown by investment, thus implying that any future would-be inflations should be quickly self-terminating.

These results provide vivid illustrations of the inherent dangers in any macroeconomic forecast utilizing econometric methods, a practice that, unfortunately for the government, was gaining wide acceptability in Iranian planning circles around 1973.

POLICY IMPLICATIONS

In terms of the nature of the savings-investment equilibrating process at the time, the government should have restrained its expenditures after 1973, thus avoiding disequilibrium in the first place. In retrospect, perhaps because the instability in these key macroeconomic relationships was not suspected, the government's half-hearted attempts at stabilization in 1974 and 1975 can be understood.

It is always hard to determine the real motivation for policies in Iran, however, especially those concerning government expenditures. Elsewhere it has been speculated that high officials in the regime made fortunes for both themselves and their cronies through controlling various development projects in Tehran and other major cities. If true, this might explain to some extent the initial lack of enthusiasm on the part of most officials at suggestions regarding the need to restrain public sector spending and easy credit to the private sector.

Table 11.1. Macroeconomic Adjustment Equations

Equation	Dependent Variable	Independent Variables DNOXNP	DGDPNP	INFC	INFW	DMSDCP	SNPL	Intercept	r^2	F
(1)	TINP	1.47		20.92		0.20		-11.57		
		(2.24)		(4.83)		(0.84)		(26.74)	0.925	53.67
(2)	MITP	0.86		13.32		0.09		-4.84		
		(2.15)		(4.32)		(0.63)		(-0.28)	0.9200	49.86
(3)	CITP	0.61		7.67		0.11		-7.21		
		(2.44)		(3.99)		(1.13)		(-0.68)	0.922	51.09
(4)	MITP		0.06	18.95		0.34		8.82		
			(0.22)	(10.12)		(2.41)		(0.37)	0.892	35.78
(5)	CITP		0.02	11.67		0.29		3.92		
			(0.10)	(9.64)		(3.16)		(0.26)	0.886	33.66
(6)	TINP		0.09	30.54		0.63		12.81		
			(0.20)	(10.16)		(2.75)		(0.33)	0.894	36.52
(7)	SNP		1.26		18.93		0.82	-103.42		
			(3.73)		(3.04)		(8.47)	(-2.48)	0.963	87.56
(8)	SNP		1.57	13.67			0.75	-99.03		
			(3.66)	(1.69)			(3.96)	(-1.88)	0.945	57.32
(9)	SNP	2.77		16.38			0.27	-83.21		
		(4.76)		(2.35)			(1.31)	(-2.07)	0.961	81.46
(10)	SNP	(2.17)			19.14		0.49	-86.72		
		(4.85)			(3.65)		(4.85)	(-2.72)	0.974	124.17

(continued)

Table 11.1. Macroeconomic Adjustment Equations (continued)

Equation	Dependent Variable	Independent Variables DNOXNP	DCP1	DWP1	DMSDCP	DGDPNP	Intercept	r^2	F
(11)	PIMP	0.30 (1.80)	2.37 (4.00)		0.14 (2.01)		1.09 (0.14)	0.901	39.56
(12)	CCIP		2.94 (16.41)		0.10 (3.43)	0.07 (1.10)	12.40 (2.55)	0.955	92.71
(13)	PCIP	0.09 (1.01)	2.52 (9.31)		0.05 (2.64)		14.02 (3.55)	0.968	131.45
(14)	TINP	1.24 (3.11)	10.77 (7.61)		0.34 (2.09)		13.45 (0.73)	0.967	125.24
(15)	TINP	1.96 (2.11)		11.09 (2.23)	0.01 (0.04)		-4.71 (-0.13)	0.868	28.50
(16)	TINP		14.36 (14.91)		0.61 (3.80)	0.39 (1.20)	25.94 (0.99)	0.948	78.24
(17)	MITP	0.69 (2.91)	6.98 (8.37)		0.19 (2.04)		11.49 (1.06)	0.969	137.87
(18)	MITP		8.96 (16.40)		0.33 (3.66)	0.25 (1.13)	16.51 (1.11)	0.956	93.66
(19)	CITP	0.56 (2.92)	3.81 (5.63)		0.15 (1.90)		1.51 (0.17)	0.949	81.28
(20)	PITP	0.47 (2.21)	4.82 (6.37)		0.21 (2.38)		12.50 (1.28)	0.949	82.22

Note: See text for identification of variables.

Unfortunately, restraints on public expenditures: (1) conflicted directly with the regime's long run plans for rapidly converting the country into a modern industrial nation; and (2) were contrary to the generally accepted (in Iran) thesis that, unless the country achieved sufficient growth momentum by the mid-1980s, the likely decline in oil production and revenues at that time would condemn the country to a permanent state of semidevelopment.

Perhaps for these reasons, the government did not seriously consider enough the option of investing abroad high incremental amounts of its post-1973 oil revenues. F. Vakil, an official in the government, at the time lamented this deficiency in the country's financial management in several semiofficial publications.(4) His warnings were largely unheeded.

In this regard, it is obviously necessary to distinguish inflationary forces that may appear to be one-shot affairs and those that threaten continued or accelerating contributions to the rate of price increases. Clearly, benefits of fighting each are quite different. In this sense, the spectacular rise in oil prices during 1973-74 was probably seen by the government as a one-shot affair with little benefit in fighting the battle.

In any case, the government was determined to maintain an increased level of investment (which was greater than the willing release of factors through voluntary savings). When inflation began threatening this objective, the government's first inclination was to impose arbitrary controls on prices. When the government took this action, the post-1973 inflation changed from that of an open one to one of repression.

POTENTIAL ADVANTAGES OF REPRESSED INFLATION

While the discussion that follows will largely deal with the disruptive effects stemming from the period of repressed inflation in the mid-1970s, it is clear that some good effects (given the government's determination to proceed with their expenditure programs) were expected to come from the strategy. While it is difficult to say for sure how many of these considerations underlay the government's price control program, several must have played an important part in the authorities decision to move ahead with the controls.

1. Repressed inflation could aid in preventing the shift in real income from the lower income groups to the higher income groups, thus avoiding the redistribution of wealth in favor of the higher income groups that usually takes place during a period of open inflation.

2. The real standard of living of the lower income groups not only might be protected under the repressed inflation but could conceivably be increased, i.e., the government's new social services and subsidized food programs during periods of controlled prices might shift wealth from upper to lower income groups.

3. Repressed inflation might enable the government to force through a much greater investment program than would be possible otherwise, particularly one that could be attempted in an open inflation.

4. Repressed inflation might encourage investment and capital formation in low cost mass producing industries, and thus increase productivity through the introduction of modern equipment. If, in fact, mass markets could be created by repressed inflation, firms might be induced to shift from quality to quantity production.

5. Labor scarcity created by the repressed inflation might promote the use of substitute factors and, therefore, induce producers to seek modern methods for increasing production.

In large part, the government attempted to repress the inflation as a means of increasing real savings. Price ceilings were set and permits of various sorts were allocated by government agencies, investment expenditures were guided and aimed at increasing output in other development areas, and imports were increased to relieve the inflationary pressure.

The presence of these controls must be looked upon as not only a means of controlling inflation but, simultaneously, one designed to increase the amount of real monetary claims available for the government's development efforts. Clearly, it was critical for the government to stabilize the real value of money if laborers and entrepreneurs were to be induced to continue exchanging their services for savings.

It must be realized that the inflation experienced after 1973 was the result of conscious policy on the part of the government to increase the country's development potential. Increased capital formation was best achieved in these circumstances through transferring factors to development projects in exchange for expanding factor incomes. Direct controls were the most powerful weapons the government could employ to carry this out, since they had the potential of curtailing consumption while maintaining the value of money.

If the Iranian economy were typified by state control of all prices and factor allocations, if foreign commerce were prohibited, and if the government protected society from the uncomfortable redistributive effects of technological change and shifting preferences by freezing the existing productive relations, there would not have been a problem. There could have been a rising real wage with a controlled expansion of investment and no unemployment. Productivity gains, if any, could have been absorbed by lowering prices. The reality of the goals of the Iranian government, however, were quite different, embracing a more complex set of objectives. Inflation control was correspondingly a more complicated affair. Within the institutional set-up of the country, therefore, simple solutions to the control of inflation were almost certain to be either wrong, too costly, or both.

PRICE CONTROLS

One of the fundamental economic truths that has emerged from the last thirty or so years of national economic experience is that there is not a costless way of controlling inflation in a market economy. Although prices and incomes policies may conceivably have some effect in reducing inflationary expectations, and manpower policies may be used to improve the efficiency of labor markets, neither is an alternative to deflationary monetary and fiscal policy. From the available evidence, it seems that inflation cannot be controlled within the framework of a system of free markets without both a temporary rise in unemployment and a temporary check to the rate of growth of the economy. Instead of accepting this as an inevitable consequence of a market economy and attempting to devise policies which both reduce the cost and ensure that the burden is borne more equitably, the government decided to gradually impose price controls after 1973.

Price controls had a long history in Iran, but their effect upon the private sector was not strongly felt until 1975. Prior to 1973, the Ministry of Economy's Department of Price Review simply monitored the prices of goods and services purchased by government departments. Alarmed over rising prices, the government established the Price Commission (PC) in October 1973 as an independent body of the Ministry of Commerce. The commission's job was to review and advise how prices should be fixed, with the stipulation that, unless justified cause was shown, prices were to be rolled back to their June 1973 level. Because of the limited staff accorded to the PC, the policy had little impact.(5)

In 1974, though, the prices of 2,236 items were fixed by the commission while actual price reductions were specified for 966 additional items. Presumably, raw materials used to produce these products and the reduced import taxes made these reductions possible. The prices of the rest of the items were either stabilized or adjusted in an effort to prevent further increases in the prices of manufactured goods.

In addition to price fixing, four other major elements in the government's program toward inflation during 1974 and

1975 can be identified:(6) (1) the introduction or substantial expansion of direct subsidy payments on a wide range of goods and services; (2) the introduction or expansion of indirect subsidies through the pricing policies of public enterprises (including those responsible for electricity, water, and refined petroleum products for domestic use); (3) the reduction or elimination of several categories of domestic taxation (particularly import duties); and (4) the abolution of user charges for a number of government supplied services in health, education, and other areas.

More specifically, one of the first steps taken by the government along these lines was to subsidize the prices of basic commodities such as wheat, meat, sugar, and some types of raw materials and intermediate goods. The subsidies were explicitly intended to keep the prices of these goods low at the consumer level. In 1974 alone, approximately 45 billion rials were spent by the government for this purpose.

Other early programs were the granting of funds to the Tehran United Bus Company and the Iranian Railways Corporation. By stabilizing prices and keeping water and electricity rates from rising, the government was able to prevent price increases in these areas from either eroding consumer incomes or being incorporated into the economy's cost structure.

A Rents Adjustment and Stabilization Law was enacted with the hope of controlling rent increases. Moreover, in order to reduce imported inflationary pressures, import costs were lowered to an unprecedented extent by reducing the commercial profit tax and the import registration fees and deposits. That this particular policy was immediately effective is evidenced by the fact that the ratio of import taxes to the total value of imports fell from an average of 24 percent from 1970 to 1973 to approximately 30 percent in 1974. The import subsidies and price support programs, while in principle relatively sophisticated, were more often than not based on poor data which, in turn, led to poor food import planning and increasing shortages.

All in all, the initial attempts at price control were of very limited success; the rapid rise in money incomes during 1973 and 1974 quickly increased effective demand and the inflationary pressures that had been building up for several years. Effective demand accelerated due to the government's massive investment program together with the sharp rise in credits to the private sector all during 1974. These expansionary factors caused the private sector liquidity to grow particularly rapidly during the second half of 1974 - increasing from 35 percent in August 1974 and 57 percent in March 1975 and finally reaching 59 percent in June 1975 (compared with comparable rates for the previous year).

At the same time, the supply of domestically produced goods rose by 18.6 percent in 1975 (as compared with 17.9

percent in the previous year), while imports expanded by 61.6 percent (compared with 22.9 percent in 1974). Aggregate supply thus increased by 27.8 percent versus an 18.9 percent increase the previous year. The relatively rapid increase in imports compared with domestically produced goods resulted in the share of imported goods in aggregate supply increasing from 21 to 27 percent.

In early 1975 the government continued to introduce new measures stabilizing prices. This involved: fixing official prices for more than 600 categories of commodities, freezing of wholesale prices of manufactures, requiring government approval for all price increases, and limiting profit margins. Many of these programs were consolidated when, on August 6, 1975, the government assumed explicit responsibility for reviewing production costs and supervising "fair pricing" by making this activity the fourteenth principle of the White Revolution. The fourteenth principle called for a nationwide crusade against inflation on a constructive and sustained basis.

The Price Intelligence Center (PIC), previously established to monitor import prices and those of certain major domestic products, was given greatly expanded powers and responsibilities. Through the PIC, an extensive price control program dealing with excessive pricing and illegal profiteering was initiated. A cabinet level committee was set up in mid-1975 to formulate measures to deal with the problems of high prices and high rents. The committee coordinated with the PIC to produce a long list of items whose prices were to be rolled back to their January 1974 level. In a related February 1976 action, the Ministry of Commerce opened a Commodity Price Center where daily prices of 160 internationally traded basic products and raw materials were quoted.(7)

Under the program, a Rastakhiz party committee (composed mostly of students), the National Commission for Consumer Protection, and the Guild Chambers (which had the power to fine, close down, or send to court offending shopkeepers) established themselves as the watchdogs for the PC whose job was to investigate cases of infractions that these bodies forwarded to it. Guilty parties could be tried by a military tribunal set up for the occasion; this resulted in the imprisonment or deportation of many. Since November 1975, the PC has investigated reasons for the shortages of foods or price increases when reported by government authorities and has recommended prices at the request of industrial concerns that sought price increases due to rising costs.

Under the new provisions, the prices of locally produced goods were to be determined on the basis of their production costs together with a "fair" profit margin (equal to a maximum return of 20 percent on capital and reserves). Profits on imported goods were determined on the basis of their c.i.f.

cost, customs duties, and related charges, with prices set so as to generate an average profit of around 15 percent. The agencies acted swiftly for, by the end of 1975, the prices of some 16,000 items were being administered.

To buttress its price control measures and alleviate shortages of essential goods, the government took steps: to discourage withholding of goods from the market, by establishing new marketing and distribution channels and directing the importation and subsidization of basic food items and other essential products.

While these measures may have seemed at the time a reasonable approach to the inflationary problem, they ran into a number of significant obstacles. First, the controls created a number of disincentives for the private sector but this proved a costly failure. The supply of vital commodities such as eggs, chickens, meat, bread, onions, and sugar was severely curtailed or, at times, blocked completely. A black market was quick to develop where many food items and other essential goods were traded at prices that, as in the case of cement, were at least ten times the official rate.

Secondly, in order to maintain its price control policy, the government was compelled to intervene increasingly in the economy, even in such areas as retail trade. Interference with the actions of private firms took such forms as anticartel measures. The government found itself involved in price fixing of consumer goods, including even such unlikely articles as wedding dresses. Special courts had to be established just to prosecute price control offenders. Early in January 1977, the Minister of Commerce admitted that these courts were no longer capable of handling the number of alleged violators brought before it. At that time, the average load of 1,500 cases of overcharging held daily, only 300 could be dealt with. Clearly, these and other administrative problems made the whole price control system ineffectual.

The application of the law seemed to be geared in these instances toward several objectives. First, it served to underscore what could be the possible consequences should businessmen not make a show of following the guidelines of the government reform movement. Second, it was a political move attempting to show to the average consumer that the government policy was seriously directed toward safeguarding real income. In actuality, however, it was impossible to elicit voluntary compliance or strict enforcement because no guidelines were ever established delineating the range over which profits were considered "fair."

It was generally believed that profit margins were to be set at 10 to 15 percent above cost. However, this figure had no foundation in the law and was only the product of misinformed press reports. In general, the antiprofiteering law had been used to attack persons selling everyday consumer items, such as food, meals in restaurants, and flowers. Prices on items that were not significant components of daily consumption were not effectively controlled. The auto industry, in fact, was granted an explicit exemption from the price laws. Nevertheless, the very inflated black market prices of automobiles were well known. Persons buying cars through regular channels, indeed, had to wait months for their purchase because the black market buyers had first priority.(8)

PROBLEMS OF REPRESSED INFLATION

In addition to the operational problems involved in its implementation, repressed inflation has a number of other limitations. For convenience, these problems are divided into the following subheadings: (1) the lack of comprehension; (2) inability to equate supply and demand; (3) the fall in investment; and (4) agricultural stagnation.

Lack of Comprehension

A major limitation with the July 1975 price controls was that housing rentals were not included despite the fact that these accounted for between 30 and 60 percent of most urban workers' salaries and wages. The rent increases reflected the pressure on housing and continued land speculation. Without dealing with the rental situation, it proved nearly impossible to control wages. Wages rose 35 to 45 percent in 1975 and were rising at about the same rate in 1976. These increases were in direct defiance of a government-imposed limit of 1 percent and Rls 20 per day (28 cents). Clearly, employers did not believe it was realistic to attempt to enforce a wage freeze. By 1976, industrial wages were so high that some industrialists were speculating that it was too late for Iranian labor to ever be competitive with their foreign counterparts.

Because housing rents were not controlled, funds flowed into the construction sector. All through 1976, as had been the case in 1975, the construction sector enjoyed an extraordinary expansion, with value added rising by 43 percent. This rate was much higher than that for the other sectors and was apparently somewhat unanticipated. The tremendous increase in income levels coupled with the rapid growth in urban population had expanded the demand for housing at an unprecedented level.

As noted earlier, the housing boom was instrumental in diverting a major part of private savings and bank credits toward the construction-real estate sectors. As a result, land prices as well as prices of building materials and labor went up and very rapidly with the wage levels for construction workers, for example, rising by 47 percent in 1975 and 39 percent in 1976.

During this same period, land prices in urban areas rose on the average of 78 percent. The rapid increase in construction workers' wages had the twin effect of raising the cost of construction by 34 percent and attracting a number of workers from manufacturing and agriculture into construction activities. Consequently, a shortage of labor in both the industrial and agricultural sectors was clearly felt.

Inability to Equate Supply and Demand

Under the direct controls, effective demand and money incomes continued to outpace the economy's productive capacity. For example, although the growth in aggregate demand fell from 39 percent in 1975 to 27 percent in 1976, the decline in the growth of total supply was much higher - from 26 to 13 percent. This was due exclusively to the fall in the growth of imports from 53 to 3 percent. Supply from domestic production actually rose by 16 percent, but failed to compensate for the fall in the growth of imported goods.

The fall in imports in 1976 is something of a puzzle. Despite the continuation in that year of the government's policies to facilitate imports, foreign exchange payments for imports rose at a considerably lower rate than the rate for the preceding year. More specifically, demand for imports in the first half of the year showed a marked decline compared to the demand for imports in the first half of 1975. Bank Markazi's explanation of this pattern was that the rapid increase in growth for imports during 1974 and 1975 (which caused bottlenecks in the ports and transport system) had "increased the stock of goods in the country beyond the absorptive capacity of the domestic market." If this were in fact the case, why did prices keep on increasing? It would seem that lack of confidence on the part of the private sector on the motives and ability of the government is the only logical explanation.

In any case, the growth rate for import registration by the private sector declined from 35 percent in 1975 to 13 percent in 1976. Also, the growth in foreign exchange payments in which had grown by 55 percent in 1975 actually declined by 3 percent in 1976. Consequently, the overall growth of current foreign exchange payments fell from 54 to 6 percent.

Fall in Private Investment

Investment by the private sector began to slacken in 1975 and, in general, was quite disappointing considering the growth of the economy and the availability of foreign exchange. While the government continued to produce a number of different indicators (such as the number of new factory licenses granted, or the demand for loans by the specialized banks) in an attempt to prove that the private sector was dynamic and enthusiastically participating in the development, a closer examination of the national income accounts shows a much different picture. In fact, private investment was very one-sided, stimulated largely by a heavy concentration in housing construction and the continued flow of government money into key industrial sectors such as oil, petrochemicals, and steel.

By 1976, industrialists were opting for simply completing their existing projects but refraining from major new investment. Presumably, this was due to the uncertainties over the government's policies regarding price controls, wage decrees, share participation, etc. Many began preferring to put their money abroad or into what has proved the most profitable ventures - property and construction. Private sector investment in urban construction projects rose 62 percent in the first nine months of 1976-77 (amounting to $2.6 billion).

Many of the uncertainties plaguing the business community originated in July 1975 when the government unveiled its plan to require many firms to distribute 49 percent of their share holdings to their employees and the public. At that time, 320 companies were selected to begin the scheme. The government's aim was to promote wider ownership, attempt to give employees a greater feeling of identity with their companies, and encourage the companies themselves to modernize their management techniques. The industrialists, on the other hand, distrusted what was seen as totally arbitrary and unnecessary government influence in areas that historically had been their exclusive prerogatives. They were also afraid the plan would dilute their control or let outsiders look into their affairs. Most importantly, they were afraid that the price put on their shares would not reflect their value. Foreign companies concerned (there were under 20) seemed to feel that their rate of return would be affected along with their ability to maintain control of management.

While most of these fears did prove groundless (by mid-1977 only 151 companies had distributed 20 percent of the total 49 percent with companies being permitted to complete the operation in three phases), it was the seemingly arbitrary nature of government power that concerned businessmen the most. The result was that the share participation scheme initiated a decline in investment confidence. This trend was accelerated with the imposition of price controls at a time when wages were rising on the average over 35 percent a year, land costs by over 60 percent a year, and import costs by over 20 percent a year. Profit margins began to be eroded to the point where losses were experienced by many companies. Worse affected in this regard seem to have been the foreign companies who, in general, had not built a large margin of error into their costs.

The issue of price control was undoubtedly the biggest single negative factor affecting business confidence, again because of its capricious nature, erratic enforcement, and uncertainty as to its duration. The net effect was that real private investment in machinery declined from 63.4 percent in 1975 to -1.7 percent in 1976 and -17.9 percent in 1977. This was occurring while the sector's investment in construction was maintaining its expansion at 35.7, 32.6, and 14.9 percent per annum for 1975, 1976, and 1977, respectively (table 8.8, chap. 8).

The sharp fall in private investment in machinery was particularly surprising to the authorities, especially in light of the fact that expanded public investment and the increased provision of overhead services were seen by them as providing the private sector with further inducements for capital formation. In fact, real government investment in machinery was increasing at rates of 38.7, 11.8, 33.8, and 16.5 percent per annum during 1974-1975, while that of public investment in machinery was growing at 25.2, 40.1, 24.8, and 9.0 percent during the same years (table 8.8, chap. 8).

The logical explanation for the private sector's investment behavior simply lies in the fact that, in contrast to the neoclassical world of perfect and costless information, actual savings and investment decisions in Iran were subject to changing whims and subjective expectations. In that environment, the expectations of any individual investor were influenced greatly by what other investors were doing. Since the activities of foreign enterprises and government were fairly conspicuous in this regard, the actions of these groups played a crucial role of providing signals of confidence in the economy (or lack thereof) to other potential investors.

The neoclassical assumptions of full information and vigorously competitive markets are especially critical to the process of efficient capital formation: it places pressures on individual firms to undertake investments in their continuous struggle to keep ahead of the competition as a key element in the growth process. The strength of these assumptions was undoubtedly much weaker in Iran than in many countries during this period. The monopolistic environment created by high levels of production meant that investments in new technology were rarely regarded by firms as necessary for survival.

Once again, there were strong features of disequilibrium working. When the country was successful in attracting foreign investment (as in the early 1970s), it also found it easy to attract additional investors at relatively low cost. The investment climate operated like a self-fulfilling prophecy. As long as the climate was generally thought to be favorable, foreign enterprises were confident about future prospects and were willing to bring substantial investments into the economy. On the other hand, as local conditions began to become less favorable and the investment climate considered unfavorable due to uncertainty over possible changes in government policies, many enterprises began repatriating as much capital as they could and even phasing out their operations in the country.

With regard to private savings, the fact that capital markets were much more imperfect in Iran than in the developed countries meant internal sources of finance were very important in ultimately facilitating investment. It was, of course, precisely in such circumstances that the motivations for savings became intertwined with those for investment.

Empirical research in various countries has tended to support the view that savings respond to longer-term considerations such as outlined in the permanent income or life cycle theories of the consumption function. These motives have been verified for Iran in several extensive studies on the economy's consumption patterns.(9) Apparently, the firms and households found it expensive to make major adjustments in their consumption patterns in the face of year to year changes in their incomes. Their expenditures, therefore, tended to be rather inflexible in the shortrun and more loosely related to expected levels of income. Each such sector tends to save a substantial portion of its income only during periods of income expansion (and growing sufficiently rapidly to outstrip expectations).

In other words, the only sure way to generate a sizable domestic savings rate in Iran was to induce rapid growth. Clearly, this point confirms the theme emphasizing the role of momentum in economic development. Once the economy was growing, it was relatively easy to keep it going as long as expectations were bouyant. Once expectations were slowed by uncertainty over government antiinflationary policy, however, savings quickly declined. By and large, then, the forces which affected private capital formation in Iran were extremely fragile, inducing households and businesses to save and invest large sums when their respective incomes were growing rapidly, but causing it to quickly stagnate once growth and/or expectations slackened.

The actual inflation experience of the country may support the view that any decline in price expectations will tend to be short lived if not produced by policies involving a direct reduction in domestic demand and liquidity. In this regard, the government policy of repressed inflation can be considered as attacking only the symptoms of inflation. In retrospect, the authorities should have selected policies that offered a reduction in inflationary expectations while, at the same time, addressing themselves more directly to the underlying causes of the inflationary pressures. Undoubtedly, a program along these lines would have been much less damaging to the confidence and expectations of the private sector than the somewhat capricous price fixing strategy actually adopted.

Agricultural Stagnation

Another problem related to repressed inflation was the country's increasing dependence on imports of food. From a position of virtual agricultural self-sufficiency in the late 1960s, Iran was one of the world's largest importers by 1976, with agricultural imports around $1.4 billion in 1975 and nearly $2 billion in 1976. By 1977, a number of forecasts were being made of the cost of the country's agricultural imports reaching $4 billion in the early 1980s.(10)

In addition to the $3 billion spent each year on subsidies and imports, over $1 billion worth of farm products was estimated to have been wasted (according to an Imperial Commission set up in the summer of 1976 to look into the problem). According to the Ministry of Agriculture, 40 percent of the grape production, 30 percent of tomatoes, and up to 20 percent of meat (just to name a few) were being lost somewhere along the chain from farm to retail store. Losses of this magnitude could only have been caused by a massive diversion of final products to the black market.(11)

Most authorities argued that, given current crop prices and increased profitability in farming, imports could soon be cut in half. The trouble was that the government was committed politically to keeping down the price of stable goods. Subsidies of $1.25 billion were given in 1977 for five or six basic products. This amounted to around 8 percent of the government's already overextended current account expenditures. At the same time, the government was continuing with its policy of eliminating the rural middleman and the bazaar dealer as much as possible by buying up over 750,000 tons of surplus wheat, the net effect being increasing intervention and higher duplication of unnecessary expenditure to the producer and the consumer.

Certainly, many of the sector's problems were long term. Rapid industrial development inevitably meant that population would be drawn from the countryside to the cities. Yet, the magnitude of these movements and the relative speed toward stagnation of the agricultural sector in the 1970s must certainly have been influenced by the government's price programs. For example, according to official statistics, people had been leaving the land at a rate of 250,000 annually from the mid-1950s through the mid-1970s, but this was also a period during which the price of wheat, for instance, only doubled while the prices paid for inputs into the sector increased much more rapidly, and productivity for most farms expanded marginally at best.

What was clearly antagonizing the agricultural sector was the low profitability of investment in farming activities, and it was the government's pricing policies that were particularly troubling for the farming community. In particular, the contrast between the price for home goods and imported commodities was a major source of irritation in rural areas. For example, in late 1976, farmers received around 10 rials a kilogram for wheat. This was widely regarded as barely adequate to cover the costs of cultivation, let alone provide a reasonable living. At the same time, the government was paying 18 rials a kilogram for imported wheat. Policies of this type were apparently the source of so much anger that they drove tea farmers in some parts of the country to burn their crops while forcing a number of poultry farmers to close their businesses.(12) It was clear that the farming community could continue to carry their burdens only at the cost of lower productivity. Quality began slipping noticeably in the fruit and vegetable markets, and an increasing number of farmers began to vocally criticize what they considered to be outrageous government pricing programs.

POLICY SHIFT

Despite the ever-increasing scope of the price control program, price levels began to rise rapidly in early 1976 and continued until the end of the year. During the year, the average consumer price index rose by 16.6 percent and the wholesale price index by 13.5 percent (compared with the indices for 1975). The housing group increased by 36 percent and had a major share - around 50 percent - of the overall increase of the price index. The index for food items rose by 13 percent.

To sum up, by 1976, a coherent antiinflationary strategy had not been formulated. In general, the government seemed somewhat reluctant to act. Outside the monetary field, the measures taken in addition to the price controls were not very sophisticated (e.g., blocking bills to contractors by the ministries, most of which were finally paid off). As the inefficiencies and the disruptive nature of the controls were increasingly recognized, the government began to look into the possibilities of demand-oriented monetary and fiscal anti-inflationary policies. While, as noted earlier, the Bank Markazi began to tighten credit in mid-1975, given the magnitude of the suppressed inflationary pressures, the liquidity of the private sector, and remaining bottlenecks, consumer prices started accelerating from 9.9 percent in 1975 to 16.6 percent in 1976, and finally to 25.1 percent in 1977. During this period, growth of domestic value added started declining.

Following the October 28, 1976, Kayhan interview, a number of measures were adopted consistent with a more sober and restrained approach. A Special Imperial Commission with eight committees was set up in November 1976 to monitor progress in all sectors of the economy. The commission, which was linked to the Imperial Inspectorate, the Shah's special investigative body, to the security organization, Savak, and to the ministries, was charged with exposing waste and inefficiency.

Second, workers were informed they could no longer expect bonuses at the end of the year if their company was not making a profit. Up to mid-1977, workers had been receiving up to three months extra pay as official policy, even if a plant was operating at a loss. The new labor code had been drafted where great emphasis was put on defining discipline - a means of achieving higher output and a sort of carrot and stick approach appears to have been adopted to promote greater productivity.

According to the director of the Plan and Budget Organization, Abdol Majid Majidi, the new Sixth Five Year Plan to be announced in October 1977 and to begin in March 1978 was to begin a period of austerity. The government was to gradually eliminate the massive food subsidies which cost $1.2 billion a year (equivalent to 9 percent of current account). Bank credit had already been tightened and efforts were being made to redirect investment away from construction which had been absorbing almost half of the total commercial credit. It was also possible that the government was thinking of curbing import demand for luxury consumer goods.

Overall production costs were still rising rapidly, as were wages and salaries. In his Kayhan interview, the Shah referred to Iranian engineers being paid more than German engineers, even though Germany's per capita income was three times that of Iran. Production per worker had risen 10 percent a year over the past three years, but labor costs rose three and four times as fast, according to the Industrial and Mining Development Bank report for 1976-77. The report also notes that the steep rise in labor costs over the period between 1974 and 1977, which was conservatively estimated at an annual average of 20 percent and probably nearer 30 percent, had played a major role in raising the price of domestically produced goods.

The Shah's point was that oil alone enabled the government to subsidize food prices, provide free education, and the trappings of a welfare state; and one day in the not too distant future this oil would run out. Unless people were prepared to work harder, produce more, and pay higher taxes, there would be nothing to replace oil.

Privately, most officials acknowledged by now that the government's excessive domestic spending was largely responsible for the country's inflation. The leveling off in oil revenues, in any case, would have forced the authorities to control expenditures more in accordance with the absorptive capacity of the economy.

The rate of increase in total government expenditures declined from a record high of 125 percent in 1974 to 35 percent in 1975 to 13 percent in 1976 (table 11.1). How much of this pattern can be attributed to stabilization concerns and how much was a response to fluctuating oil revenues is impossible to discern. Officially at least, it was late 1976 before the government announced publically its decision to use fiscal restraint in its antiinflation program.

Political considerations inevitably appeared. And the government was faced with questions such as:

1. To what extent could the government risk alienating the growing urban/industrial workforce by clamping down on wages and cutting food subsidies when inflation was running high and housing costs were outpacing all wage demands?
2. To what extent could the authorities afford to alienate the growing middle class, the future of his industrialized society, by freezing product prices and so discouraging investment?
3. To what extent could the military budget be pruned without upsetting the military who are the ultimate guarantors of power?

Before there was enough money to please everyone, but now aspirations were aroused and could not be sustained without major changes.

Table 11.1. Fiscal Trends
Current Prices
(billion rials)

	Revenues			Expenditures		Deficit (-)
	Total	Petroleum	Non-Petroleum	Current	Capital	Surplus (+)
1959	31.3	8.2	23.1	30.5		0.8
1960	37.0	9.2	27.8	31.7	-	-0.1
1961	38.0	8.1	29.9	38.9	-	-0.9
1962	42.8	13.8	29.0	41.6	-	1.2
1963	60.7	27.7	33.0	48.3	18.6	-6.2
1964	69.1	36.4	32.7	53.5	26.7	11.1
1965	91.3	50.0	41.3	58.3	42.5	-9.5
1966	99.2	47.4	51.8	62.7	47.0	-11.5
1967	107.8	54.0	53.8	82.4	54.0	-28.3
1968	127.3	61.8	65.5	98.8	69.9	-41.4
1969	149.1	76.4	72.7	114.4	82.8	-48.1
1970	172.3	84.7	87.6	135.2	96.6	-59.5
1971	258.9	155.3	103.6	176.7	115.1	-32.9
1972	302.1	178.2	123.9	227.3	131.8	-57.0
1973	464.8	311.2	153.6	316.8	161.2	-13.2
1974	1394.4	1205.2	189.2	727.8	348.7	140.0
1975	1582.1	1246.8	335.3	929.3	526.8	12.7
1976	1836.4	1241.5	414.9	1047.3	591.6	-37.6
1977	2034.3	1497.8	536.5	1223.0	921.6	-388.5

Source: Bank Markazi, Iran, *Annual Report*, various issues.

CONCLUSIONS

What comes through the analysis is the fact that the country's inflationary situation was aggravated by the fact that neither the price rises themselves nor income growth operated in a conventional stabilizing manner. On the contrary, both the rate of inflation and increases in income induced further increases in investment, thus causing the demand-pull inflation to feed upon itself. This pattern was aggravated by the fact that, during upswings in economic activity, the country's underdeveloped financial institutions were not capable of effecting an increase in savings nearly commensurate with the increased investment. Increases in the supply of real credit further added to the investment boom and increasing inflationary pressure. The failure of the Bank Markazi to adequately contain credit ultimately undermined any possibilities for returning to a stable growth path.

One might easily argue that tight credit control immediately after the oil price increases would have created an even worse set of problems than actually developed. Credit provided working capital and thus helped determine the degree to which the country's stock of physical capital was utilized. Consequently, there was a possibility that a drastic reduction in private credit for purposes of macroeconomic adjustment might have had high costs in terms of aggregate income and employment growth. Clearly, the optimal antiinflationary policy was controlled government expenditures. Instead, the government responded with price controls and antiprofiteering legislation. Both did much to interfere with allocative efficiency and reduced private confidence. By supplanting the market mechanism by bureaucratic decision making, the price controls proved an inferior stabilizing instrument lacking coherence, coordination, and consistency. While it may be argued that stability per se has no intrinsic value, the dislocation and waste caused by the country's post-1973 inflationary experience was hardly worth whatever short-run gains were achieved in terms of high investment rates.

Unfortunately for Iran, 1976-77 did not see the end of its inflationary pressures. New pressures soon arose, some from causes similar to those which existed in 1974-75, and others from completely different sources. In contrast to a policy of repressed inflation, chief reliance was finally put on fiscal and monetary policy to stem the new inflationary pressures. Of course, these actions were too late for the survival of the government, which must credit its demise largely to measures used to combat rising prices.

12 An Optimal Control Solution

INTRODUCTION

In order to examine the consequences of the increased oil revenues, a number of forecasting models were developed in Iran after 1973. The econometric models developed at the Plan and Budget Organization were designed with the premise that:

> Oil revenues may well be a mixed blessing, depending on the size of the annual liquidity injections relative to the availability of complementary factors of production. Indeed, these revenues are on the one hand like the blood of the economy carrying badly needed investment resources to particular areas for purposes of expanding productive capacity and on the other they are capable of producing an excessive liquidity situation, if capital resources become suddenly out of line with other complementary factors of production (such as skilled labor, technology, organizational skills, natural resources or general infrastructure services). This duality renders the planning task all the more difficult under conditions of financial surplus, since it requires a shift of emphasis in the planning circles, from an allocation of resources according to the now abundant factor to an allocation of resources according to the real scarce factor.(1)

Using these models for forecasting over a twenty year period, several important difficulties associated with the country's development were identified.(2)

- The prospect of a recession during the period 1980-87
- The existence of impending difficulties in adjusting from oil induced growth to consumption induced growth
- High inflation anticipated during the decade 1972-82, as well as a highly uneven impact on various social and economic groups
- The need to identify areas of comparative advantage in the industrial and mining sectors
- The prospect of a serious balance of payments disequilibrium beginning around 1987
- The prospect of an unusual widening of urban-rural income disparities with little hope of a self-adjusting mechanism
- Identification of the correct role of the public sector in a mixed enterprise economy undergoing rapid change.

Interestingly enough, when this particular forecast was tested for the sensitivity of these results to an increase in government revenues, it was found that a 4.4 percent increase in revenues spread over 20 years (1972-82) did not have a significant impact in terms of the endogenous variables. Also apparent was that an increase in oil revenues without any correcting policy considerations contributed to urban-rural income disparities. Out of this analysis several scenarios were drawn.

The basic policy problems brought to light by the initial forecasts were therefore that:

1. a do-nothing approach to urban-rural disparities would not bring out a self-adjusting mechanism (and, therefore, something needed to be done);
2. the level of disparities implied by the do-nothing approach was such that the social fabric would be able to withstand it only under a very tight control situation;
3. the disparities would encourage rural-urban migration at a rate which might be untenable given the existing amount of urban infrastructure;
4. for a more balanced society more acceptable targets had to be set, even if the effects of such targets were reduced growth and increased inflation.(3)

Thus, on the argument that oil was a depletable resource and that its wealth must be conserved in financial terms to serve future generations, a spending policy was derived. A number of simulations of the economy were made to determine if it was possible to:

1. avoid the forecasted recessions of 1979-87;
2. extend the protective financial umbrella of oil-based resources out in time;

3. smooth out Iran's growth path over the next 20 years;
4. avoid excessive inflationary pressures in the initial years;
5. avoid exceeding the absorptive capacity of investment;
6. solve the anticipated balance of payments crisis of 1987-92;
7. leave future generations beyond 1992 with a certain size of capital stock.

In general, these were found to be compatible goals and a number of policy recommendations were made on the basis of the Plan and Budget Organization's econometric model and forecasts.(4)

The use of econometric models for quantitative analysis of macroeconomic policy was thus a major development in Iranian planning. Using these econometric models, it was possible for planners to make projections of key economic variables. Given a set of proposed future values for the policy variables or instruments at the government's disposal, planners were then able to examine the nature of these projections in order to evaluate policy proposals. While a productive start in the right direction, this approach to policy analysis was deficient for two reasons.

First, the dynamic response of the economic variables to a particular course assigned to the policy was complicated and unpredictable. The selection of policy by a trial and error process was, therefore, extremely inefficient. What was needed was the specification of a loss function of the key economic variables and the minimization of its value with respect to the policy instruments included in the model. The specification of an objective or loss function and the derivation of a policy solution by optimization would have given the planners a much clearer picture of the extent to which the country's economic performance could have been improved upon. There was no assurance that the trial and error methods actually used came anywhere close to forecasting the economy's optimal growth path.

The second, and perhaps more important, deficiency stemmed from the uncertainty inherent in the projections. Given the proposed time paths for the policy variables, it is impossible to rely on an econometric model to make perfect predictions of which values important economic variables should assume. Uncertainty not only makes it difficult to evaluate a given policy path, but it makes the evaluation of such a path unrealistic and irrelevant.(5)

The former difficulty can be resolved by stochastic simulations which incorporate random elements in the econometric model in making projections; the means and variances of the future paths can then be calculated. Because of uncertainty in the economy, it would have been unrealistic to expect the government to adhere to a fixed plan irrespective of future developments; future decisions were made on the basis of future observations of the economy. Hence, it was unrealistic and irrelevant for the Plan and Budget Organization to evaluate the consequences of a preassigned sequence of policy actions. A more realistic policy would have taken the form of a reaction function, or a feedback control equation permitting the values of the policy variables to be determined according to future economic observations.

In sum, the policy analysis at this time not only lacked optimization but it was also not conducted in a setting capable of yielding feedback as to the impact of policy actions. It is puzzling why several of the more sophisticated and insightful mathematical models available at the time were not used. In particular, since the Plan and Budget Organization's econometric models were linear with an additive random disturbance, it would have been best to minimize the expected value of a quadratic loss function for T periods according to the methods developed some time earlier by Herbert Simon(6) and Henri Theil(7), i.e., that of optimal control.

METHOD OF OPTIMAL CONTROL

An optimal control problem consists of:

1. a set of differential or difference equations that represent a system that is to be controlled;
2. a set of constraints on the variables of the system;
3. a set of boundary conditions on the variables; and
4. cost functional or performance index which is to be minimized.

The essential idea of optimal control is precisely to derive the optimal policy in order to steer the economy to a specified set of targets. A necessary step in this regard is to specify an objective function or a welfare loss function by which the outcome associated with the optimal policy or its alternatives can be evaluated. Given this welfare loss function and a dynamic model, a policy sequence can be found minimizing the expectation of the welfare loss for a given time horizon. For example, the solution to the optimal control problem with unknown parameters using a quadratic loss function can be written as:

$$(1)\ y(t) = A(t)y(t+1) + C(t)x(t) + b(t) + u(t)$$

where $y(t)$ is a vector of endogenous variables at time t; $x(t)$ is a vector of policy variables at time t; $b(t)$ is a vector combining the effects of all exogenous variables not subject to control. The matrices $A(t)$, $C(t)$, and $b(t)$ consist of unknown parameters whose probability distribution is assumed to be given, and u(t) is a vector of random disturbances having mean 0, co-variance matrix V, and being serially uncorrelated. Endogenous variables and policy variables with higher order lags can be eliminated by defining new endogenous variables so as to retain the form (1) of a system of first order linear stochastic difference equations in which only the current control variables x(t) appear. We can include the policy variables in the vector y(t) so that x(t) need not be an argument of the loss function.(8) The loss function can be depicted as:

$$(2)\ W = \sum_{t-1}^{T} (yt - at)^{1} K_t (yt - at)$$

where a(t) is a vector of targets for the variables y(t), and K(t) is a diagonal matrix giving the relative penalties for the squared deviations of the various variables from their targets. The problem becomes essentially one of minimizing the expected value of the loss function for T periods by choosing a strategy for x(1), and x(2) . . . x(T). The control variables will be selected sequentially, the vector x(t) for each period being determined only after the up-to-date information is available. This information consists mainly of y(t-1) which includes the observations of all past endogenous variables and policy variables affecting the current endogenous variables at time (t).

It may be argued that decisions of the planners in Iran, particularly after the oil price increases, were not made in a context of marginal optimization. However, the manner in which the planning authorities approached their responsibilities can be approximated by the optimization of a well-defined objective function. After all, the responsible officials on the regime's High Economic Council were all reasonably knowledgeable men and concerned with national income, the price level, the balance of payments, and so on. Clearly, a deviation between actual developments and the desired ones in any of these aspects can be regarded as having caused disutility to this group.

The application of optimal control to the problem of planning a development strategy after 1972 is presented below.(9) The approach is straightforward. Based on the analysis in previous chapters, the economic system is represented by an econometric model, namely, a set of difference equations. There are constraints; for example, inflation is not allowed to increase over a certain rate. The boundary conditions are the initial values of the variables while real non-oil GDP is maximized for 1980 in the objective function.

A MODEL OF THE IRANIAN ECONOMY

The model consists of a series of identities and estimated equations and draws on the analysis contained in earlier chapters. For clarity, a rough outline shows the major relationships (table 12.1). The model incorporates a foreign sector, the domestic banking system, the government, and the private sector (the basic identities of each are depicted in equations 1-4 of the table, respectively).

Each of the first three sectors involves income as well as financial transactions, whereas the income transactions of the banking system are considered to be negligible. An increase in the deficit or a reduction in the non-financial net savings is assumed to result in either an increase in its financial liabilities or a decrease in its holdings of financial assets or both. Furthermore, given its non-financial savings or deficit, a sector can acquire more of one financial asset only at the expense of accumulations to its holdings of one or more alternative financial assets or in exchange for increases in one or more financial liabilities.(10) The account for each sector is assumed balanced at the end of the year. The model, therefore, contains a set of sectoral balance sheet constraints. As usual in models of this type, certain behavior relations are required to explain the economic and financial activities of various sectors.

The model's construction was constrained by lack of data on several variables. In particular, there are no figures on private savings or the capital stock. As an approximation, the capital stock was simply assumed to be a summation of the total gross domestic capital formation in the current and two prior years:

(3) KPL = TINP + TINPL + TINPL2

where TINP = PITP + GITP (total private investment plus total government investment).

For convenience, non-oil GDP (equation 8) is specified in linear form in the optimum control exercises. Both the real capital (KP) stock and labor force (L) were assumed to make independent contributions to real non-oil (NOXNP) output.

The price level (equation 9) was assumed to reflect excess real demand, monetary factors, and world prices. Excess demand is measured as the ratio of liquidity to real output (M/NOXNP), while the export price index of the developed countries (EUVICA) was used as an approximation of world price trends. Since specification for the price level incorporates a disequilibrium relationship, it is easily converted into an inflation equation for empirical estimation. As noted earlier, import prices are an important determinant of

Table 12.1. A Macroeconomic Framework

Equation	Structural Specification
1	ΔMSFAP = EXR - ZNP + GFP + PFP
2	ΔMZP = ΔMSFAP + ΔMSDCP
3	ΔMSGCP = GCNP + GITP - GREUP - GFP - ΔGB
4	PITP = SP + ΔPCP + PFP - ΔM2P - ΔB
5	ΔPCP = ΔMSDCP - ΔGCP
6	SP = NOXNP - NOREUP - PCNP
7	KP = KPL + PITP + GITP - DEP
7^1	KP = TINP + TINPL + TINPLZ
8	NOXNP = KP + L
9	P = EXCESS + EUUICA
10	MIP = NOXNP + INF
11	MZ = BMRM
12	ZNP = PC + PTINP + ΔWPI
13	NOREUP = PENANP
14	PCNP = NOXNP - ΔCPI
15	EXPECTNA = EUUCP + CCP
16	GEXPTNAP = GREUP

Note: See text for description of symbols.

domestic prices. As formulated here, an increase in import prices may cause upward pressure on domestic prices mainly through their effect on the costs of production, and the substitution of domestic for imported goods (which creates demand pressure on domestic resources).

The demand for liquidity (equation 10) simply states that the transaction demand (depicted by real non-oil GDP) as reinforced by the rate of inflation (or requirement for additional cash to finance expenditures during periods of price increases) determines desired real money (MIP) holdings.

The positive sign for inflation reflects the lack of attractive non-financial assets that the public could acquire during this period as the opportunity cost of holding money increased (due to the price increases).(11)

Imports (equation 12) are assumed to be related largely to the importation of machinery by both the public (PIMP) and the government (GIMP). This view of imports (ZNP) accepts the two-gap theory assumptions that, given the nature of Iran's import substitution strategy and the lack of a domestic capital goods industry, the country required a certain minimal amount of imports just to maintain a given level of income. The change in wholesale prices obviously indicates a shift away from domestic producers to cheaper foreign suppliers (of non-machinery goods) as local prices increase.

The limited non-oil government revenues (equation 13) were largely duties of one sort or another, plus the income tax. They are assumed to be largely a function of private expenditure (PENANP).

Private consumption (equation 14) is a function of real non-oil output. Consumption was also assumed to be affected by government activity whereby stepped up government purchases may preempt a certain amount of expenditures, either through a forced savings mechanism or "crowding out" effect through tightening of credit availability.(12)

Exports (equation 15) are largely a function of crude petroleum production (CCP) and the price of oil in world markets (depicted by the export price of oil EUVCP). Non-oil exports were largely disregarded (but are included in EXPTNA).

The main characteristics of the model include: (1) integration of the domestic economy with that of the world economic system; (2) an active role played by both the banking system and government; (3) the use of non-oil output and the rate of inflation as the optimal control targets; (4) the adaptation of changes in the private banking system; and (5) government investment in machinery as the control variable.(13)

The major objective in formulating an optimal control simulation of the economy for the 1972-77 period is to examine whether and to what extent the government's stabilization program could have been more successful in controlling inflation in a manner that would have been less disruptive on the private sector than was actually the case.

The main tasks in formulation of the simulation were: (1) estimating the structural equations; (2) establishing desirable end point (1977) targets (level of real non-oil GDP, inflation); and (3) estimating the required levels of the policy instruments year-by-year to attain these targets (with inflation treated as the welfare loss function).

The results of the econometric two-stage estimation of the structural equations are encouraging and need little further comment (see table 12.2). The equations used in the actual simulations are the first one listed for each variable; the primed equations for each were alternates and are included here because they depict an interesting aspect of the variable. The optimal control steps involved:

1. Setting the values for the exogenous variables at their historical values. Exogenous variables were:

- CPP - index of crude petroleum production;
- EUVIC - export price index industrial countries;
- EUV - Iranian export price index; and
- lagged variables in the estimated equations.

2. With (1) simulating values for the endogenous variables over the 1972-77 period.
3. Setting two values for 1977 for real non-oil GDP (NOXNP) to be optimized (Rls. 1,650 billion and Rls. 1,800 billion as opposed to the actual historical figures of Rls. 1,453.8 billion).
4. Simultaneously the rate of increase of the consumer price index was set at equal or less than 10 percent per annum for the 1971-77 period as a whole (the historical rate was 13.54 percent).
5. Two instrument variables, government investment in machinery (GIMP) and private credit from the banking system (PCP), were selected for control purposes.
6. No constraints were placed on government investment in machinery or private consumption although this could be introduced with no problem once a basis for their lower limit was established.

Logically, four policy variables could be chosen in the context of the stabilization model outlined above. In addition to the change in net domestic credit (private sector) of the banking system and government capital expenditure, government construction and government consumption expenditures were possible instruments of fiscal policy. Regardless of their choice, the policy instruments included in the model must be well coordinated since the various sectors are interacting with one another. It can be seen from the simulation model that a change in the rate of credit expansion would influence foreign

Table 12.2. Macroeconomic Simulation Model
(Two-Stage Least Sources Estimates)

Equation		
	Non-oil GDP (constant price)	
(1)	NOXNP = 0.91 + 0.04L - 132.22 (10.78) (2.06) (-0.89)	r^2 = 0.997 F = 1541.73
(1a)	NOXNP = 4.86PIMP + 4.46GIMP = 15.50 TIME + 140.05 (5.11) (3.85) (2.27) (3.71)	r^2 = 0.990 F = 281.06
(1b)	NOXNP = 0.94KP + 7.41TIME + 130.65 (12.83) (1.90) (7.19)	r^2 = 0.9970 F = 1490.81
(1c)	NOXNP = 0.89KP + 0.013POP - 134.45 (10.04) (2.15) (-0.98)	r^2 = 0.997 F = 1628.99
(1d)	NOXNP = 1.07KP - 14.39ICOR + 198.96 (62.05) (-2.66) (15.99)	r^2 = 0.998 F = 1932.27
	Private Consumption (constant price)	
(2)	PCNP = 0.64NOXNP - 1.62ΔCPI + 59.08 (20.57) (-2.67) (4.60)	r^2 = 0.995 F = 192.64
(2^1)	PCNP = 0.69NOXNP - 0.14GENANP + 52.18 (9.42) (-2.30) (2.67)	r^2 = 0.994 F = 734.28
	Private Expenditures	
(3)	PENANP = 0.25NOXNP + 1.51PCP + 145.45 (2.29) (3.30) (4.33)	r^2 = 0.997 F = 445.55
	Total Savings	
(4)	FSNP = 1.09EXR - 28.73 (68.79) (-6.49)	r^2 = 0.9981 F = 4731.42

(continued)

Table 12.2. Macroeconomic Simulation Model (continued)
(Two-Stage Least Sources Estimates)

Equation		
	Private Investment in Machinery	
(5)	PIMP = 0.32ΔNOXNP + 0.11PCPL - 0.72	
	(2.85) (1.78) (-0.21)	r^2 = 0.939 F = 61.61
(5a)	PIMP = 0.82ΔM1P + 0.25ΔNOXNP + 4.88	
	(3.56) (3.21) (1.99)	r^2 = 0.967 F = 117.74
(5b)	PIMP = 0.16ΔNOXNP + 0.53ΔM2P + 4.86	
	(2.26) (5.04) (2.55)	r^2 = 0.980 F = 192.64
	Private Investment in Construction	
(6)	PICP = 0.16ΔGENANP + 0.52ΔPCP + 18.27	
	(9.19) (7.14) (11.61)	r^2 = 0.965 F = 111.49
(6a)	PICP = 0.06ΔGENANP + 0.14PCP + 13.13	
	(2.84) (8.55) (7.28)	r^2 = 0.975 F = 154.69
(6b)	PICP = 0.06GENANP + 0.13ΔNOXNP + 14.52	
	(4.06) (3.52) (3.98)	r^2 = 0.983 F = 229.61
	Government Consumption	
(7)	GCNP = 0.15GREVP + 0.80GREVPL - 6.19	
	(8.54) (17.53) (-1.73)	r^2 = 0.998 F = 2098.63
(7a)	GCNP = 1.06GREVPL + 0.36GDEFP - 6.87	
	(24.62) (3.68) (-0.93)	r^2 = 0.992 F = 553.81
	Government Investment in Machinery	
(8)	GZMP = -0.28GDEFP + 0.11GREUP - 2.18	
	(-4.39) (10.18) (-0.66)	r^2 = 0.951 F = 78.05

(continued)

Table 12.2. Macroeconomic Simulation Model (continued)
(Two-Stage Least Sources Estimates)

Equation		
	Government Investment in Construction	
(9)	GICP = -0.66GDEFP + 0.24GREUP - 1.87 (-5.00) (10.80) (-0.28)	r^2 = 0.954 F = 83.40
(10)	Total Government Investment	
	GTTP = 0.31GREVPL + 0.43GREVPL2 - 8.48 (1.75) (1.83) (-1.25)	r^2 = 0.970 F = 127.92
	Imports	
(11)	ZNP = 0.72PCP + 0.07EXW + 8.39 (4.57) (2.80) (0.64)	r^2 = .0.970 F = 128.59
(11a)	ZNP = 0.86PCP + 0.28BMFAP + 6.63 (12.23) (5.10) (0.78)	r^2 = 0.986 F = 281.10
(11b)	ZNP = 1.49PIMP + 2.86GIMP + 63.48DFWPA (5.47) (9.06) (1.85)	r^2 = 0.9953 F = 556.98
	Exports (deflated with export deflator)	
(12)	EXR = 0.42VAG + 1.31EUVP - 7.44 (35.44) (7.73) (-0.74)	r^2 = 0.998 F = 1994.38
(12a)	EXR = 0.26 VAD + 6.83RUVICA - 249.35 (8.28) (7.21) (-5.70)	r^2 = 0.997 F = 1764.29
	Exports (deflated with world price deflator)	
(13)	EXW = 0.95VAD + 2.97EUVP - 17.14 (35.54) (7.77) (-0.75)	r^2 = 0.998 F = 2007.05
(13a)	EXW = 0.60VAO + 15.53EUVICA - 567.29 (8.29) (7.22) (-5.72)	r^2 = 0.998 F = 1768.33

(continued)

Table 12.2. Macroeconomic Simulation Model (continued) (Two-Stage Least Sources Estimates)

Equation		
	<u>Exports (deflated with world price deflator)</u> (continued)	
(13b)	EXW = 12.83EUVICA + 0.66EXPTNA - 453.87 (6.12) (9.74) (-4.75)	r^2 = 0.992 F = 1983.4
	<u>Exports (current price)</u>	
(14)	EXPTNA = 1.04VAO + 15.94 (86.69) (2.75)	r^2 = 0.9988 F = 7515.16
(14a)	EXPTNA = 3.95EUVCP + 14.22CPP - 280.66 (4.95) (13.85) (-5.94)	r^2 = 0.996 F = 6983.41
	<u>Private Sector Credit from Banking System</u>	
(15)	PCP = 0.88BMRMP + 0.47PCPL + 1.98 (2.91) (1.96) (0.44)	r^2 = 0.994 F = 612.70
(15a)	PCP = 0.39ΔNONXNP + 0.97PCPL + 0.68 (2.48) (10.92) (0.14)	r^2 = 0.992 F = 525.35
	<u>PC (current price)</u>	
(16)	PC = 2.70BMRMP - 58.60 (26.41) (-5.76)	r^2 = 0.986 F = 697.54
(16a)	PC = 1.12BMRM + 0.15NOXNP - 38.22 (16.75) (5.16) (-4.23)	r^2 = 0.999 F = 4232.63
	<u>Balance of Payments Current Account (current price)</u>	
(17)	CURE = 0.41EXW - 13.74 (26.63) (-1.39)	r^2 = 0.986 F = 708.99

(continued)

Table 12.2. Macroeconomic Simulation Model (continued)
(Two-Stage Least Sources Estimates)

Equation		
	CUREP (constant price)	
(18)	CUREP = 0.47EXWL - 23.82 (27.56) (-3.69)	r^2 = 0.987 F = 759.72
	Government Oil Revenues	
(19)	OREVP = 1.11EUVP + 7.06CPP - 103.46 (15.28) (80.55) (23.31)	r^2 = 0.999 F = 6688.93
(19a)	OREVP = 0.46VAO + 5.38 (22.99) (0.56)	r^2 = 0.983 F = 528.33
(19b)	OREVP = 5.86CPP + 13.82CPPL - 214.08 (7.73) (2.86) (-3.58)	r^2 = 0.9911 F = 444.23
	Government Non-Oil Revenues	
(20)	NOREVP = 0.17PENANP - 16.38 (17.23) (-3.27)	r^2 = 0.971 F = 297.03
(20a)	NOREVP = 0.20PENANP - 1.50INFC - 27.74 (15.08) (-3.12) (-5.45)	r^2 = 0.987 F = 298.55
	Government Deficit	
(21)	GDEFP = 1.07CUREP + 0.68GREUP - 12.40 (-5.10) (-6.34) (-1.61)	r^2 = 0.926 F = 50.28
	Bank Markazi Revenue Money	
(22)	BMRM (current price) BMRM = 0.64GENANP - 9.99 (17.21) (-1.07)	r^2 = 0.971 F = 296.08

(continued)

Table 12.2. Macroeconomic Simulation Model (continued)
(Two-Stage Least Sources Estimates)

Equation		
	<u>Bank Markazi Reserve Money (constant price)</u>	
(23)	BMRMP = 0.04EXR + 0.27PENANP - 45.71	
	(-4.80)	r^2 = 0.998
		F = 253.97
	<u>Bank Markazi Net Foreign Assets</u>	
(24)	BMRMFAP = 0.560REUP - 0.227ZNP + 8.91	
	(14.89) (-2.54) (1.05)	r^2 = 0.990
		F = 411.68
	<u>Supply of Narrow Money (current price)</u>	
(25)	M1 = 1.09BMRM + 16.15	
	(65.26) (6.31)	r^2 = 0.998
		F = 4258.5
	<u>Supply of Broad Money (current price)</u>	
(26)	M2 = 2.34BMRM - 4.72	
	(55.40) (-0.73)	r^2 = 0.997
		F = 3069.47
	<u>Demand for Narrow Money</u>	
(27)	M1P = 0.22NOXNP + 1.70INFC - 17.09	
	(12.87) (2.15) (-2.44)	r^2 = 0.991
		F = 442.44
	<u>Demand for Broad Money</u>	
(28)	M2P = 0.49NOXNP + 3.33INFC - 84.75	
	(27.98) (4.00) (-11.51)	r^2 = 0.998
		F = 2014.39
	<u>Bank Markazi Currency in Circulation</u>	
(29)	BMCP = 2.22BMCPL + 0.05GENANP - 16.83	
	(2.08) (1.64) (2.85)	r^2 = 0.833
		F = 22.46

(continued)

Table 12.2. Macroeconomic Simulation Model (continued)
(Two-Stage Least Sources Estimates)

Equation		
	Value Added by Oil Sector	
(30)	VAO = 14.23CPP + 3.29EUVCP - 263.02 (15.14) (4.51) (-6.09)	r^2 = 0.986 F = 273.39
	Value Added by Oil Sector (continued)	
(30a)	VAO = 3.91CPP + 2.06VAOL - 136.83 (1.92) (6.61) (-7.46)	r^2 = 0.992 F = 501.79
	Wholesale Price Index	
(31)	WPI = 193.82EXCESSA + 0.06M2L + 66.08 (3.17) (2.16) (6.94)	r^2 = 0.987 F = 342.70
(31a)	WPI = 183.11EXCESSA + 0.13M1L + 65.39 (2.95) (2.30) (7.53)	r^2 - 0.988 F = 359.08
	Consumer Price Index	
(32)	CPI = 87.92EXCESSD + 0.21M1L + 101.75 (2.79) (7.12) (87.50)	r^2 = 0.994 F = 729.60
(32a)	CPI = 0.07M2L + 0.69EUVICA + 81.09 (4.69) (4.22) (14.08)	r^2 = 0.995 F = 960.92
(32b)	CPI = 0.07M2L + 1.18EUVICAL + 59.45 (4.61) (4.74) (5.98)	r^2 = 0.996 F = 1085.03
	Wholesale Price Inflation	
(33)	INFW = 0.19GM2L + 0.33GM2L2 + 0.35WINF - 6.54 (2.51) (2.97) (4.06) (-4.08)	r^2 = 0.903 F = 31.78

(continued)

Table 12.2. Macroeconomic Simulation Model (continued)
(Two-Stage Least Sources Estimates)

Equation	
	Consumer Price Inflation
(34)	INFC = 17.94EXCESSD + 105.74EXCESSDL + 0.18WINF - 1.18 (2.65) (12.42) (2.11) (-1.40) r^2 = 0.995 F = 71.14
	Excess Demand (M1/NOXNP)
(35)	EXCESSA = 0.00078M2L - 0.0003NOXNPL + 0.22 (7.76) (-3.65) (11.23) r^2 = 0.984 F = 267.43
	Excess Demand (/ M2/NOXNP)
(36)	EXCESSD = 0.0012ΔM1 + 0.00028ΔGENANP + 0.00067ΔPCP + 0.026 (10.52) (2.40) (4.34) (4.02) r^2 = 0.995 F = 478.83
	Agriculture Sector Output
(37)	AGP = 0.097NOXNP + 68.81 (4.58) (5.53) r^2 = 0.678 F = 21.02
	Manufacturing Sector Output
(38)	MANP = 0.23NOXUP - 25.94 (31.36) (-6.14) r^2 = 0.989 F = 983.71
	Construction Sector Value Added
(39)	CONP = 0.038NOXNP + 8.09 (3.96) (1.46) r^2 = 0.610 F = 15.66
	Value Added by Water and Power Sectors
(40)	WPP = 0.046NOXNP - 10.63 (31.50) (-12.55) r^2 = 0.9900 F = 992.31

(continued)

Table 12.2. Macroeconomic Simulation Model (continued)
(Two-Stage Least Sources Estimates)

Equation		
	Value Added in Transport and Communications Sectors	
(41)	TCP = 0.065NOXNP + 8.12 (16.58) (3.52)	r^2 = 0.965 F = 275.04
	Value Added in Trade Sector	
(42)	TP = 0.086NOXNP + 2.23 (9.71) (0.43)	r^2 = 0.904 F = 94.24
	Value Added by Ownership of Dwellings	
(43)	ODP = 0.052NOXNP + 5.37 (13.35) (2.38)	r^2 = 0.947 F = 178.35
	Value Added by Private Services	
(44)	PRIVP = 0.068NOXNP - 6.12 (12.24) (-1.88)	r^2 = 0.937 F = 149.84
	Value Added by Public Services	
(45)	PUBP = 0.20NOXNP - 33.79 (15.17) (-4.36)	r^2 = 0.958 F = 229.98
	Incremental Capital-Output Ratio	
(46)	ICOR = 14.82GNOXNP + 4.04 (-2.88) (7.93)	r^2 = 0.455 F = 8.35

Note: See text for description of symbols.

reserves, output, and prices through imports and investment. The change in output would also have an effect on imports and tax revenues and, hence, the balance of payments and the budget of the government. At the same time, the change in credit and domestic liquidity through a change in the demand for money resulting from the changes in real income and in domestic credit creation would have affected imports and, thus, investment and the rate of growth.

ASSESSMENT OF RESULTS

The results of the optimal control exercise (see table 12.3) were very satisfactory in that they confirmed the following facts concerning economic policy in Iran during the 1970s.

1. Both government investment in machinery (total government investment could have been used as a policy variable just as easily) and private credit would have been sufficient in obtaining considerably higher rates of real non-oil GDP than was actually obtained.
2. The fall in government investment in machinery was not excessive in the high NOXNP target case (optimal II), averaging 24.17 percent per year increase (1971-77) versus the historical rate of 25.67. However, in reducing non-oil GDP from 1800.0 in 1977 to 1650.0 would require a drastic fall in government investment in machinery (real growth falling from 24.17 to 5.38) and not an appreciable reduction in inflation (10.00 to 9.77).
3. Private credit had to bear most of the burden in controlling inflation, falling from the actual annual rate of growth of 17.87 percent to 7.67 percent and 11.28 percent for the 1650.0 NOXNP and 1800.0 NOXNP, respectively. The fall in growth was needed largely to control the inflation associated with these rates.
4. The overall importance of the private and government sectors was not altered in moving from 1453.8 to 1650.0 and 1800.0 NOXNP in 1977 with the actual increase in real private expenditure (PENANP) of 15.28 percent falling to 15.24 percent or increasing to 17.27 percent in optimal I and optimal II, respectively, whereas the increase in real government expenditure (GENANP) fell from an actual 23.71 to 21.83 in optimal I, and was 23.52 in optimal II.
5. While the overall levels of government and private sector expenditures are not altered significantly in the optimal paths over their actual values, their compositions are with the most significant being a shift away from private construction (PICP) to private consumption (PCNP) with real private construction falling from an actual 28.76 per-

Table 12.3. Actual and Optimal Growth Rates, 1971-1977 (Billions of Rials)

	Actual 1971	Actual 1972	Simulated 1973	Actual 1977	Optimal I 1977	Optimal II 1977	Average Annual Growth 1971-77 Actual	Optimal I	Optimal II
NOXNP	635.8	735.7	710.6	1453.8	1650.0	1800.0	14.78	17.23	18.94
PCNP	440.6	504.4	496.0	884.9	1053.0	1169.9	12.32	15.63	17.67
PICP	38.1	48.7	43.9	173.6	47.6	57.3	28.76	3.78	7.04
PIMP	34.0	57.1	47.9	144.6	142.1	151.3	27.29	26.92	28.25
PCP	159.0	195.4	195.4	426.3	247.7	310.8	17.87	7.67	11.82
PITP	72.1	105.8	91.8	318.1	189.8	208.6	28.07	17.51	19.37
GIMP	29.8	25.8	25.9	117.4	40.8	109.2	25.67	5.38	24.17
GICP	66.1	66.1	79.5	314.7	314.7	314.7	29.70	29.70	29.70
GCNP	147.2	185.6	185.6	439.8	439.8	439.8	20.01	20.01	20.01
GITP	96.0	105.3	105.3	432.1	355.5	355.5	28.49	24.38	24.38
ZNP	159.4	195.6	190.5	600.9	529.6	578.2	24.25	22.15	23.96
SNP	164.7	214.7	221.2	865.4	865.3	865.3	31.85	31.85	31.85
TINP	168.4	211.1	197.2	750.3	545.3	632.5	28.28	21.63	24.68
EXR	192.5	226.3	253.8	732.8	854.8	854.8	24.96	28.21	28.21
EXW	437.4	514.2	522.3	1665.3	1866.8	1866.8	24.96	27.36	27.36
EXPTNA	240.6	308.5	366.8	1815.2	1804.7	1804.7	40.05	39.91	39.91
RP	439.2	517.5	503.6	2016.7	1475.1	1691.2	28.92	22.38	25.20
M1P	120.4	157.5	145.2	273.6	347.6	390.1	14.66	19.33	21.64
M2P	240.6	307.6	284.1	618.7	745.3	842.1	17.05	20.74	23.22
BMRMP	102.0			300.2	286.9	317.5	19.71	18.81	20.83
BMFAP	37.5			369.7	367.1	358.1	46.43	46.26	45.66
M1	154.93	214.33	207.7	668.0	554.4	601.4	27.58	23.67	25.36
INFC	4.24	6.47	5.70	27.31	8.07	8.59	-	-	-
PENANP	512.7	610.2	596.2	1203.1	1200.8	1333.3	15.28	15.24	17.27
GENANP	243.2	290.9	209.9	871.9	795.3	863.7	23.71	21.83	23.52
OREUP	120.7	130.9	138.6	613.4	836.9	836.9	31.12	38.09	38.09
NOREUP	80.5	90.8	88.0	219.7	209.7	236.3	18.21	17.30	19.60
GDEFP	-25.6	-41.9	-54.7	-159.1	-260.0	-241.1	35.59	47.16	45.32
GREUP	201.2	221.9	226.7	833.1	1046.5	1073.2	26.72	31.63	32.18
CPI	136.07	144.88	144.29	290.36	238.09	241.06	13.47	9.77	10.00

Note: See text for description of symbols.

cent over the 1971-77 period to 3.78 and 7.04 percent, respectively, in optimal I and optimal II; and PCNP increasing from a historical 12.32 percent to 15.63 percent in optimal I and 17.67 percent in optimal II.

More generally (and despite the size and simplicity of the econometric model), the experimental results do provide at least some crude lessons for stabilization policy in Iran. For example, when government consumption and construction expenditures were permitted to remain at their desired levels, private credit had to be cut back fairly drastically to contain inflation within a range of 10 percent per annum. Apparently the lag between money and prices that existed in Iran at that time required policy instruments to be applied in strong bursts.

One might argue that lags were a distinguishing factor between monetary and fiscal policy and should in practice have determined the proper mix and timing of the two. In actuality, monetary and fiscal policy in Iran were probably not substitutes, but complements, and should have been used in combination.

In any case, it is clear why the authorities were frustrated in stabilizing the price level. In addition to being related to liquidity, inflation was also affected by world price trends. There were, therefore, natural limits below which further reductions in the inflation rate were not productive.

The results indicate that the practical design of stabilization policies during this time were critically dependent on the proper phasing of monetary and fiscal policy. It was clearly not just a question of how much monetary restraint or fiscal austerity were desirable but more importantly at what point in time each should have been altered. Fiscal policy appears to have operated with short lags and monetary policy over a longer period of time.

From what we know of the mechanisms at work in the Iranian economy involving the relationships between credit, money, and the balance of payments, it appears that the Bank Markazi, through monitoring reserves and controlling private credit, was able to perform all of the functions necessary for successful stabilization of the economy.

CONCLUSIONS

Even with the aid of econometric models in the early 1970s, policy formulation in Iran remained suboptimal. A major problem stemmed from the fact that all of the models developed for policymaking were structured for the analysis of medium and long-term problems. Apparently, no short-run models existed that systematically accounted for the incorporated financial flows stemming from the monetary impacts of alternative budgets on inflation.

The absence of a systematic treatment of the inflationary impacts of domestic expenditures was undoubtedly a holdover from the 1960s when inflation was not a real problem and growth was the primary consideration of policymakers. At that time, the government's efforts were largely concentrated on obtaining the financial resources with which to implement their development plans. Foreign exchange was relatively scarce, and thus Iran's international creditworthiness did not permit significant capital inflows on a scale capable of creating serious inflationary pressures.

Because the country's decision makers apparently did not have a clear view of the inflationary and balance of payments impacts on the government budget, stabilization policy after the oil price increases continued to be conducted on largely an ad hoc intuitive basis as in the past.

The second problem facing decision makers (even after the development of the large-scale economy-wide models) was the fact that the means of determining what policy was in some sense "best" remained unclear.(14) Part of the problem was that of quantifying the objectives of the policy in a precise way (assuming that the objectives of the policy were indeed known). Because the Plan Organization models never incorporated an objective function to be maximized, policymakers and other officials were forced (again on an ad hoc basis) to choose among a number of feasible scenarios without the knowledge of if and how each of these options could be improved upon. While computer simulations were often used to learn more about the dynamic behavior of the economy and to study the effects of different policies on its key variables, they represented an extremely inefficient effort in this regard.

In retrospect, it is clear that, after 1973, Iranian planners should have focused on shorter-run stabilization issues and contributed more actively to the budgetary decision making process. This is true with regard not only to the longer-run supply effects of the government's programs but also the shorter-run demand and stabilization difficulties posed by the rapidly accelerating level of expenditures.

Secondly, the planners should have clarified more precisely the goals of the regime and together with the constraints facing the economy developed an objective cost or utility function for the near term.

Finally, given that both monetary and fiscal actions had a fairly strong impact on the major macroeconomic aggregates, there should have been much closer cooperation between the Bank Markazi and the Treasury. As noted earlier, too much pressure at too late a point in time was placed on the central bank to control inflation.

13 Income Distribution

INTRODUCTION

It is clear now that income inequality in Iran generally increased in the 1960s and 1970s, among both rural and urban households. Also clear is the fact that the economic development of the 1960s benefited the top income groups relatively more than the poorer segments of the population. It wasn't until the early 1970s, however, that government officials and economists in Iran began to show much interest in these income movements in income distribution.(1) One aspect of this interest probably stemmed from the political implications stemming from the fact that particular socioeconomic groups and geographic regions were hardly benefiting at all from the country's sustained economic growth. In addition, there was apparently increasing awareness in official circles that further increase in overall income inequality might result in slack demand for many of the key manufactured products the country's planners were counting on as ultimately replacing oil as the country's chief generator of wealth.

CHANGING PATTERN OF INCOME DISTRIBUTION

The first in-depth analysis of the country's income distribution was undertaken as part of the ILO comprehensive strategy mission (which visited Iran from November 1971 to January 1972). Through a detailed assessment of the consumption, expenditure, and income distribution figures for urban and rural households in 1969-70, the ILO team identified an extremely concentrated distribution of income for the country as a whole (Gini coefficient as high as 0.6 and 0.7) with extensive dissavings in the rural lower income groups, and extensive positive savings in the urban higher income groups.(2)

In their 1974 report on Iran, the World Bank constructed profiles of households classified as poor (those households which in 1971 that effectively spent less than $800).(3) A major finding was that more than half of the households in Iran at that time were poor, with poor households much more numerous in the rural than urban areas. As one might expect, the poor households were also characterized as being headed by self-employed agricultural workers and those living in the less naturally endowed areas of the country. Urban poor, on the other hand, were generally either construction workers or held odd jobs in other low wage manufacturing sectors.

In contrast to the ILO and World Bank studies, M. H. Pesaran of the Bank Markazi concentrated on assessing the income distributional trend between 1959 and 1974 in both urban and rural areas. His results tend to show increasing income inequality during the period 1959-60 to 1971-72, with some signs of stabilization in the subsequent years, 1971-72 to 1973-74.(4) An additional finding was that income inequality in any given region during this period was positively related to (1) the level of government development expenditure in the region, (2) the overall educational attainment of the household, and (3) urban/rural disparities.

Additional insights as to the pattern of income distribution in Tehran can be derived from studies on the nutritional levels of the city's inhabitants.(5) These provide evidence that as late as 1965 more than 25 percent of the city's households received nutritionally inadequate diets (a condition apparently stemming more from low incomes than from a lack of nutritional education).

Finally, a later ILO study found that:(6)

1. The country's urban/rural dichotomy was an important determinant of income expenditure inequality (and more so than were geographic disparities).
2. Apart from Tehran where inequality is the highest, income appeared to be distributed more equally in large rather than small cities. However, taken together, urban areas showed a higher degree of inequality than rural areas.
3. The urban/rural disparities tended to be higher in the southwestern regions (where natural resources were poor) and lower in the northwestern regions (where natural resources were richer).
4. Both the status and sector of employment accounted for larger portions of income inequality than the urban/rural division.

5. The employment patterns were more important in the urban than rural areas in accounting for income disparities.
6. Incomes tended to be most concentrated among households with employers as heads (as opposed to those headed by government workers, self-employed workers, or wage and salary earners).
7. Inequality appeared to be higher in the less labor intensive sectors (manufacturing and services) than in the more labor intensive sectors (construction and agriculture).

In sum, the picture obtained from these initial studies is one of the country's income disparities being determined to a greater extent by the type of employment than by geographic location. Type of employment apparently played a larger role in the urban areas, while regional factors were more important in the rural sections of the country.

Bank Markazi initiated studies on income distribution for the government and found substantial changes in the distribution of income from 1959 onwards.(7) The bank's raw data was for urban expenditures, and this shows the Gini coefficient of inequality increasing throughout most of the 1959-74 period: in 1959-60 the coefficient was 0.4552, increasing to 0.4945 in 1973-74. In 1971-72 the Gini value was exceptionally high at 0.5051.

These studies show that the process which contributed to the growing inequality was one involving shifts in the percentage shares of total expenditures of the three major groups of households. The bank's analysis shows:

1. The income share of the bottom 40 percent of households decreased from 13.90 percent in 1959-60 to 11.65 percent in 1971/72 (but gradually reversed its trend in the following years).
2. The share of the top 20 percent continually increased from the already high level of 51.99 percent in 1959-60 to an extremely high value of 55.56 percent in 1973-74.
3. The share of total consumption for the middle expenditure group steadily decreased from 34.31 percent in 1959-60 to 32.48 percent in 1973-74.

There appears to have been a structural change in the pattern of the urban distribution in 1971-72. Prior to that time, increasing inequality was associated with a steady shift in expenditures from the middle and bottom groups to the top group. However, after 1971-72, middle expenditure groups seem to have lost ground to both the top and bottom income groups. Unfortunately, Bank Markazi figures include only urban households. Some comparisons with rural groups can, however, be made with data compiled by the Plan and Budget Organization (PBO).

The PBO results indicate that expenditure distribution was substantially and uniformly less concentrated among the rural (than urban) households.(8) In part, this result is to be expected simply because rural household expenditures are mainly on basic requirements, the distribution of which has a low variance. In terms of trends, the share of total expenditures of both the top 20 percent and the bottom 40 percent of rural income groups increased initially (table 13.1). After 1970-71, however, the distributional pattern seems to have changed (as indicated by the rise of the share of the middle expenditure group accompanied by a decline of the share of the top group and a mixed trend for the bottom group). Overall, the pattern of the Gini coefficients seem to indicate that rural inequality generally increased despite the rising share of the middle expenditure group.

Table 13.1. Distribution of Consumption Expenditures in Rural Areas

Year	Share of Bottom 40 Percent	Share of Middle 40 Percent	Share of Top 20 Percent	GINI Coefficient
1969-70	18.03	37.09	44.88	0.3559
1970-71	18.17	35.98	45.85	0.3685
1971-72	17.55	36.78	45.67	0.3899
1972-73	18.40	38.01	43.59	0.3659

Sources: Household Budget Surveys, Statistical Center of Iran, Plan and Budget Organization; M. H. Pesavan, "Income Distribution and its Major Determants in Iran" Tehran, Bank Markazi (August 1975) Table 4, p. 8. (Mimeo).

Another pattern of importance is that of urban/rural disparities. Apparently the gap between these groups substantially widened during the period 1959-72, with the average consumption per head in the urban areas (which was about twice that of the rural areas in 1959-60) growing to more than three times by 1971-72.

Together with the Bank Markazi surveys for the urban areas, the PBO surveys for the rural areas present a fairly clear picture of growing inequality during the country's high growth years of the 1960s and early 1970s.

Realistically, there is not enough data of sufficient quality to make a definitive statement as to which of the general explanations may be most applicable. One factor that does stand out is that the widening urban/rural gap was closely accompanied by decreasing productivity in the agricultural sector relative to that of the non-agricultural sector. The ration of gross domestic product per economically active member of agriculture relative to non-agriculture sectors generally increased during the period 1959-72. This pattern was in line with the movement of the urban/rural consumption ratio (table 13.2).

Table 13.2. Urban-Rural Consumption Ratios

Year	Ratio
1959-60	2.13
1960-61	2.20
1961-62	2.14
1962-63	2.16
1963-64	2.18
1964-65	2.09
1965-66	2.00
1966-67	2.25
1967-68	2.35
1969-69	2.50
1969-70	2.60
1970-71	2.79
1971-72	3.06

Source: Bank Markazi Iran, National Income of Iran (1959-72).

The deterioration of agriculture's terms of trade was undoubtedly a major cause of the increased urban/rural income disparity. What evidence there is shows that the quantity of agricultural goods necessary for exchange with a fixed amount of nonagricultural products increased throughout the years under consideration.

Yet another factor which may help to explain the increasing disparity between urban and rural households was the disproportionate allocation of development expenditures among the various sectors. As noted earlier, the development budget of the Fourth Five Year Plan, for example, allocated only 13.5 percent of its total to agriculture (while simultaneously spending 66.0 percent on industry).

The distribution of assets must have also been a prime determinant of both the level and trend in the country's income distribution. The land reform program (initiated in 1962) and the subsequent completion of the third stage of the land redistribution seems on the surface to contradict this conclusion. An examination of the pattern of credit and other forms of government assistance show that these programs tended to benefit the richer rural groups relative to the poorer. For example, the average rural cooperative loan was about 3,000 rials in 1963-64. By 1972-73, however, it was more than 8,500 rials (table 13.3). Similarly, the average amount loaned by the Agricultural Cooperative Bank quadrupled during the same period (from about 10,000 rials in 1963-64 to more than 50,000 rials in 1972-73) suggesting that, increasingly, the richer farmers obtained the bulk of rural credits.

Of particular importance is the fact that recent analyses appear, contrary to Marxist belief, to have established that poverty did not increase in Iran during the 1970s prior to the revolution.(9) This conclusion is based on a poverty definition adopted by the World Bank placing Iranian poverty at below US $800/household/year or 5,050 rials per month in 1971. Between 1971-72 and 1975-76, the Iranian consumer price index rose by 50 percent so that the poverty in nominal figures had risen to 7,575 rials per month by the latter period. On this basis, both the percentage and total amount of poor households diminished considerably; in 1971-72 about 54 percent of households could be classified as poor, declining to 28 percent in 1975-76. The corresponding percentages for urban households were, respectively, 34 percent and 15 percent. For rural households the corresponding rates were 68 and 41 percent, respectively. As a result, middle income households in rural areas increased from 30 to 53 percent, and rich households in urban areas from 8 to 17 percent.(10)

Table 13.3. Average Size of Agriculture Loans
(Rials)

Year	Rural Co-operatives Corporation	Agriculture Co-operating Bank
1963-64	3,338	10,709
1964-65	4,359	6,851
1965-66	4,816	10,000
1966-67	8,988	20,672
1967-68	6,058	15,866
1968-69	6,821	15,028
1969-70	6,816	15,471
1970-71	6,992	42,024
1971-72	7,776	41,125
1972-73	8,579	54,681

Source: Ministry of Co-operatives and Rural Affairs.

CONCLUSIONS

In sum, while one might make a good case for an increasing disparity of income during the 1960s and 1970s, there is no evidence of increasing poverty. Quite the contrary, poverty seems to have lessened somewhat dramatically during the 1970s.

14 Economic Factors in the Iranian Revolution

INTRODUCTION

In recent years, social scientists have subjected the relatively unchartered area of internal political unrest to intensive study in an attempt to identify and quantify those factors which appear to ultimately manifest themselves in unrest and eventual revolution. In this regard, explanations for the Iranian Revolution seem to have run along at least five main lines.(1)

1. The cause of political unrest in the country stemmed from one or more sociological traits or political factors interspersed occasionally with insights taken from administrative theory.(2)
2. Psychological, future shock, mass alienation were the chief causes.(3)
3. Quantitative links between specific factors such as military spending are considered as explanatory variables of increasing discontent.(4)
4. Descriptive-historical explanations contending that the unavailability of advanced quantitative methods and/or sufficient data made other approaches unrealistic.(5)
5. The cause of the revolution can be explained by Marxist class-exploitation theories, whereby extreme poverty and economic hardships suffered by the masses brought mass political opposition and convinced even the conservative clergy that they must support the people against the regime.(6)

These approaches have provided valuable insights into the decline of the Pahlavi regime. Still, they all seem to be built on some form of tautological argument; i.e., the revolution occurred because all of the conditions for revolution were present. How do we know they were present? Because the revolution occurred. Perhaps the nature and complexity of the problem will inevitably reduce most explanations to this sort of form.

It is possible that we will never fully understand the roots of Iran's revolution, but in the search for understanding, we should not fall into traps of believing that a fundamentally tautological relationship has really "explained" anything, or of tunnel vision of single sources - Islamic revival, arms transfers, political repression, and so on, as even partial explanations of the revolution.

Recognizing these problems, the previous chapters should be viewed as a preliminary attempt in determining to what extent economic factors can be considered as prime contributing elements in affecting political unrest in Iran.

ECONOMIC EXPLANATIONS OF THE REVOLUTION

Implicit in this approach is the assumption that economic well-being rather than poverty per se was a fundamental motive for political action in general and manifest political unrest in particular. It should be noted that this hypothesis claims neither the primacy nor the exclusivity of economic factors as determinants of Iran's political unrest; it merely asserts their importance.

The hypothesis that the process of economic growth is related to sociopolitical unrest has been supported by research on other countries. In his analysis of some of the problems that are associated with economic growth, especially when it is rapid, Mancur Olson has suggested that both gainers and losers from economic growth may act as destabilizing influences because their position in the social order is changing.(7) Furthermore, he has argued that:

> The assumption that economic growth ameliorates social discontent is in addition to its other shortcomings weakened by the fact that there is no necessary connection between rapid economic growth and short run increases in the incomes of the mass of the people. And even when the incomes of the mass of the people are increasing, it does not follow that their standard of living is increasing, for the increased rate of saving concomitant with economic growth may reduce the level of consumption.(8)

Income distribution would seem to be the most logical variable to use in correlating economic factors with political violence.

The data for Iran, besides being somewhat suspect, are not complete for the 1970s. In addition, different sources tend to give a somewhat different picture of both the levels of and changes in inequality over time.

Movements in the balance of payments is another variable that has been suggested in predicting political violence.(9) The advantage of the balance of payments as a variable stems from the fact that its change from year to year is dependent upon a number of external (e.g., foreign investment loans) and domestic (e.g., production of export items, budget) factors. Thus, it should be a relatively sensitive measure of the country's economic life. Presumably, when the balance of payments was not at a satisfactory level, pressures (often external) forced the government to respond with some sort of stabilization program.

The usual steps taken by the government were harsh and included: (1) increases in taxation; (2) budgetary cutbacks, particularly for development spending; (3) ending of protective subsidies and other trade "distortions," import and export regulations of both goods and money; and (4) generally, a global shift of the economy from an inflationary to a deflationary gap. The effect of these steps was to cut back the level of economic activity. The end product was often unemployment, shortage of consumer goods, decreased income after taxes, decreased welfare, and continued rise in the cost of living over the short run (both because of the lag time in the inflationary process and because of subsidy cutbacks and import restrictions).

From the discussion in previous chapters (especially chapters 2, 8, and 11) when used together with the cost of living index, movements in the balance of payments might be expected to give a fairly good indicator of impending political violence. One would imagine sociopolitical unrest in Iran to have been the greatest when a peak in the cost of living was coincident with a balance of payments trough. Kazemi has confirmed this pattern for Iran.(10) Using a measure of political violence defined to include mutual and collective coercion - such political assassinations, coups d'etat, demonstrations, strikes, riots, and other similar acts - Kazemi found a correlation for the period 1946-68 between the peak in the cost of living and a trough in the balance of payments, on the one hand, and political violence, on the other.

Clearly, this result is suggestive of the nature of the impact economic movements had in Iran before the revolution. It should also be noted, however, that the type and quality of political violence measured by Kazami were likely influenced by intervening variables and other factors. In the first place, a downward turn of the economy would not be expected to affect the whole population equally. At certain times, the primary burden of economic hardship may have been borne by those who were either least inclined to express their discontent in violent terms or did not have collective or organizational means at their disposal for such expression. Secondly, the magnitude of political violence is likely to have been dependent also upon the nature of the government's response to economic hardship and the degree of legitimacy which it enjoyed among the population at the time. On those occasions (such as in the late 1960s) when the regime appeared to make a concerted effort to remedy economic ills and was viewed by the majority as legitimate, the final magnitude of political violence was likely to be significantly less. Finally, there were certain political clashes resulting in violence which appear to be based purely on political rather than economic reasons. For example, the 1956 series of tribal clashes with the central government were probably unrelated to the economy's performance at the time.(11)

Clearly, therefore, econometric studies by themselves are not capable of explaining the severity of the 1977-78 violence and eventual revolution. On the other hand, a summary of the answers to the five major questions raised in the introduction:

1. What precisely was the Iranian development strategy--including its ideological foundations, rationale, and method of implementation?
2. What were the country's major economic goals?
3. What problems did the development strategy create before 1973?
4. What were the origins of the economic problems caused by the strategy and oil boom after 1973?
5. How did these problems interact to reduce the ability of the government to manage the economy?

and dealt with at length in the preceding chapters seem to provide a fairly complete explanation as to the severity of the tensions building up in the country during the 1970s.

DEVELOPMENT STRATEGY GOALS

In large part, the government's approach to the country's economic development relied on borrowing techniques, methods, and solutions that have been successful in other countries. In this regard, the authorities should have been more aware of the fallacy of eclecticism, i.e., the assumption that countries can borrow freely bits and pieces that are alleged to have been successful in other settings. Although these economies - the United States in particular - seldom are consistent in all regards, their objectives, programs, and policies tend to have certain coherent or internal logic which clearly made it difficult for Iran to benefit from their experience, particularly given that many of the Iranian regime's objectives were radically different.

In terms of the three major development strategies open to countries(12) - technocratic, reformist, and radical - it is fair to say that Iran followed the technocratic approach to development. The government's prime economic objective under the prerevolutionary regime was to increase output, either by inducing industrialists and landowners to incorporate more conventional inputs such as capital equipment in their productive processes, or, as was the case in many industries, encouraging the adoption of improved technology. Until the early 1970s at least, the country's economic system was justified essentially in terms of a liberal capitalist ideology, with the government implicitly assuming that private property, competition, and free markets were sufficient conditions (together with state investment in key sectors and infrastructure) for achieving its major economic objectives. In practice, property ownership was highly concentrated and this was reflected in the movement toward large corporate farms and various types of tenancy arrangements.

In this system, the benefits of technical change and higher output accrue, at least in the first instance, to the owners of property. Inequality of income, far from being deplored, was welcomed, since the authorities seemed to assume that the rich would save a large proportion of their extra income and, thereby, contribute to faster accumulation and growth. In other words, the concentration of income and wealth was one of the ways whereby the output objective was expected to be achieved.

Clearly, the regime rejected the radical strategy since it is largely supported by the ideology of socialism. The objective of this strategy is first and foremost to achieve rapid social change and a redistribution of political power. Next in priority comes a redistribution of wealth and income (in that order), and lastly higher production. In short, the objectives of the radical strategy involve greater mass participation, economic equality, and faster growth. No conflict is seen by its advocates between the first two objectives; indeed, they are merely viewed as different aspects of the same thing (and these, in turn, need not conflict with the third). If there is a conflict, however, most radicals would prefer that the growth objective give way to the quest for social, political, and economic equality.

Finally, a reformist strategy or compromise between the two extremes' positions could have been adopted. In general, reformist governments tend to place priority on redistributing income to some sections of the community and, accordingly, attribute a lower priority than the technocratic strategy to increasing output. Attempts are made to reconcile greater equity with faster growth through various institutional changes. The government's apparent lack of concern over income distributional issues and its preoccupation with growth rates per se justify its classification as technocratic.

In retrospect, the government should have had a relatively easy time in meeting its economic objectives through the use of a more reformist strategy. More precisely, recent analyses(13) utilizing a macroeconomic model and input-output framework(14) have shown that reducing the disparity of income (in terms of the Gini coefficient) during the 1970s would have increased the country's average propensity to consume at the expense of the average propensity to save. The net result would have led to a higher gross domestic product as well as higher employment or lower underemployment and unemployment. In terms of the composition of output, the demand for agricultural products and processed food would most likely have shown a significant increase. This would, in turn, have lowered underemployment in rural areas (under the assumption that the domestic output and not imports of food would increase).

On the other hand, a more equal distribution of income would have probably slowed down the expansion of services (due to the reduction in income of the rich). While the model gave large-scale industry (and in particular heavy industry) using imported modern technology little chance of creating significant employment opportunities for the redundant unskilled labor force, it was found that there was ample scope for large establishments creating new markets for small-scale (labor-intensive) industry.

The net result of a more equal distribution of income in favor of the middle income classes was to generate sufficient demand for self-propelled growth in the consumer goods industry. Such development of domestic market for industrial products would most likely create better preconditions for a diversification of exports which, at the time, depended too much on the production of crude oil. The general conclusion of these studies is that, in the short or even medium term, it is unlikely that industrialization stimulated by broadly based demand (through income redistribution) would be sufficient in and of itself to solve the country's employment problems. In the long term, however, industrialization appeared to be the only way to create enough jobs for the large number of young people who would appear on the labor market.(15)

One reason that growth would have likely been accelerated under a reformist type income redistribution scheme stems from the fact that Iran was one of the few populated developing countries which could carry out an industrialization program without a foreign exchange constraint. This situation was in marked contrast to most developing countries at a similar level of development where income redistribution could have reduced growth due to increased import demand.(16) The technocratic strategy would seem to make the most sense in a country such as Brazil where the government, given a limited tax base, would be forced to rely on increased private savings for the bulk of investment funds.

Oil revenues, as in Iran's case, should have made it unnecessary to tolerate increased inequality on the grounds of resource mobilization. The adaption of the technocratic model to the Iranian situation, while consistent with the regime's ideology, was clearly unwise in light of the unnecessary inequalities and dislocation it caused. In addition, whatever the relative theoretical merits or limitations of the technocratic strategy, the government planners proved incapable within its framework of dealing with the problems presented by:

- a real decline in oil revenues beginning in 1977, with a decline in output projected to occur in the mid-1980s, and little prospect of finding alternative sources of foreign exchange on a comparable scale;
- an inefficient bureaucracy, without a proper planning apparatus, replete with corruption and an inability to implement equitable social and economic reforms;
- low productivity in the industrial sector, rendering Iranian manufactured goods noncompetitive on international markets, and unending reliance of both public and private industrial sectors on government funding;
- a continually growing inequality in incomes, within urban areas and between urban and rural populations;
- a real decline in agricultural production necessitating massive food imports and controls;
- an ever increasing defense budget necessary to sustain and modernize existing military forces and support the Shah's foreign policies;
- a return to balance of payments and fiscal deficits, with little prospect of future revenue surpluses due to overly ambitious development plans and rapidly increasing current expenditures.

The failures of many government policies have been documented in the previous chapters. For the man in the street, the end result is summed up in the following statement.

> Nobody really believed that the government had a firm grip on economic matters any longer. "It's a crisis of confidence," remarked one Iranian. "I mean, the confidence of the people in the Government. If the person telling you that agriculture is all-important is the same person who told you yesterday that industry was all-important, why should you believe him?"(17)

PROBLEMS CREATED BY THE TECHNOCRATIC STRATEGY

Even before 1973, many of the tensions that eventually led to the demise of the regime could be traced to the mindless implementation of the technocratic strategy. For example, in the 1960s, many Iranian planners began subscribing to the theory that traditional industries could only be developed by replacing their existing production processes with Western-type techniques. Yet, the cost of such modernization was often overlooked, even though, in many cases, the expense and waste were obvious to the most casual observer. One striking and unfortunately typical example occurred in 1972 when it was decided to modernize Tehran's bakeries. This was to be accomplished not only by mechanizing traditional breadmaking but by replacing local bread with French baguettes and English processed bread. Iranian consumer's tastes were apparently totally ignored in this decision, as were the dietary merits of the traditional bread, which was unquestionably superior to its European equivalents. The closure of the existing small bakeries would mean the loss of 12,000 bakery workers' jobs; and, given the fact that each Iranian worker had an average of four dependents, a maximum of 50,000 people could have been affected. Fortunately, however, only half these jobs were lost, because many Iranians chose to eat the bread they were used to and refused to purchase the new bread.(18)

This incident highlights the country's problems in technology transfer. There is little doubt that the planners' insensitivity to traditional tastes in their drive for sweeping modernization prompted a reaction among the people. This led to anti-Western feelings being expressed and may be a factor in the Islamic revival as well as a possible cause of the widespread unrest and discontent. The focus of this discontent was often the city bazaar where workers and residents increasingly felt their existence threatened by technological progress and the Westernization of traditional life.(19)

In general, the Iranian experience seems to indicate that:

- technological change is not identical to progress, and the latter has little meaning unless values are specified;
- scant progress occurred in many sectors of the economy in the sense that inequality did not diminish and the income of many individuals increased in general only slightly and in many cases not at all;
- because of the narrow class or factional support on which the government depended, the range within which policies could be varied were, in fact, rather restricted; and
- those groups which were harmed by technical change tried to protect their interests first by operating through existing institutions and, when that was unsuccessful, outside the established law.

Similarly, the consequences of the government's stabilization strategy in 1977 led to mass alienation resulting from the following:

- The construction industry, a major source of employment for unskilled rural labor, underwent a severe contraction. Rural migrants as a whole suffered the greatest decline in living standards because of inflation, food shortages, and the need to use a large portion of their income for rents.
- The bazaar merchants, dependent on state credits to finance many of their activities and thereby affected by inflation, came to feel their economic role in society increasingly threatened by the regime's development strategy, a strategy that was perceived by them as openly hostile and one designed to reduce their upward social mobility.
- Small industrialists joined by the merchants expressed their opposition to price controls; antiprofiteering campaigns and a plethora of government decrees placed limits on their incomes and stifled any possibilities they might have for socioeconomic advancement.

CONCLUSIONS

The great majority of people who offer economic advice to governments assume that the economic system is self-equilibrating and that there is a basic harmony of interests among the individuals and groups who comprise the system. When interests diverge, it is assumed that they can be reconciled relatively easily through minor policy adjustments, and when the system moves out of equilibrium, it is assumed that automatic forces tend to restore it to the previous position. This vision of the economic system is strongly entrenched in economic theory. It is reflected in Adam Smith's benevolent "hidden hand" which reconciles private self-interest with the general welfare; and in Alfred Marshall's theory of markets which expounds the calculus of an optimizing self-adjusting economy.

The Iranian experience seems a clear exception to this general view. In Iran's case, it is safe to assume a number of interests were in conflict - the government, many smaller industrialists, various agricultural groups, and of course the religious groups. Clearly, many of these conflicts were long standing. With no automatic adjustments in sight, it appears the policy options were seen by the government (especially during periods of increasing balance of payments deficits and/or inflationary pressures) in terms of which groups were to be favored. In addition, there was no observable tendency for a countervailing power to arise when one group found itself at a disadvantage vis a vis another. With the possibility of cumulative movements quite high, those who were harmed by change naturally attempted to respond.

15 Conclusions

Realistically, any study of this sort cannot be completely devoid of judgmental elements. On the basis of the analysis in the previous chapters, it appears that:

1. The Pahlavi regime's concern for upgrading the lot of the majority of Iranians was genuine.
2. The development strategy followed by the government was sound from a theoretical point of view.
3. However, given the limited information on the nature of economic forces at work and the impossibility of closely monitoring most macroeconomic developments, the strategy was of an extremely high risk.
4. The implementation of the strategy was ill-conceived with few of the institutional reforms for its necessary success actually made.
5. The failure of the strategy was due in part to its initial success and the inability of the government to recognize the extent of the resentment generated by the short-run inequities and dislocations caused by the economic programs associated with the strategy.

The strategy referred to the need to complete major investments in infrastructure and in the industrial sector by the time oil revenues ran down in the 1990s. The creation of a prosperous, healthy, literate, well-housed, and largely (90 percent) urban society was the strategy's ultimate objective with industry emerging as the employer of perhaps 40 percent of the labor force. If successful the strategy anticipated that: (1) the industrial sector would be bolstered through its performance as an export sector, while agriculture was expected to move rapidly toward the goal of 80 percent self-sufficiency in foodstuffs by 1992; (2) agriculture would be completely transformed by the 1990s with only a small proportion (10-15 percent) of the labor force employed there; (3) the dislocations associated with rural to urban migration would have become a thing of the past; and (4) with most of the population situated in urban areas, a national demographic transition would have been well underway.(1)

One of the main reasons for the failure of the development strategy was that there were several conceptual deficiencies surrounding the country's development plans, in particular, there was a lack of any relationship between development objectives and programs and current policy problems. In disequilibrium economies suffering from inflation, this relationship can only be established by integrating stabilization and development programs and policies. Such integration in Iran appears to have been obstructed by those in the government who believed inflation was a temporary phenomenon which could and should be allowed to decelerate. When that approach did not work, shock therapy with all of its consequent ramifications was tried.

It has been argued in the previous chapters that the economic and institutional distortions introduced by inflation in Iran were so serious that permanent solutions could only be achieved by coherent and persistent action on a broad policy front over a sufficiently long period of time. Development plans and programs should have been constrained by stabilization programs.

Unfortunately, existing planning models and techniques were not particularly suitable for this purpose. The relationships between financial and growth variables were not specified in these models, and existing planning models did not take into account the problems of timing and uncertainty which were crucial elements in controlling Iran's inflationary pressures. Instead of a coherent, consistent, and integrated growth-stabilization plan, the government operated on a short-run crisis management approach toward the economy.

By this time, a number of possible connections between developments in the economy and the deterioration in popular support for the regime should be apparent. Of the factors listed above, the deterioration of income distribution would seem to be the key in explaining the mass discontent that erupted in 1977-78.

Notes

CHAPTER 1

1. George Lenczowski, "Iran: The Awful Truth," The American Spectator (December 1979), p. 12.

2. Farid Abolfathi et al., The OPEC Market to 1985 (Lexington, Mass.: Lexington Books, 1977), p. 109.

3. Martin Zonis, "He Took All the Credit, Now He Gets All the Blame," New York Times (Jan. 14, 1979), p. 27.

4. Lenczowski, "Iran: The Awful Truth."

5. Robert Looney, A Development Strategy for Iran Through the 1980s (New York: Praeger, 1977), Ch. 4.

6. Fred Halliday, "Iran: The Economic Contradictions," MERIP Reports (July - August 1978), p. 13.

7. Bank Markazi Iran, Annual Report, 1978.

8. Ibid.

9. Fred Halliday, Iran: Dictatorship and Development (New York: Penguin Books, 1979), p. 173.

10. Julian Bharier, Economic Development in Iran 1900-1970 (London: Oxford University Press, 1971), p. 140-41.

11. Fred Halliday, Iran: Dictatorship and Development, p. 173.

12. Nikki Keddie, "Oil, Economic Policy, and Social Conflict in Iran," Race and Class (1979), pp. 13-29.

13. James Petras and Morris Morley, "Development and Revolution: Contradictions in the Advanced Third World Countries -

Brazil, South Africa and Iran," Studies in Comparative International Development (Spring 1981), pp. 31-33.

14. New York Times Magazine (Dec. 17, 1978), pp. 134-35.

15. Robert Looney, Income Distribution Policies and Economic Growth in Semi-Industrialized Countries (New York: Praeger, 1975), p. 97.

16. Bank Markazi Iran, Annual Report, 1979, p. 15.

17. Ruth Sivard, World Military and Social Expenditures (Leesburg, Va.: World Priorities, 1980), p. 22.

18. New York Times (Jan. 14, 1979), p. 2.

19. New York Times (Dec. 2, 1979), p. 3.

20. Yair Hirschfeld, "Decline and Fall of the Pahlavis," The Jerusalem Quarterly (Summer 1979), pp. 20-33.

21. Ibid., p. 31.

22. See for example Dudley Seers, "A Theory of Inflation and Growth in Underdeveloped Economies Based on the Experience of Latin America," Oxford Economic Papers (June 1962) for a description of the structuralist approach.

CHAPTER 2

1. The first three periods are those identified by the former Iranian Minister of State in Charge of Planning and Budget, Abdol-Majid Majidi, in his "Iran 1980-85: Problems and Challenges of Development," The World Today (July 1977), p. 267.

2. Farhad Daftary, "Development Planning in Iran: A Historical Survey," Iranian Studies (Autumn 1973), p. 177.

3. Cf. A. Banani, The Modernization of Iran: 1921-1941 (Stanford, Calif.: Stanford University Press, 1961), Ch. 7.

4. A. K. S. Lambton, "Persia," Journal of the Royal Central Asian Society (January 1944), p. 14.

5. See particularly George Baldwin, Planning and Development in Iran (Baltimore: Johns Hopkins University Press, 1967), Ch. 2.

6. Henry Bruton, "Notes on Development in Iran," Economic Development and Cultural Change (July 1961), pp. 625-29.

7. Ibid.

8. Jahangir Amuzegar, "Iran's Economic Planning Once Again," Middle East Economic Papers (1957), p. 3.

9. Ibid., p. 4.

10. A. Waterson, *Development Planning: Lessons of Experience* (Baltimore: Johns Hopkins University Press, 1956), pp. 61-63.

11. Daftary, "Development Planning in Iran," p. 82.

12. P. Bjorn Olsen and N. Norregaard Rasmussen, "An Attempt at Planning in a Traditional State: Iran," in *Planning Economic Development*, edited by E. Hagen (Homewood, Ill.: Richard D. Irwin, 1963), pp. 227-28.

13. Cf. Bruton, "Notes on Development in Iran," for an excellent, detailed discussion of these points.

14. Baldwin, *Planning and Development in Iran*, p. 58.

15. William Bartsch, "The Impact of the Oil Industry on the Economy of Iran," in *Foreign Investment in the Petroleum and Mineral Industries*, edited by Raymond F. Mikesell (Baltimore: Johns Hopkins University Press, 1971), pp. 256-57.

16. Amuzegar, "Iran's Economic Planning," p. 5.

17. Bruton, "Notes on Development in Iran," p. 640.

18. Thomas Walton, "Economic Development and Revolutionary Upheavals in Iran," *Cambridge Journal of Economics* (September 1980), p. 278.

CHAPTER 3

1. Plan Organization, *Review of the Second Seven Year Plan* (Tehran, 1960), pp. 15-18.

2. Bank Markazi Iran, *Annual Report*, various issues.

3. Nasrollah Vagar, "Economic Development in Iran and the Financing of the Gap in the Third Plan," *Middle East Economic Papers* (1964), p. 111.

4. Farhad Daftary, "Development Planning in Iran: A Historical Survey," *Iranian Studies* (Autumn 1973), p. 18.

5. Thomas Walton, "Economic Development and Revolutionary Upheavals in Iran," *Cambridge Journal of Economics* (September 1980), p. 278.

6. Nasrollah Vagar, "An Analysis of Iran's Foreign Trade and the Causes of the Stagnation of Its Exports," *Middle East Economic Papers* (December 1969), p. 91.

7. Ibid., p. 103.

8. This is an expanded version of Avramovie's list; cf., Dragoslav Avramovie, "Industrialization of Iran: The Records,

the Problems and the Prospects," Tahqiqat-e eqtesadi (Spring 1970), pp. 14-47.

9. Computed from Ministry of Economy, Annual Industrial Survey, various issues.

10. Cf. C. Michalopoulos, "Interindustry Relations, External Economies and Regional Economic Development," in Industrial Location and Regional Development, Proceedings of an Interregional Seminar, Minsk, August 14-26, 1968 (New York: United Nations, 1971).

11. R. L. Chawla, "Economic Development of Iran," India Quarterly (April/July 1979), p. 168.

12. Ibid., p. 170.

13. Walton, "Economic Development and Revolutionary Upheavals in Iran," p. 280.

14. George Baldwin, Planning and Development in Iran (Baltimore: Johns Hopkins University Press, 1967), p. 138.

CHAPTER 4

1. Ann Schultz, "Iran's New Industrial State," Current History (January 1977), p. 18.

2. An example based on M. A. Katouzian, "Oil Versus Agriculture: A Case of Dual Resource Depletion in Iran," The Journal of Peasant Studies (April 1978), p. 362. Also see his excellent discussion of agriculture's problems in The Political Economy of Modern Iran: 1926-1979 (London: Macmillan, 1981), Ch. 15.

3. Abdolmajid Majidi, "Iran 1980-1985: Problems and Challenges of Development," The World Today (July 1977), p. 268.

4. Nikki Keddie, "Oil, Economic Policy and Social Conflict in Iran," Race and Class (Summer 1979), p. 24.

5. Farhad Khamsi, "Land Reform in Iran," Monthly Review (June 1969), p. 21.

6. Ibid., p. 22.

7. M. A. Katouziam, "Land Reform in Iran: A Case Study in the Political Economy of Social Engineering," Journal of Peasant Studies (June 1974), p. 228.

8. A. K. S. Lambton, The Persian Land Reform: 1962-1966 (Oxford: Oxford University Press, 1969), p. 147.

9. M. Parvin and A. Zamani, "Political Economy of Growth and Distribution: A Statistical Interpretation of the Iranian Case," Iranian Studies (Winter-Spring 1979), p. 51.

10. Hossein Askari, John Cummings and Bassam Harik, "Land Reform in the Middle East: A Note on Its Redistributive Effect," Iranian Studies (Autumn 1977), pp. 267-79.

11. Thomas Walton, "Economic Development and Revolutionary Upheavals in Iran," Cambridge Journal of Economics (September 1980), pp. 280-81.

12. Leonard Binder, "Iran," in Joint Economic Committee, Congress of the United States, The Political Economy of the Middle East: 1973-1978 (Washington: U.S. Congress, 1980), pp. 163-64.

13. For an excellent account of this analysis see Grace Goodell, "How the Shah De-Stabilized Himself," Policy Review (Spring 1981), pp. 55-72.

14. Cf. M. A. Katouziam, pp. 358-61.

15. D. Craig, "Thc Impact of Land Reform on an Iranian Village," The Middle East Journal (1978), p. 153.

16. Keddie, "Oil, Economic Policy and Social Conflict in Iran," p. 25.

17. See, for example, the excellent study by O. Aresvick, The Agricultural Development of Iran (New York: Praeger, 1976) for details of these policies.

18. Business International, Operating in Iran (New York: Business International, 1977), p. 340.

19. Samuel Liberman, "Development and Population Growth in Iran," Population and Development Review (June 1979), pp. 302-03.

20. Ibid.

21. Cf. S. Thomas Stockley and B. Najafi, "The Effectiveness of Foreign Corporations in Iran," Tahqiqat-e eqtesadi (Winter 1971), pp. 18-28.

22. Parvin and Zamani, "Political Economy of Growth and Distribution."

23. Ibid.

24. James Bill, The Politics of Iran: Groups, Classes and Modernization (Columbus, Ohio: Charles Merrill, 1972), p. 146.

25. Binder, "Iran," p. 163.

26. Ibid.

CHAPTER 5

1. For an excellent critique of the relevance of neoclassical economics to understanding the problems of less developed countries, see Jeffrey Nugent and Pan Yotopoulos, "What Has Orthodox Development Economics Learned from Recent Experience?" World Development (June 1979), pp. 541-51.

2. For other descriptions of the country's macroeconomic trends, see Firouz Vakil, Determining Iran's Financial Surplus, 1352-1371 (Tehran: The Institute for International Political and Economic Studies, 1975); Ahmad Shahshahani and T. Malcolm Dowling, Jr., "An Econometric Model Forecast of Iran 1975-1985," The Journal of Energy and Development (Autumn 1976), pp. 148-62; W. A. Dellalfar and J. K. Shirazi, "An Analysis of the Dynamics of Growth in Iran: 1959-73," Journal of Economic Development (July 1979), pp. 143-70; Robert Looney, Iran at the End of the Century (Lexington, Mass.: Lexington Books, 1977); Robert Looney, A Development Strategy for Iran Through the 1980s (New York: Praeger, 1977); and Jahangir Amuzegar, Iran: An Economic Profile (Washington: The Middle East Institute, 1977).

3. Unless otherwise specified, the macroeconomic data used here is from the Bank Markazi Iran, Annual Report, various issues.

4. For a detailed description of this methodology and the assumptions that underlie it, see J. Vanek, Estimating Foreign Resource Needs (New York: McGraw-Hill, 1967).

5. A similar pattern occurred at the same time in Saudi Arabia. Cf. Arthur Smithies, The Economic Potential of the Arab Countries (Santa Monica, Calif.: Rand, 1978), p. 41.

6. The following adopts the methodology developed in Luis Landau, "Saving Functions in Latin America," in Studies in Development Planning, edited by Hollis B. Chenery (Cambridge, Mass.: Harvard University Press, 1971), pp. 316-19, to the Iran situation.

7. Ibid.

8. An excellent study along these lines is Ahmad Kader, "The Contribution of Oil Exports to Economic Development: A Study of the Major Oil Exporting Countries," The American Economist (Spring 1980), pp. 46-51.

9. H. Chenery and L. Taylor, "Development Patterns: Among Countries and Over Time," The Review of Economics and Statistics (November 1968), p. 396. See also H. Chenery, "Patterns of Industrial Growth," American Economic Review (September 1960), pp. 624-54.

10. Gobind Nankani, "Development Problems in Mineral Exporting Countries," World Bank Staff Working Paper No. 354 (August 1979), pp. 13-18.

11. Jeffrey Nugent, "Momentum for Development and Development Disequilibria," Journal of Economic Development (July 1977), pp. 31-52.

12. Ibid., pp. 35-36.

13. All data were from the World Bank, World Development Report, 1980 (New York: Oxford University Press, 1980).

14. For a technical description of the procedure and the computational methods used, see Michael R. Anderberg, Cluster Analysis for Applications (New York: Academic Press, 1973).

15. See, for example, Eprime Eshag, "Quantification of Disruptive Effects of Export Shortfalls," Tahqiqat-e eqtesadi (Winter 1971), pp. 29-64.

16. Ibid.

17. Nugent, "Momentum for Development," p. 36.

18. Ibid., pp. 36-48.

CHAPTER 6

1. For a discussion of the relative strength of petroleum linkages in different environments, see William Bartsch, "The Impact of the Oil Industry on the Economy of Iran," in Foreign Investment in the Petroleum and Mineral Industries, edited by R. F. Mikesell, (Baltimore: Johns Hopkins University Press, 1971), pp. 237-63; William Harris, "The Impact of the Petroleum Export Industry on the Pattern of Venezuelan Economic Development," in ibid., pp. 129-56; and Scott Pearson, Petroleum and the Nigerian Economy (Stanford, Calif.: Stanford University Press, 1970).

2. See E. J. Chambers and D. E. Gordon, "Primary Products and Economic Growth: An Empirical Measurement," Journal of Political Economy (August 1966); R. F. Emery, "The Relation of Exports and Economic Growth, Kyklos (1967); and M. H. Watkins, "The Staple Theory Revisited," Journal of Canadian Studies (Winter 1977).

3. Raymond Mikesell, "The Contribution of Petroleum and Mineral Resources to Economic Development," in Foreign Investment in the Petroleum and Mineral Industries, pp. 3-28.

4. See M. Ali Fekrat, "Growth of OPEC-Type Economies: A Preliminary Theoretical Inquiry," Economia Internazionale (February 1979), pp. 77-98.

5. Jahangir Amuzegar and M. Ali Fekrat, Iran: Economic Development Under Dualistic Conditions (Chicago: University of Chicago Press, 1971), Ch. 3.

6. Gobind Nankani, "Development Problems of Mineral Exporting Countries," World Bank Staff Working Papers, No. 354 (August 1979), p. 6.

7. Ibid., p. 7-8.

8. Farid Abolfathi et al., The OPEC Market to 1985 (Lexington, Mass.: Lexington Books, 1977), p. 112.

9. Fereidun Fesharaki, Revolution and Energy Policy in Iran (London: The Economist Intelligence Unit, 1980), pp. 15-16.

10. Harry Johnson, "The Ideology of Economic Policy in the New States," in Chicago Essays in Economic Development, edited by David Wall (Chicago: University of Chicago Press, 1972), p. 33.

11. Cf. Ahmad Kader, "The Contribution of Oil Exports to Economic Development," The American Economist (Spring 1980), pp. 48-49.

12. Saul Pleeter, Economic Impact Analysis: Methodology and Applications (Boston: Martinus Nijhoff, 1980), p. 11.

13. See also M. M. Metwally and H. V. Tamaschke, "Oil Exports and Economic Growth in the Middle East," Kyklos (1980) pp. 499-522, for an analysis of several other Middle Eastern countries.

14. Cf. L.M. Koyck, Distributed Lags and Investment Analysis (Amsterdam: North Holland, 1954) for a description of the procedure.

CHAPTER 7

1. Ragaei El Mallakh and Jacob Atta, The Absorptive Capacity of Kuwait (Lexington, Mass.: Lexington Books, 1981), p. 1.

2. Ibid., p. 2.

3. The classic work is John Adler, Absorptive Capacity, the Concept and Its Determinants (Washington, D.C.: Brookings Institution, 1965). See also Richard Eckaus, "Absorptive Capacity as a Constraint Due to Maturation Processes," in Development and Planning, edited by J. N. Bhagwati and R.

S. Eckaus (Cambridge, Mass.: MIT Press, 1973); and Taher El Jehaimi, "The Absorptive Capacity of Libya: A Constrained Expenditure Approach," The Journal of Energy and Development (Spring 1976), pp. 326-47.

4. Ahmad Shahshahani and Mihssen Kadhim, "Development Problems of an Energy Economy: Iran," Journal of South Asia and Middle East Studies (1979), p. 70.

5. Ibid., p. 68.

6. Firouz Vakil, "Iran's Basic Macroeconomic Problems: A Twenty Year Horizon," Economic Development and Cultural Change (July 1977), p. 716.

7. Christopher Gebelein, "Forecasting Absorptive Capacity for Oil Revenues: Practical Techniques for Policy Analysis," in U.S. and World Energy Resources: Prospects and Priorities, edited by Ragaei El Mallakh and Carl McGuire (Boulder, Colorado: International Research Center for Energy and Economic Development, 1977), p. 107.

8. M. A. Fekrat, "Growth of OPEC-Type Economies: A Preliminary Theoretical Inquiry," Economia Internazionale (February 1979), p. 82.

9. "The Shah's Americans: In Iran for Beaucoup Bucks," The Washington Post (May 12, 1977), p. A-10. Quoted in Farkat, "Growth of OPEC-Type Economies," p. 82.

10. Keith Griffin, Underdevelopment in Spanish America (Cambridge, Mass.: MIT Press, 1969), p. 132.

11. An approach somewhat similar to that developed in Taher El Jehaimi, "The Absorptive Capacity of Libya."

12. The limitations of the capital output ratio as a measure of productivity are well known. Cf. W. B. Reddaway, The Development of the Indian Economy (Homewood, Ill.: Richard D. Irwin, 1962), pp. 207-08; and especially Willy J. Stevens, Capital Absorptive Capacity in Developing Countries (Leiden, The Netherlands: A. W. Sijthoff, 1971).

13. A similar approach has been proposed by Ragaei El Mallakh and Mihssen Kadhim "Absorptive Capacity, Surplus Funds, and Regional Capital Mobility in the Middle East," Revista Internazionale di Scienze Economiche e Commerciali (April 1974), pp. 310-11.

14. Cf. T.Y. Shen, "Technological Diffusion, Substitution and Efficiency," Econometrica (March 1973).

15. A theme developed by M. Kaldor, Strategic Factors in Economic Development (Ithaca, N.Y.: Cornell University Press, 1967).

16. K. Arrow, "The Economic Implications of Learning by Doing," Review of Economic Studies (June 1962), pp. 155-73.

17. Cf. Edwin Luck, "Port Congestion," The Financial Times (July 28, 1975), p. 26; and Robert Graham, "Power Shortage Plays Havoc with Industry," The Financial Times (July 25, 1977), p. 15.

18. Robert Graham, "State A Barrier to Investment," The Financial Times (July 25, 1977), p. 17.

19. Cited in Graham, "Power Shortage."

20. Ibid.

21. H. Askari, J. T. Cummings, and G. Richter, "Efficiency of LDC Trading Patterns: The Case of Iran," American Economic Review (May 1979), pp. 191-95.

22. Ibid.

23. "Farming Lags Behind," The Financial Times (July 25, 1977), p. 19.

24. Ibid.

25. Fekrat, "Growth of OPEC-Type Economies," p. 83.

CHAPTER 8

1. Brian Griffiths, Inflation: The Price of Prosperity (New York: Holmes & Meier, 1976), p. 3.

2. Firouz Vakil, "Iran's Basic Macroeconomic Problems: A Twenty-Year Horizon," Economic Development and Cultural Change (July 1977), p. 722.

3. For a discussion of the Fisher theory as relevant for developing countries, see Milton Friedman, "Monetary Policy for a Developing Society," Bank Markazi, Iran, Bulletin (March-April 1971).

4. Bank Markazi, Iran, Annual Report, 1975 (Tehran: Bank Markazi, 1975), p. 69.

5. A partial list (including non-Iranians) together with their writings include: Nikki Keddie, "The Iranian Village Before and After Land Reform," Journal of Contemporary History (July 1968); and her "The Midas Touch: Black Gold, Economics and Politics in Iran Today," Iranian Studies, (August 1977), pp. 243-66; M.A. Katouzian The Political Economy of Modern Iran, 1926-1979 (London: Macmillan, 1981); M.A. Katouzian "Land Reform in Iran: A Case Study in the Political Economy of Social Engineering," Journal of Peasant Studies (January 1974), pp. 220-39; and H. Katouzim, "Oil Versus Agriculture:

A Case Study of Dual Resource Depletion in Iran," Journal of Peasant Studies (April 1978); and A. Ashraf, "Historical Obstacles to the Development of a Bourgeoisie in Iran," Iranian Studies (Spring-Summer 1979).

6. This framework has been developed in much more detail in the context of Latin America. See D. Seers, "A Theory of Inflation and Growth in Underdeveloped Economies Based on The Experience of Latin America," Oxford Economic Papers (June 1962); and R. F. Mikesell, "Inflation in Latin America," in Latin America: Problems in Economic Development, edited by C. Nisbet (New York: Free Press, 1969).

7. Cf. the references to H. Katouzim above.

8. C. H. Kirkpatrick and F. I. Nixson, "The Origins of Inflation in Less Developed Countries: A Selective Review," in Inflation in Open Economies, edited by Michael Parkin and George Zis (Manchester, England: Manchester University Press, 1976), p. 132.

9. Ibid.

10. Fred Halliday, "Iran: Trade Unions and the Working Class Opposition," MERIP Reports (October 1978), pp. 7-14.

11. As documented in Gail Cook Johnson, High-Level Manpower in Iran: From Hidden Conflict to Crisis (New York: Praeger, 1980).

12. Based on the models developed in H. Chenery and M. Bruno, "Development Alternatives in An Open Economy: The Case of Israel," Economic Journal (March 1962), pp. 79-103; and H. Chenery and A. Strout, "Foreign Assistance and Economic Development," American Economic Review (September 1966), pp. 679-733.

13. See Milton Iyoha, "Inflation and Openness in Less Developed Economies: A Cross Country Analysis," Economic Development and Cultural Change (October 1973), pp. 31-38. See, however, criticisms of this study in M. A. Akhtar, "An Empirical Note on Inflation and Openness in Less Developed Economies," The Philippine Economic Journal (1976), pp. 636-49; and Kirkpatrick and Nixson, "The Origins of Inflation," pp. 158-59.

14. Iyoha, "Inflation and Openness," p. 33.

15. Kirkpatrick and Nixson, "The Origins of Inflation," p. 158.

16. Ministry of Labor figures from Nicholas Cumming-Bruce, "Budget: Battling the Legacy of Overspending and Infrastructural Jams," Middle East Economic Digest, Special Report on Iran (February 1977), p. 5.

17. Ibid.

18. Robert Graham, "Time for Tighter Belts," The Financial Times, (July 25, 1977), p. 11.

19. Development Planning Division, ESCAP Secretariat, "The Iranian Economy: Oil Development in the First Half of the 1970s," Economic Bulletin for Asia and the Pacific (December 1978), p. 42.

20. Ibid.

21. Robert Graham, "State as a Barrier to Investment," The Financial Times (July 25, 1977), p. 12.

22. Several possible explanations for the movements in skill differential are given in International Labor Office, Employment and Income Policies for Iran (Geneva: ILO, 1973), p. 25-26.

23. Ibid., pp. 21-36.

24. See Nicholas Cumming-Bruce, "Ports and Transport," Middle East Economic Digest, Special Survey on Iran (February 1977), pp. 21-24.

25. Edwin Luck, "Port Congestion," The Financial Times (July 28, 1975), p. 26.

26. Development Planning Division, ESCAP Secretariat, "The Iranian Economy," p. 44.

27. Robert Graham, "Power Shortage Plays Havoc with Industry," The Financial Times (July 25, 1977), p. 15.

28. Ichiro Otani, "Inflation in An Open Economy: A Case Study of the Philippines," International Monetary Fund, Staff Papers (1975), pp. 750-74.

29. See E. J. Sheehey, "On the Measurement of Imported Inflation in Developing Countries," Weltwirtschaftliches Archiv (1979), pp. 68-79 for a critique of this method.

CHAPTER 9

1. For a clear, concise statement of the theory together with its contrast to other views on the inflationary process, see Harris Johnson, "Monetary Theory and Policy," American Economic Review (June 1962), pp. 335-84.

2. J. A. Schumpeter, The Theory of Economic Development: An Inquiry into Profits, Capital, Credit, Interest and the Business Cycle, translated version by Redvers Opie (Cambridge, Mass.: Harvard University Press, 1934).

3. For an early criticism of this narrow view of the development process, see Richard Benedick, Industrial Finance in Iran (Cambridge, Mass.: Harvard University Press, 1964).

4. Ibid., Chap. 7.

5. Here, monetarist will refer largely to the statements issued by the Bank Markazi, although the bank was quite careful in its official statements not to appear overly critical of the government and advocates of an alternative approach toward the country's development.

6. Cf. Jacob Frenkel and Harry Johnson, "The Monetary Approach to the Balance of Payments: Essential Concepts and Historical Origins," in The Monetary Approach to the Balance of Payments, edited by Jacob Frenkel and Harry Johnson (London: George Allen & Unwin, 1976), pp. 22-45.

7. M. Mussa, "A Monetary Approach to Balance of Payments Analysis," Journal of Money, Credit and Banking (August 1974), p. 338.

8. B. Putnam and D. Sykes Wilford, The Monetary Approach to International Adjustment (New York: Praeger, 1978), p. 74.

9. See also the evidence presented by Robert McNown and Myles Wallace, "International Reserve Flows of OPEC States: A Monetary Approach," The Journal of Energy and Development (Spring 1977), pp. 267-78.

10. A point developed and substantiated by Robert M. Dunn, "Exchange Rates, Payments Adjustments and OPEC: Why Oil Deficits Persist," Princeton Essays in International Finance (December 1979), pp. 15-17.

11. David Morgan, "Fiscal Policy in Oil Exporting Countries, 1972-78," International Monetary Fund, Staff Papers (March 1979), pp. 58-61.

12. The formulation used follows that developed by A. Harberger, "The Dynamics of Inflation in Chile," Measurement in Economics, edited by C. Christ (Stanford, Calif.: Stanford University Press, 1963), pp. 219-50.

13. Cf. Benedick, Industrial Finance in Iran.

14. R. McKinnon has developed a theory of monetary policy around this type of situation. See R. McKinnon, Money and Capital in Economic Development (Washington: Brookings Institution, 1973), p. 38.

CHAPTER 10

1. As done in David Morgan, "Fiscal Policy in Oil Exporting Countries, 1972-78," International Monetary Fund, Staff Papers (March 1979), pp. 55-86.

2. Farideh Mehran and Hamid Mehran, "Monetary Policies of the Oil Exporting Countries," Paper presented at the Western Economic Association Annual Meetings, San Francisco, July 4, 1981, p. 1.

3. An excellent discussion of this process is given in Jahangir Amuzegar, Iran: An Economic Profile (Washington: The Middle East Institute, 1977), Ch. 15.

4. The following sections summarizing monetary policy year by year have been culled from the Bank Markazi, Annual Reports. The specific policy actions on the part of the bank listed here are documented in those reports.

5. Ronald I. McKinnon, Money and Capital in Economic Development (Washington: The Brookings Institution, 1973).

6. Michael Bruno, "Stabilization and Stagnation in a Semi-Industrial Economy," in International Economic Policy: Theory and Evidence, edited by Rudiger Dornbusch and Jacob Frenkel (Baltimore: Johns Hopkins University Press, 1979), pp. 270-88.

7. McKinnon, Money and Capital.

8. This follows the model developed by Basant Kapur, "Alternative Stabilization Policies for Less Developed Economies," Journal of Political Economy (August 1976), pp. 777-95.

9. Ibid.

CHAPTER 11

1. Kayhan, October 28, 1976, p. 2.

2. Bank Markazi Iran, Annual Reports, 1978, p. 9.

3. See N. Leff and K. Sato, "Macroeconomic Adjustment in Developing Countries: Instability, Short Run Growth, and External Dependency," The Review of Economics and Statistics (May 1980), pp. 170-79, for a detailed discussion of this process.

4. See Firouz Vakil, Determining Iran's Financial Surplus 1352-1371: Some Management Concepts (Tehran: The Institute for International Political and Economic Studies, 1975), pp. 36-47.

5. Gail Cook Johnson, High-Level Manpower in Iran: From Hidden Conflict to Crisis (New York: Praeger, 1980), p. 33.

6. As reported in Bank Markazi Iran, Annual Report, 1975; Annual Report, 1976.

7. Jahangir Amuzegar, Iran: An Economic Profile (Washington: The Middle East Institute, 1977), pp. 231-33.

8. Johnson, High Level Manpower, p. 33.

9. Alan Brown, "A Note on the Consumption Function in Iran," Oxford Bulletin of Economics and Statistics (February 1978), pp. 1-9.

10. "Farming Lags Behind," Financial Times (July 25, 1977), p. 19.

11. Ibid.

12. Ibid.

CHAPTER 12

1. Firouz Vakil, "Iran's Basic Macroeconomic Problems: A Twenty Year Horizon," Economic Development and Cultural Change (July 1977), pp. 715-16.

2. Planometrics Bureau, A Twenty Year Macro-Economic Perspective for Iran, 1351-1371 (Tehran: Planning Division: Plan and Budget Organization, May 1974), p. 89.

3. Ibid., pp. 58-59.

4. Ibid., pp. 69-93.

5. Gregory Chow, "Control Methods for Macroeconomic Policy Analysis," American Economic Review (May 1976), p. 341.

6. H. A. Simon, "Dynamic Programming Under Uncertainty with a Quadratic Criterion," Econometrica (January 1956), pp. 74-81.

7. H. Theil, "A Note on Certainty Equivalence in Dynamic Planning," Econometrica (April 1957), pp. 346-49.

8. A complete description is given in G. C. Chow, Analysis and Control of Dynamic Economic Systems (New York: McGraw Hill, 1975).

9. It should be noted that the nature of the problem dealt with here is one of short-run stabilization over a period with known exogenous variables. For a longer-run forecast of the economy suing an optimal control approach see Homa Motamen, Expenditure of Oil Revenue: An Optimal Control Approach with Application to the Iranian Economy (New York: St. Martin's Press, 1979).

10. See C. H. Wong and O. Pettersen, "Financial Programming in the Framework of Optimal Control," Weltwirtschaftliches Archiv (1979), pp. 20-37, for a detailed discussion of these assumptions.

11. See Vicente Galbis, "The Demand for Money, Investment and Growth in Latin America, 1961-1973," Economic Development and Cultural Change (March 1979) for an empirical test of this assumption.

12. An example of of this mechanism and related ones for another country is described in E. V. K. Fitzgerald, "Capital Accumulation in Mexico," Development and Cultural Change (July 1980), pp. 391-418.

13. Government capital expenditure is probably a more effective tool than consumption in the Iranian context because consumption was undoubtedly less amenable to control. Moreover, government capital expenditure not only constitutes a component in the aggregate demand but enabled the economy to mitigate demand pressure.

14. A discussion of this problem for the United States is given in L. R. Klein, "Political Aspects of Economic Control," in Theory for Economic Efficiency: Essays in Honor of Abba Lerner, edited by H. Greenfield et al. (Cambridge, Mass.: MIT Press, 1979), pp. 76-91.

CHAPTER 13

1. Farhad Mehran, "Income Distribution in Iran: The Statistics of Inequality," International Labor Office, World Employment Programme Research, Working Papers (October 1975), pp. 2-3.

2. Harry Oshima, "Income Distribution," Mission Working Papers No. II, Employment and Income Policies in Iran (Geneva: World Employment Programme, International Labor Office, 1973).

3. International Bank for Reconstruction and Development, The Economic Development of Iran, Vol. I, The Mann Report, Report No. 378a-IRN, (June 1974).

4. Summarized in M. H. Pesaran and F. Gahvary, "Growth and Income Distribution in Iran," in Econometric Contributions to Public Policy, edited by Richard Stone (New York: St. Martin's Press, 1978), pp. 231-45.

5. H. Ghassemi and Martin Massoudi, "Food Budgeting for Adequate Nutrition in Tehran, Iran," Journal of the American Dietetic Association (1971), pp. 219-24.

6. Mehran, "Income Distribution," p. 4.

7. See M. H. Pesaran, "Income Distribution Trends in Rural and Urban Iran," Bank Markazi Iran (March 1974), mimeo; M. H. Pesaran, "Income Distribution and Its Major Determinants in

Iran," Bank Markazi Iran (August 1975), mimeo; and M. H. Pesaran, "Income Distribution in the City of Tehran," Bank Markazi, Iran (April 1974), mimeo.

8. Quoted in Pesaran and Gahvary, "Growth and Income Distribution."

9. Wouter van Ginneken, "Some Methods of Poverty Analysis: An Application to Iranian Data, 1975-76," World Development (September 1980), pp. 639-46.

10. Ibid., p. 640.

CHAPTER 14

1. Leonard Binder, "Iran," in Joint Economic Committee, Congress of the United States, The Political Economy of the Middle East: 1973-78 (Washington: U.S. Government Printing Office, 1980), p. 154.

2. See Naomi Caiden and Aaron Wildavsky, Planning and Budgeting in Poor Countries (New York: John Wiley, 1974), for a general discussion of the problem; and George Baldwin, Planning and Economic Development (Baltimore: Johns Hopkins University Press, 1967), for a specific case study on Iran.

3. See William Griffith, "The Revival of Islamic Fundamentalism: The Case of Iran," International Security (Summer 1979), pp. 132-38; Fred Halliday, "Theses on the Iranian Revolution," Race and Class (Summer 1979), pp. 81-90; James Bill, "The American Analysis of Iranian Politics," Iranian Studies (Summer 1977), pp. 164-95.

4. See Theodore Moran, "Iranian Defense Expenditures and the Social Crisis," International Security (Winter 1978/79), pp. 178-92.

5. See Younes Benab, "Tabriz in Perspective: A Historical Analysis of the Current Struggle of Iranian Peoples," The Review of Iranian Political Economy and History (June 1978), pp. 1-42; Nikki Keddie, "Oil Economic Policy and Social Conflict in Iran," Race and Class (Summer 1979), pp. 13-30; Sepher Zabih, Iran's Revolutionary Upheaval: An Interpretive Essay (San Francisco: Alchemy Books, 1979).

6. See James Petras and M. Morley, "Development and Revolution: Contradictions in the Advanced Third World Countries - Brazil, South Africa and Iran," Studies in Comparative International Development (Spring 1981), pp. 3-43; Shahrzad Azad, "Workers' and Peasants' Councils in Iran," Monthly Review (October 1980), pp. 14-29; and Eqbal Ahmad, "The Iranian Revolution: A Landmark for the Future," Race and Class (Summer 1979), pp. 3-13.

7. Mancur Olson, "Rapid Growth as a Destabilizing Force," Journal of Economic History (December 1963), pp. 529-52.

8. Ibid., p. 541.

9. I. Zartman et al., "An Economic Indicator of Socio-Political Unrest," International Journal of Middle Eastern Studies (October 1971), p. 295.

10. Farhad Kazemi, "Economic Indicators of Political Violence in Iran," Iranian Studies (Winter-Spring 1975), pp. 70-86.

11. Ibid., p. 82.

12. A somewhat different but not conflicting classification is given in Jahangir Amuzegar, "Ideology and Economic Growth in the Middle East," The Middle East Journal (Winter 1974), pp. 1-9.

13. Cf. Robert Looney, Iran at the End of the Century (Lexington, Mass.: Lexington Books, 1977), Ch. 6; and Jiri Skolka and M. Garzuel, Changes in Income Distribution, Employment and Structure of the Economy: A Case Study of Iran. (Geneva: International Labor Office, 1976).

14. Skolka and Garzuel, "Changes in Income Distribution."

15. Ibid., p. 45.

16. Robert Looney, A Development Strategy for Iran Through the 1980s (New York: Praeger, 1977), Ch. 10.

17. "The Day the Magic Carpet was Rolled up and Packed Away," Euromoney (December 1978), p. 138.

18. From Rodney Wilson, "Technology Transfer Threatens Traditional Industries," Middle East Economic Digest (November 3, 1981), p. 3.

19. Ibid.

CHAPTER 15

1. Samuel Liberman, "Prospects for Development and Population Growth in Iran," Population and Development Review (June 1979), pp. 312-13.

Bibliography

Abolfathi, Farid et al. The OPEC Market to 1985. Lexington, Mass.: Lexington Books, 1977.

Adler, John. Absorptive Capacity, the Concept and Its Determinants. Washington, D.C.: Brookings Institution, 1965.

Ahmad, Eqbal. "The Iranian Revolution: A Landmark for the Future." Race and Class, Summer 1979.

Akhtar, M. A. "An Empirical Note on Inflation and Openness in Less Developed Economies." The Philippine Economic Journal, 1976.

Albrecht, Ulrich. "Militarised Sub-Imperialism: The Case of Iran." in The World Military Order, edited by Mary Kaldor. New York: Praeger, 1979.

Amuzegar, Jahangir. "Iran's Economic Planning Once Again." Middle East Economic Papers, 1957.

_________. Iran: An Economic Profile. Washington: The Middle East Institute, 1977.

Amuzegar, Jahangir and M. Ali Fekrat. Iran: Economic Development Under Dualistic Conditions. Chicago: University of Chicago Press, 1971.

Anderberg, Michael. Cluster Analysis for Applications. New York: Academic Press, 1973.

Anderson, C., and J. L. Jordon. "The Monetary Base-Expansion and Analytical Use." Federal Reserve Bank of St. Louis Review, August 1968.

Aresvick, O. The Agricultural Development of Iran. New York: Praeger, 1976.

Argy, Victor. "Rules vs. Discretion in Monetary Management and Short Term Stability." Journal of Money, Credit and Banking, February 1971.

_________, and P. Kouri. "Sterilization Policies and the Volatility of International Reserves." In National Monetary Policies and the International Financial System, edited by Robert Z. Alben. Chicago: University of Chicago Press, 1974.

Arrow, K. "The Economic Implications of Learning by Doing." Review of Economic Studies, June 1962.

Ashraf, A. "Historical Obstacles to the Development of a Bourgeoisie in Iran." Iranian Studies, Spring-Summer, 1979.

Askari, Hossein, J. Cummings and B. Harik. "Land Reform in the Middle East: A Note on Its Redistributive Effect." Iranian Studies, Autumn 1977.

_________, J. T. Cummings, and G. Richter. "Efficiency of LDC Trading Patterns: The Case of Iran." American Economic Review, May 1979.

Avramovie, Dragoslav. "Industrialization of Iran: The Records, the Problems and the Prospects." Tahqiqat-e eqtesadi, Spring 1970.

Azad, Shahrzad. "Workers' and Peasants' Councils in Iran." Monthly Review, October 1980.

Balbach, A. B., and A. E. Burger. "Derivation of the Monetary Base." Federal Reserve Bank of St. Louis Review, November 1976.

Baldwin, George. Planning and Development in Iran. Baltimore: Johns Hopkins University Press, 1967.

Banani, A. The Modernization of Iran: 1921-1941. Stanford, Calif.: Stanford University Press, 1961.

Bank Markazi Iran. Annual Report, various issues.

Barnaby, Frank. "The Scale of World Military Expenditures." In Disarmament and World Development, edited by Richard Jolly. Oxford: Pergamon Press, 1978.

Bartsch, William. "The Impact of the Oil Industry on the Economy of Iran." In Foreign Investment in the Petroleum and Mineral Industries, edited by R.F. Mikesell. Baltimore: Johns Hopkins University Press, 1971.

Benab, Younes. "Tabriz in Perspective: A Historical Analysis of the Current Struggle of Iranian Peoples." The Review of Iranian Political Economy and History, June 1978.

Benedick, Richard. Industrial Finance in Iran. Cambridge, Mass.: Harvard University Press, 1964.

Benoit, Emile. Defense and Economic Growth in Developing Countries. Lexington, Mass.: Lexington Books, 1973.

_________. "Growth and Defense in Developing Countries." Economic Development and Cultural Change 26 January 1978: 271-80.

Bharier, Julian. Economic Development in Iran 1900-1970. London: Oxford University Press, 1971.

Bill, James. The Politics of Iran: Groups, Classes and Modernization. (Columbus, Ohio: Charles Merrill, 1972).

_________. "The American Analysis of Iranian Politics." Iranian Studies, Summer 1977.

Binder, Leonard. "Iran." In Joint Economic Committee, Congress of the United States, The Political Economy of the Middle East: 1973-78. Washington: U.S. Government Printing Office, 1980.

Bronfenbrenner, M. "Statistical Tests of Rival Monetary Rules." Journal of Political Economy, February 1961.

_________. "Monetary Rules: A New Look." Journal of Law and Economics, October 1965.

Brown, Alan. "A Note on the Consumption Function in Iran." Oxford Bulletin of Economics and Statistics, February 1978.

Bruno, Michael. "Stabilization and Stagnation in a Semi-Industrial Economy." In International Economic Policy: Theory and Evidence, edited by Rudiger Dornbusch and Jacob Frenkel. Baltimore: Johns Hopkins University Press, 1979.

Bruton, Henry. "Notes on Development in Iran." Economic Development and Cultural Change, July 1961.

Business International. Operating in Iran. New York: Business International, 1977.

Caiden, Naomi, and Aaron Wildavsky. Planning and Budgeting in Poor Countries. New York: John Wiley, 1974.

Chambers, E. J., and D. E. Gordon. "Primary Products and Economic Growth: An Empirical Measurement." Journal of Political Economy, August 1966.

Chawla, R. L. "Economic Development of Iran." India Quarterly, April/July 1979.

Chenery, Hollis. "Patterns of Industrial Growth." American Economic Review, September 1960.

_________. "Targets for Development." In The Widening Gap, edited by Barbara Ward. New York: Columbia University Press, 1971.

Chenery, Hollis, and M. Bruno. "Development Alternatives in An Open Economy: The Case of Israel." Economic Journal, March 1962.

Chenery, Hollis, and A. Strout. "Foreign Assistance and Economic Development." American Economic Review, September 1966, pp. 679-733.

Chenery, Hollis, and L. Taylor. "Development Patterns: Among Countries and Over Time." The Review of Economics and Statistics, November 1968.

Chow, G. C. Analysis and Control of Dynamic Economic Systems. New York: McGraw Hill, 1975.

_________. "Control Methods for Macroeconomic Policy Analysis." American Economic Review, May 1976.

Craig, D. "The Impact of Land Reform on An Iranian Village." The Middle East Journal, 1978.

Crockett, Andrew and Owen Evans. "Demand for Money in Middle Eastern Countries." International Monetary Fund, Staff Papers, September 1980.

Cummings-Bruce, Nicholas. "Budget: Battling the Legacy of Overspending and Infrastructural Jams." Middle East Economic Digest, Special Report on Iran, February 1977.

_________. "Ports and Transport." Middle East Economic Digest, Special Survey on Iran, February 1977.

Daftary, Farhad. "Development Planning in Iran: A Historical Survey." Iranian Studies, Autumn, 1973.

Dagli, V. The Public Sector in India. Bombay: Vira, 1969.

Dailami, Mansoor. "The Determination and Control of Money Supply in an Oil Exporting Country: The Iranian Experience." MIT Energy Laboratory, Working Paper No. MIT-EL 78-027WP, July 1978, revised February 1979.

"The Day the Magic Carpet was Rolled Up and Packed Away." Euromoney, December 1978.

Dellalfar, W. A., and J. K. Shirazi. "An Analysis of the Dynamics of Growth in Iran: 1959-73." Journal of Economic Development, July 1979.

Development Planning Division, ESCAP Secretariat. "The Iranian Economy: Oil and Development in the First Half of the 1970s." Economic Bulletin for Asia and the Pacific, December 1978.

Dorfman, Robert. "A Comment on Professor Benoit's Conundrum." International Development Review 14 (January 1972): 10-12.

Dunn, Robert M. "Exchange Rates, Payments Adjustment and OPEC: Why Oil Deficits Persist." Princeton Essays in International Finance, December 1979.

Eckaus, Richard. "Absorptive Capacity as a Constraint Due to Maturation Processes." Development and Planning, edited by J.N. Bhagwati and R.S. Eckhaus. Cambridge, Mass.: MIT Press, 1973.

Eckstein, Harry. "Theoretical Approaches to Explaining Collective Political Violence." In Handbook of Political Conflict, edited by Ted R. Gurr. New York: The Free Press, 1980.

Emery, R. F. "The Relation of Exports and Economic Growth." Kyklos, 1967.

Eshag, Eprime. "Quantification of Disruptive Effects of Export Shortfalls." Tahqiqat-e eqtesadi, Winter 1971.

"Farming Lags Behind." The Financial Times, July 25, 1977.

Fekrat, M. Ali. "Growth of OPEC-Type Economies: A Preliminary Theoretical Inquiry." Economia Internazionale, February 1979.

Fesharaki, Fereidun. Revolution and Energy Policy in Iran. London: The Economist Intelligence Unit, 1980.

Fitzgerald, E. V. K. "Capital Accumulation in Mexico." Development and Cultural Change, July 1980.

Forbis, William. Fall of the Peacock Throne: Story of Iran. New York: Harper & Row, 1980.

Frenkel, Jacob, and Harry Johnson. "The Monetary Approach to the Balance of Payments: Essential Concepts and Historical Origins." In The Monetary Approach to the Balance of Payments, edited by Jacob Frenkel and Harry Johnson. London: George Allen & Unwin, 1976.

Friedman, Milton. A Program for Monetary Stability. New York: Fordham University Press, 1959.

__________. "Monetary Policy for a Developing Society." Bank Markazi, Iran, Bulletin, March-April 1971.

Galbis, Vicente. "The Demand for Money, Investment and Growth in Latin America, 1961-1973." Economic Development and Cultural Change, March 1979.

Gates, Gregory F. "An Analysis of the Impact of American Arms Transfers on Political Stability in Iran." M. A. thesis, Naval Postgraduate School, 1968.

Gebelein, Christopher. "Forecasting Absorptive Capacity for Oil Revenues: Practical Techniques for Policy Analysis." In U.S. and World Energy Resources: Prospects and Priorities, edited by Ragaei El Mallakh and Carl McGuire. Boulder, Colorado: International Research Center for Energy and Economic Development, 1977.

Ghassemi, H., and Martin Massoudi. "Food Budgeting for Adequate Nutrition in Tehran, Iran." Journal of the American Dietetic Association, 1971.

Graham, Robert. "Power Shortage Plays Havoc with Industry." The Financial Times, July 25, 1977.

_________. "Times for Tighter Belts." The Financial Times, July 25, 1977.

Griffin, Keith. Underdevelopment in Spanish America. Cambridge, Mass.: The MIT Press, 1969.

Griffith, William. "The Revival of Islamic Fundamentalism: The Case of Iran." International Security, Summer 1979.

Griffiths, Brian. Inflation: The Price of Prosperity. New York: Holmes & Meier, 1976.

Gurr, Ted. "A Causal Model of Civil Strife: A Comparative Analysis Using New Indices." The American Political Science Review, December 1968.

_________. Why Men Rebel. Princeton: Princeton University Press, 1970.

Halliday, Fred. "Iran: The Economic Contradictions." MERIP Reports, July-August 1978.

_________. "Iran: Trade Unions and the Working Class Opposition." MERIP Reports, October 1978.

_________. Iran: Dictatorship and Development. New York: Penguin Books, 1979.

_________. "Theses on the Iranian Revolution." Race and Class, Summer 1979.

_________. "The Genesis of the Iranian Revolution." Third World Quarterly, October 1979.

Harberger, Arnold. "The Dynamics of Inflation in Chile." In Measurement in Economics, edited by C. Christ. Stanford, Calif.: Stanford University Press, 1963.

Harris, William. "The Impact of the Petroleum Export Industry on the Pattern of Venezuelan Economic Development." In

Foreign Investment in the Petroleum and Mineral Industries, edited by R.F. Mikesell. Baltimore: Johns Hopkins University Press, 1971.

Hirschfeld, Yair. "Decline and Fall of the Pahlavis." The Jerusalem Quarterly, Summer 1979.

Hirschman, H. O. "The Changing Tolerance for Income Inequality in the Course of Economic Development." Quarterly Journal of Economics, November 1973.

Howe, Charles. Natural Resource Economics. New York: John Wiley, 1979.

International Bank of Reconstruction and Development. The Economic Development of Iran. Vol. I. The Mann Report. Report No. 378a-IRN, June 1974.

________. World Tables: 1976. Washington: International Bank for Reconstruction and Development, 1978.

International Labor Office. Employment and Income Policies for Iran. Geneva: ILO, 1973.

Iyoha, Milton. "Inflation and Openness in Less Developed Economies: A Cross Country Analysis." Economic Development and Cultural Change, October 1973.

Jehaimi, Taher El. "The Absorptive Capacity of Libya: A Constrained Expenditure Approach." The Journal of Energy and Development, Spring 1976.

Johnson, Gail Cook. High-Level Manpower in Iran: From Hidden Conflict to Crisis. New York: Praeger, 1980.

Johnson, Harris. "Monetary Theory and Policy." American Economic Review, June 1962, pp. 335-84.

Johnson, Harry. "The Ideology of Economic Policy in the New States." In Chicago Essays in Economic Development, edited by David Wall. Chicago: University of Chicago Press, 1972.

Jordan, J. L. "Elements of Money Supply Determination." Federal Reserve Bank of St. Louis Review, October 1969.

Kader, Ahmad. "The Contribution of Oil Exports to Economic Development: A Study of the Major Oil Exporting Countries." The American Economist 7 (Spring 1980): 46-51.

Kaldor, Mary. Strategic Factors in Economic Development. Ithaca, N.Y.: Cornell University Press, 1967.

________. "The Military in Development." World Development, June 1976.

Kapur, Basant. "Alternative Stabilization Policies for Less Developed Economies." Journal of Political Economy, August 1976.

Katousiam, Homa. "Land Reform in Iran: A Case Study in the Political Economy of Social Engineering." Journal of Peasant Studies, June 1974.

________. "Oil Versus Agriculture: A Case Study of Dual Resource Depletion in Iran." Journal of Peasant Studies, April 1978.

________. The Political Economy of Modern Iran, 1926-1979. London: Macmillan, 1981.

Kayhan, October 28, 1976, p. 2.

Kayhan International (Tehran), March 8, 1975.

Keddie, Nikki. "The Iranian Village Before and After Land Reform." Journal of Contemporary History, July 1968.

________. "The Midas Touch: Black Gold, Economics and Politics in Iran Today." Iranian Studies, August 1977, pp. 243-66.

________. "Oil, Economic Policy, and Social Conflict in Iran." Race and Class, 1979.

Khamsi, Farhad. "Land Reform in Iran." Monthly Review, June 1969.

Kirkpatrick, C. H., and F. I. Nixson. "The Origins of Inflation in Less Developed Countries: A Selective Review." In Inflation in Open Economies, edited by Michael Parkin and George Zis. Manchester, England: Manchester University Press, 1976.

Klein, L. R. "Political Aspects of Economic Control." In Theory of Economic Efficiency: Essays in Honor of Abba Lerner, edited by H. Greenfield et al, Cambridge, Mass.: MIT Press, 1979.

Lambton, A. K. S. "Persia." Journal of the Royal Central Asian Society, January 1944.

________. The Persian Land Reform: 1962-1966. Oxford: Oxford University Press, 1969.

Landau, Luis. "Saving Functions in Latin America." In Studies in Development Planning, edited by Hollis B. Chenery. Cambridge, Mass.: Harvard University Press, 1971.

Leff, N., and K. Sato. "Macroeconomic Adjustment in Developing Countries: Instability, Short Run Growth, and External Dependency." The Review of Economics and Statistics, May 1980.

Lenczowski, George. "Iran: The Awful Truth." The American Spectator, December 1979.

Liberman, Samuel. "Development and Population Growth in Iran." Population and Development Review, June 1979.

________. "Prospects for Development and Population Growth in Iran." Population and Development Review, June 1979.

Looney, Robert E. Income Distribution Policies and Economic Growth in Semi-Industrialized Countries. New York: Praeger, 1975.

________. A Development Strategy for Iran Through the 1980s. New York: Praeger, 1977.

________. Iran at the End of the Century. Lexington, Mass.: Lexington Books, 1977.

Luck, Edwin. "Port Congestion." The Financial Times, July 28, 1975.

Majidi, Abdol-Majid. "Iran 1980-85: Problems and Challenges of Development." The World Today, July 1977.

El Mallakh, Ragaei, and Jacob Atta. The Absorptive Capacity of Kuwait. Lexington, Mass.: Lexington Books, 1981.

El Mallakh, Ragaei, and Mihssen Kadhim. "Absorptive Capacity, Surplus Funds, and Regional Capital Mobility in the Middle East." Revista Internazionale di Scienze Economiche e Commerciali, April 1974.

Mayer, T. "The Lag Effect in Monetary Policy: Some Criticisms." Western Economic Journal, September 1967.

McDermott, Anthony, and Andrew Whitley. "Iran Without the Shah." The Financial Times, January 17, 1979.

McKinnon, Ronald I. Money and Capital in Economic Development. Washington: The Brookings Institution, 1973.

McNown, Robert, and Myles Wallace. "International Reserve Flows of OPEC States: A Monetary Approach." The Journal of Energy and Development, Spring 1977.

Mehran, Farhad. "Income Distribution in Iran: The Statistics of Inequality." International Labor Office. World Employment Programme Research, Working Papers, October 1975.

Mehran, Farideh and Hamid Mehran. "Monetary Policies of the Oil Exporting Countries." Paper presented at the Western Economic Association Annual Meeting, July 4, 1981, San Francisco, Calif.

Metwally, M. M., and H. V. Tamaschke. "Oil Exports and Economic Growth in the Middle East." Kyklos, 1980.

Michalopoulos, C. "Interindustry Relations, External Economies and Regional Economic Development." In Industrial

Location and Regional Development, Proceedings of an Interregional Seminar, Minsk, 14-26 August 1968. New York: United Nations, 1971.

Mikesell, R. F., "Inflation in Latin America." In Latin America: Problems in Economic Development, edited by C. Nisbet. New York: Free Press, 1969.

________. "The Contribution of Petroleum and Mineral Resources to Economic Development." In Foreign Investment in the Petroleum and Mineral Industries, edited by R.F. Mikesell et al. Baltimore: Johns Hopkins University Press, 1971.

Millspaugh, A. C. Americans in Persia. Washington: Brookings Institution, 1946.

Ministry of Economy. Annual Industrial Survey, various issues.

Modigliani, F. "Some Empirical Tests of Monetary Management and of Rules Versus Discretion." Journal of Political Economy, June 1964.

Moran, Theodore H. "Iranian Defense Expenditures and the Social Crisis." International Security, Winter 1978/79.

Morgan, David. "Fiscal Policy in Oil Exporting Countries, 1972-78." International Monetary Fund, Staff Papers, March 1979.

Motamen, Homa. Expenditure of Oil Revenue: An Optimal Control Approach with Application to the Iranian Economy. New York: St. Martin's Press, 1979.

Mussa, M. "A Monetary Approach to Balance of Payments Analysis." Journal of Money, Credit and Banking, August 1974.

Nankani, Gobind. "Development Problems in Mineral Exporting Countries." World Bank Staff Working Papers, No. 354, August 1979.

New York Times, Jan. 14, 1979, p. 2.

New York Times, Dec. 2, 1979, p. 3.

New York Times Magazine, Dec. 17, 1978.

Newman, Stephanie. "Security, Military Expenditures and Socio-Economic Developments: Reflections on Iran." Orbis, Fall 1978.

"Notes and Documents." Race and Class, Summer 1979.

Nugent, Jeffrey, and Pan Yotopoulos. "Momentum for Development and Development Disequilibria." Journal of Economic Development, July 1977.

________. "What Has Orthodox Development Economics Learned from Recent Experience?" World Development 7 (September 1979): 541-54.

Olsen, P. Bjorn, and N. Norregaard Rasmussen. "An Attempt at Planning in a Traditional State: Iran." In Planning Economic Development, edited by E. Hagen. Homewood, Ill.: Richard D. Irwin, 1963.

Oshima, Harry. "Income Distribution." Mission Working Paper No. II, Employment and Income Policies in Iran. Geneva: World Employment Programme, International Labor Office, 1973.

Otani, Ichiro. "Inflation in An Open Economy: A Case Study of the Philippines." International Monetary Fund, Staff Papers, 1975.

Parvin, Manouchester. "Economic Determinants of Political Unrest." Journal of Conflict Resolution, June 1973.

Parvin, Manouchester, and A. Zamani. "Political Economy of Growth and Distribution: A Statistical Interpretation of the Iranian Case." Iranian Studies, Winter-Spring 1979.

Pearson, Scott. Petroleum and the Nigerian Economy. Stanford, Calif.: Stanford University Press, 1970.

Pesaran, M.H. "Income Distribution Trends in Rural and Urban Iran." Bank Markazi Iran. March 1974, mimeo.

________. "Income Distribution in the City of Tehran." Bank Markazi Iran, April 1974, mimeo.

________. "Income Distribution and its Major Determinants in Iran." Bank Markazi Iran, August 1975, mimeo.

Pesaran, M.H., and F. Gahvary. "Growth and Income Distribution in Iran." In Econometric Contributions to Public Policy, edited by Richard Stone. New York: St. Martin's Press, 1978.

Petras, James, and Morris Morley. "Development and Revolution: Contradictions in the Advanced Third World Countries - Brazil, South Africa and Iran." Studies in Comparative International Development, Spring 1981.

Pierce, James. "Some Rules for the Conduct of Monetary Policy." In Federal Reserve Bank of Boston. Controlling Monetary Aggregates, June 1969.

Plan Organization. Review of the Second Seven Year Plan. Tehran, 1960.

Planometrics Bureau. A Twenty Year Macro-Economic Perspective for Iran, 1351-1371. Tehran: Planning Division, Plan and Budget Organization, May 1974.

Pleeter, Saul. Economic Impact Analysis: Methodology and Applications. Boston: Martinus Nijhoff 1980.

Putnam, B., and D. Sykes Wilford. The Monetary Approach to International Adjustment. New York: Praeger, 1978.

Quester, George. "The Shah and the Bomb." Policy Sciences, March 1977.

Reddaway, W. B. The Development of the Indian Economy. Homewood, Ill.: Richard S. Irwin, 1962.

Richardson, James. "Monetary Rules and Optimal Monetary Policy." Nebraska Journal of Economics and Business, Autumn 1975.

Rizvi, Saiyid Athar Abbas. Iran: Royalty, Religion and Revolution. Melbourne: Ma'rifat, 1979.

Saikal, Amin. The Rise and Fall of the Shah. Princeton: Princeton University Press, 1980.

Sargent, T. J., and N. Wallace. "Rational Expectations and the Theory of Economic Policy." Studies in Monetary Economics, No. 2, Research Department, Federal Reserve Bank of Minneapolis, June 1975.

Sayers, R. S. Central Banking after Bagehot. London: Oxford University Press, 1957.

Schultz, Ann. "Iran's New Industrial State." Current History, January 1977.

Schumpeter, J. A. The Theory of Economic Development: An Inquiry into Profits, Capital, Credit, Interest, and the Business Cycle, translated version by Redvers Opie. Cambridge, Mass.: Harvard University Press, 1934.

Seers, Dudley. "A Theory of Inflation and Growth in Underdeveloped Economies Based on the Experience of Latin America." Oxford Economic Papers 15 (June 1962): 172-95.

"The Shah's Americans: In Iran for Beaucoup Bucks." The Washington Post, May 12, 1977.

Shahshahani, Ahmad, and T. Malcolm Dowling, Jr. "An Econometric Model Forecast of Iran 1975-1985." The Journal of Energy and Development, Autumn 1976.

Shahshahani, Ahmad, and Mihssen Kadhim, "Development Problems of an Energy Based Economy: Iran." Journal of South Asia and Middle East Studies, 1979.

Sheehey, E. J. "On the Measurement of Imported Inflation in Developing Countries." Weltwirtschaftliches Archiv, 1979.

Shen, T. Y. "Technological Diffusion, Substitution and Efficiency." Econometrica, March 1973.

Silk, Leonard. "Lessons from Iran." New York Times, January 19, 1979.

Simon, H. A. "Dynamic Programming Under Uncertainty with a Quadratic Criterion." Econometrica, January 1956.

Sivard, Ruth. World Military and Social Expenditures. Leesburg, Va.: World Priorities, 1980.

Smithies, Arthur. The Economic Potential of the Arab Countries. Santa Monica, Calif.: Rand, 1978.

Stevens, Willy J. Capital Absorptive Capacity in Developing Countries. Leiden, The Netherlands: A. W. Sijthoff, 1971.

Stockley, S. Thomas, and B. Najafi. "The Effectiveness of Foreign Corporations in Iran." Tahqiqat-e eqtesadi, Winter 1971.

Theil, H. "A Note on Certainty Equivalence in Dynamic Planning." Econometrica, April 1957.

U.S. Arms Control and Disarmament Agency. World Military Expenditures and Arms Transfers 1967-76. Washington: ACDA, 1978.

U.S. Military Sales to Iran. Staff Study, Subcommittee on Foreign Assistance, Committee on Foreign Relations. Washington: U.S. Senate, 1976.

U.S. Arms Policies in the Persian Gulf and Red Sea Areas: Past, Present, Future. Staff Report, Committee on International Relations. Washington, D.C.: House of Representatives, 1977.

Vagar, Nasrollah. "Economic Development in Iran and the Financing of the Gap in the Third Plan." Middle East Economic Papers, 1964.

________. "An Analysis of Iran's Foreign Trade and the Causes of the Stagnation of Its Exports." Middle East Economic Papers, December 1969.

Vakil, Firous. Determining Iran's Financial Surplus 1352-1371: Some Management Concepts. Tehran: The Institute for International Political and Economic Studies, 1975.

________. "Iran's Basic Macroeconomic Problems: A Twenty Year Horizon." Economic Development and Cultural Change, July 1977.

van Ginneken, Wouter. "Some Methods of Poverty Analysis: An Application to Iranian Data, 1975-76." World Development, September 1980.

von der Mehden, Fred, and Kim Hill. "Social and Economic Conditions and Political Violence." Rice Program in Development Studies, Paper No. 32, Fall 1972.

Walton, Thomas. "Economic Development and Revolutionary Upheavals in Iran." Cambridge Journal of Economics, September 1980.

Waterson, A. Development Planning: Lessons of Experience. Baltimore: John Hopkins University Press, 1956.

Watkins, M. H. "The Staple Theory Revisited." Journal of Canadian Studies, Winter 1977.

Wilson, Rodney. "Technology Transfer Threatens Traditional Industries." Middle East Economic Digest, November 3, 1981.

Wong, C. H., and O. Pettersen. "Financial Programming in the Framework of Optimal Control," Weltwirtschaftliches Archiv, 1979.

World Bank. World Development Report, 1980. New York: Oxford University Press, 1980.

Youseffi, Manmood. "Monetary Rules in Monetary Policy." Rivista Internazionale di Scienze Economiche e Commerciali, March 1979.

Zabih, Sepher. Iran's Revolutionary Upheaval: An Interpretive Essay. San Francisco, Alchemy Books, 1979.

Zonis, Martin. "He Took All the Credit, Now He Gets All The Blame." New York Times, Jan. 14, 1979.

Index

About the Author

ROBERT E. LOONEY is associate professor of National Security Affairs at the Naval Postgraduate School, Monterey, California. He is a graduate of the University of California, Davis, and has been a faculty member of the University of California at Davis, The University of Santa Clara, and the Monterey Institute of International Studies. He has also been a development economist for the Stanford Research Institute and has served as an economic adviser to the governments of Iran, Saudi Arabia, Mexico and Panama. He is currently a consultant for the International Labor Office, Geneva. Dr. Looney has published numerous articles in professional journals and is the author of *The Economic Development of Iran* (1973), *Income Distribution Policies and Economic Growth in Semiindustrialized Countries* (1975), *The Economic Development of Panama* (1976), *Iran at the End of the Century* (1977), *A Development Strategy for Iran through the 1980s* (1977), *Mexico's Economy* (1978), *The Impact of World Inflation on Semidependent Countries* (1979) and *Saudi Arabia's Growth Potential* (1981).